CONFIDENT IN CHRIST

LIVING BY FAITH *Really* WORKS

CONFIDENT IN CHRIST

LIVING BY FAITH *Really* WORKS

ROBERT N. WILKIN

GES

GRACE EVANGELICAL SOCIETY
IRVING, TEXAS

Confident in Christ: Living By Faith Really Works
Copyright © 1999 by Grace Evangelical Society
Printed in the United States of America

Unless otherwise indicated, Scripture quotations are from *The New King James Version*, Copyright © 1979, 1980, 1982, by Thomas Nelson, Inc.

Cover and book design: Keith Yates

Library of Congress Cataloging-in-Publication Data
Wilkin, Robert N., 1952-
Confident in Christ: living by faith really works / Robert N. Wilkin.
Includes bibliographical references.
ISBN 0-9641392-3-5
1. Salvation. 2. Faith. 3. Christian life.
Library of Congress Catalog Card Number: 98-89930

Requests for information should be addressed to:
Grace Evangelical Society
PO Box 167128
Irving, TX 75016-7128

*This book is dedicated to
my wife, Sharon, and to my parents,
Bob and Jean Wilkin.
I will be forever grateful for the wonderful influence
you have had on my life.*

ACKNOWLEDGEMENT

I am indebted to Zane Hodges,
my mentor for the past twenty years,
for teaching me how to interpret God's Word
and how to walk by faith.

CONTENTS

Introduction

Saving Faith

Assurance

Eternal Security

Perseverance

Appendices

WHY I WROTE THIS BOOK

I HAD THREE major religious influences in my early life. I was christened into the Serbian Orthodox faith. My mother, nee Jana Budincich, is Serbian, and her parents immigrated to the United States. Occasionally I attended services with her, and I served as an altar boy one summer at a church camp. The second influence was the Methodist church where my dad, Robert Faris Wilkin,[1] was the head usher and where I attended Sunday School and morning worship service each week.

However, far and away the greatest influence on my life came from a small religious boy's club which met after school once or twice a week and on Saturdays. This club was founded by a maverick from a Pentecostal Holiness church who felt that the doctrines and practices of his fellow church members were not strict enough.

I was in the club from first through eighth grades. We received religious instruction in our weekly club meetings, and we also played football, basketball, and baseball. Over time I came to believe the club's teaching that salvation was only for those who were holy enough. I also accepted the teaching that if I ever did gain salvation; I would lose it forever if I committed even one sin. The club taught that sinless perfection was necessary to maintain my salvation, and that if I lost it, I could never get it back.

My parents insisted I quit the club at the start of ninth grade, and this disturbed me because I thought that staying in the club was the only way I could go to heaven. I was determined to become a club leader and spend my life serving God and ensuring my position in heaven. So, at first I openly defied my parents and went to a club meeting. When this met with quick reaction from my dad, I began to covertly go to the club meetings.

Every day I lived in fear, sure that hell existed and that most people were going there. I wasn't sure if I had been saved yet, or even how I could be sure, since there was no objective way of knowing if I was holy enough to be saved. And, even if I were saved, I wasn't sure if I was living a sinless life now, or if I could do so in the future.

The club affected my whole life. I didn't date because I had been taught that dating anyone except the girls in the club (there was also a girl's branch) would send me to hell. When I quit the club, I also quit playing competitive baseball, basketball, and football, since we were taught that participating in regular high school or college sports would cause us to go to hell. Bad company corrupts good morals, and everyone outside of the club was bad company! Though 6 foot 6 inches in height and very athletic and interested in dating, I avoided these things so that I could become worthy of eternal salvation.

My only real friend was another long-time member of the club whose parents had also forced him to quit. John and I had secretly gone to the club many times during our high school years.

John became a Christian while in college. One day late in the summer before my senior year, he appealed to my doubts when he asked, "Bob, are you sure that your understanding of the gospel is correct?" Then he invited me to a Christian meeting at his college, USC. I went and the questions began. "How is eternal security possible? Doesn't sinning mean that we lose our salvation? How can the only condition be faith in Christ?" Over the course of the next few months, one by one my questions were answered and I came to believe that Jesus guaranteed me eternal life on the sole basis of my believing in Him for it. I knew I was secure forever because I could now see the truth of His promise, "He who believes in Me has everlasting life."

I was overjoyed. It was as though I had been released from prison. I *knew* that I was set for eternity! I was so thrilled I began telling others. Soon I was involved in regular outreach on my campus, U. C. Irvine.

I gave up my plans of becoming a doctor and decided to devote my life to telling others about the wonderful grace of God. This book is a part of that devotion. I hope that you find in this book not merely an explanation of tough texts. It is my prayer that you also see the passion, love, and gratitude that I have, and that we all can have, if we are deeply touched by the wonderful grace of God.

Saving
Faith

CHAPTER 1

SAVING FAITH IN FOCUS

C ONFUSION OVER THE gospel abounds. I hear it from people all over the country and around the world. They don't know what to believe. They aren't sure what God requires. Is it turning from sins or commitment of life? Inviting Jesus into their hearts? Obeying the Golden Rule? Confessing their sins? Being baptized?

There is only one true gospel. The key is to discover and believe it. However, that isn't necessarily easy to do, because many different gospels are being preached and it is hard to determine which one is correct.

Most forms of the gospel being preached today are what I call *faith-plus* gospels. These say that faith in Christ for eternal life is *necessary*, but that it is *not enough*.[1] Works must accompany faith, according to faith-plus gospels, in order for a person to make it to heaven. There are two versions of the faith-plus gospel.

• *Salvation by faith plus works.* Some say that one must have faith plus works in order to obtain salvation. A person lacking sufficient good works, or guilty of major sins, will not make it to heaven, even if he believes in Christ.[2]

• *Salvation by faith that works.* Others say that one must have faith that works. They claim that one is saved by faith in Christ plus nothing, but that *true* faith in Christ results in commitment, obedience, turning from sins, etc.[3] This may sound significantly different than salvation by faith plus works. However, it is actually another way of saying the same thing.

There is no real difference between saying that to be saved you must turn from sins, commit your life to Christ, and believe in Him, and saying that believing in Christ necessarily results in turning from your sins and committing your life to Him. Both insist that

3

turning from sins and commitment of life are necessary to obtain final salvation.

• *Salvation apart from faith or works.* In addition to faith-plus gospels, there is one gospel requiring no faith at all! That is the gospel of universalism, which teaches that all are already saved, or will ultimately be saved. According to this view no one will spend eternity apart from God, even those who never believed in Christ. This view can surface anywhere, even in very conservative, evangelical churches. The motive may seem to be good—an abhorrence of people going to hell—but it is a direct contradiction of God's Word. The way to keep people from hell is by proclaiming the true gospel that they might believe it and be saved, not by distorting the gospel.

The Bible Is the Only Reliable Guide to the Gospel

Understanding the gospel is not a matter of taking a poll. The majority is rarely right and that is especially true in terms of the gospel. Jesus said, "Enter by the narrow gate; for wide is the gate and broad is the way that leads to destruction, and there are many who go in by it. Because narrow is the gate and difficult[4] is the way which leads to life, and there are few who find it" (Matthew 7:13-14). Jesus unequivocally said that the majority of people are on the wrong road. *Many* are on the broad way. *Few* are on the narrow way.

The gospel is contrary to our expectations. Very few things in life are received simply by believing. (Actually, I can't think of anything, other than eternal life, which is received by faith alone.) Thus, the gospel seems to be "foolishness to those who are perishing" (1 Corinthians 1:18).

To be saved you must resist the impulse to follow the crowd. There is only one reliable guide to spiritual truth and that is the Bible.

When the apostle Paul went to the city of Berea, he began teaching in the Jewish synagogue. Paul's traveling companion, Luke, reports that the Bereans "were more fair-minded than those in Thessalonica, in that they received the word with all readiness, and searched the Scriptures daily to find out whether these things were so" (Acts 17:11).

Every person should study the Scripture to see whether the gospel they are hearing is correct. We should all be like the Bereans, searching the Scriptures, so that we will know what to believe.

The only condition of eternal salvation is faith in Christ. Even a casual reading of the Gospel of John, the only book in Scripture whose purpose is evangelistic (John 20:31),[5] makes this clear. "He who believes in Me has everlasting life" (John 6:47). "He who believes in Him is not condemned" (John 3:18). "Most assuredly, I say to you, he who hears My word and believes in Him who sent Me has everlasting life, and shall not come into judgment, but has passed from death into life" (John 5:24). "Whoever lives and believes in Me shall never die [spiritually]" (John 11:26).

The Bible is God's Word. As such, it is without contradiction. We can be sure that if these and many other passages list faith in Christ as the sole condition of eternal life and freedom from condemnation, this is indeed true. There are no other conditions.

What Is Faith in Christ?

Let's begin by considering what *faith* is. Once we determine that, we will consider what *faith in Christ* is.

• *Faith is the conviction that something is true.* We all exercise faith every day. For example, most of us believe that George Washington was the first President of the United States because we have recognized that the evidence is convincing.[6]

Do you believe that you exist? That is, are you *convinced* that you are alive? I once met a college student who doubted his existence and that of everything in the universe. I was tempted to pinch him to give him some tangible evidence! Most rational people are certain they exist, no doubt about it. The evidence is overwhelming.

Though long past her childbearing years, Abraham's wife

5

Sarah believed that she was going to have a son. God had said she would: "By faith Sarah herself also received strength to conceive seed, and she bore a child when she was past the age, *because she judged Him faithful who had promised"* (Hebrews 11:11, italics added). Ninety-year-old Sarah was positive that God would keep His promise, and would do what He said. Abraham too was *"fully convinced* that what [God] had promised He was also able to perform" (Romans 4:21, italics added). Faith is being convinced or persuaded (the KJV has "fully persuaded" here) of the truth of something—in this case, the promise that a son would be born to an elderly couple.[7]

The key to believing something is the proof in favor of it. Thus, despite popular opinion, faith is not really a choice. You don't "choose" to believe that George Washington was the first President, that you exist, that two plus two equals four, etc. Similarly, Sarah and Abraham didn't "choose" to believe that God would keep His promise to them regarding a son. When the evidence that something is true persuades people, they believe it. When they aren't persuaded, they don't believe it.

Let's say you were on a jury. After listening to all of the evidence, you concluded that the defendant was guilty. Could you *choose to believe* that he was innocent? Of course not. You could *vote* not to convict, but that would be acting dishonestly, contrary to what you believed. The only way you could move from belief to unbelief or the other way around is if you came to perceive the testimony differently.[8]

Doesn't this mean, then, that the evidence traps us? In a sense, yes. However, two people can look at the same evidence and draw different conclusions because they have different opinions on whether the evidence is trustworthy. We are guided by our perception of the evidence. We believe evidence that we perceive as true. We don't believe evidence that we perceive as false.

Therefore, faith is not a decision. It is the conviction that something is true. It is especially important that we understand this, for much confusion about the gospel has resulted from the mistaken idea that we can be convinced that the gospel is true and yet not be saved until we decide to believe it.

• *Faith in Christ is the conviction that He is the Guarantor of eternal life for every believer.* Faith in Christ is sometimes called *saving faith*, since the Bible teaches that all who believe in Him have eternal salvation. There are many things that Jesus promised. When the Bible speaks of "faith in Christ," it is talking about believing a specific promise that He made. Jesus explained that saving promise to His friend, Martha:

> Jesus said to her, "I am the resurrection and the life. He who believes in Me, though he may die, he shall live. And whoever lives and believes in Me shall never die. Do you believe this?" She said to Him, "Yes, Lord, I believe that You are the Christ, the Son of God, who is to come into the world."
> —John 11:25-27

"Do you believe this?" Jesus' question to Martha cuts to the heart of the gospel. While Jesus promised many things in the course of His ministry, this one promise is the key to gaining eternal salvation. Jesus is claiming to be "the resurrection and the life." Anyone who believes that has eternal life and will never die.

First, as "the resurrection," He guarantees, "He who believes in Me, though he may die, he shall live." That is, He insures bodily resurrection from the dead to all who believe in Him. Since we know from other Scriptures that both believers and unbelievers will be resurrected (Daniel 12:2; John 5:29; Acts 24:15), this must refer to the resurrection of the righteous, also called the first resurrection (Revelation 20:5-6). Jesus is promising that death will not keep a believer from bodily participation in His eternal kingdom. All believers will live eternally in glorified bodies in Jesus' kingdom.

Notice that this promise has no other conditions. Many add to what Jesus said and end up with this distorted gospel: "He who believes in Me and turns from His sins and perseveres in good works,

7

though he may die, he shall live." That is not what Jesus promised. A person who believes this altered message does not believe what Jesus said.

Second, as "the life," He certifies, "Whoever lives and believes in Me shall never die." This is another way of reinforcing what He has just said. In verse 25 He confirms that *physical* death cannot keep the believer from bodily participation in the eternal kingdom. In verse 26 Jesus affirms that no believer will ever experience *spiritual* death. As "the life," Jesus is the Guarantor of eternal life: "Whoever lives and believes in Me *shall never die.*" He guarantees the believer will never lose eternal life. All who believe in Him are secure forever.

Some say, "Yes, He is the Giver of eternal life; however, to be saved takes more than just believing. You must also commit your life to Him, turn from your sins, confess Him, obey Him, be baptized, etc., etc., etc." Once again, if a person is convinced that this distorted message is true, then he doesn't believe what Jesus is saying. Jesus made it clear that the *only* condition is being convinced that He guarantees eternal life to all who believe in Him. Add anything to that and you have a different gospel.

Martha believed Jesus' promise. In answer to the question, "Do you believe this?" she said, "Yes, Lord, I believe." She then went on to acknowledge Him as "the Christ, the Son of God, who is come into the world." She knew that Jesus was the Messiah and as such, He certainly fulfills His promise to give eternal life, life that is forever secure, to every believer (compare John 20:31). Martha understood that there were no strings attached. She knew that she had eternal life and that she would never lose it because Jesus, as the Son of God, was trustworthy.

The apostle Paul sums up what Martha, and every Christian, believes when they come to faith in Christ: "However, for this reason I obtained mercy, that in me first Jesus Christ might show all longsuffering, as a pattern to those who are going to believe on Him for everlasting life" (1 Timothy 1:16). In order to be saved, we must believe on Jesus *for everlasting life*. On the basis of His death and resurrection, He always fulfills His guarantee to give everlasting life to all who believe in Him for it.

Martha did not *decide* to believe in Jesus for eternal life. She was convinced of the truth of what Jesus said and hence she believed in Him in the biblical sense.

• *Faith in Christ does not erase every problem.* It greatly saddens me when I hear some evangelists tell the unsaved to believe in Jesus for benefits other than eternal life. "Believe in Jesus and He will heal your broken marriage." "Believe in Him and He will turn your finances around." "Become a Christian and all your depression will vanish." People who believe in Jesus for a better marriage, for financial prosperity, or for emotional well being, are not guaranteed eternal salvation.

Many today think they are saved because they went forward at some meeting and gave Jesus their life, believing in Him for something other than eternal life. While it is true that He can help us with all issues in life, that is not the promise of the gospel, and the help He gives is not necessarily the deliverance we want. He doesn't guarantee a happy marriage, good finances, or freedom from depression to every believer. There are many factors other than faith in Christ, which influence these things. However, the only condition of eternal life is faith in Christ!

What Saving Faith Is Not

It is sometimes helpful to consider what something is *not*. This is particularly true of saving faith. Contrary to popular understanding, none of the following are a part of or a synonym for saving faith: believing general Bible truth, promising to serve God, praying, walking an aisle, being sorry for your sins, turning from your sins, inviting Jesus into your heart, believing with a special kind of faith, doing good works, or having heart faith.

• *Believing general Bible truth.* You can believe many biblical concepts and still miss the one truth that is saving—the truth of the gospel. For example, you can attest to Jesus' deity, His virgin birth, and His bodily resurrection, and yet not believe Jesus' promise to give you eternal life freely if you just believe in Him for it. There is only one truth that will save: Jesus'guarantee that anyone who believes in Him for eternal life has it.

• *Promising to serve God.* Promises, promises! Almost every child who goes to a Christian camp makes some sort of commitment in front of a campfire. If all the young people who promised to become missionaries had done so, there would never be a lack of workers on any mission field in the world.[9] Many have vowed to serve God in the hope that their commitment would cause God to save them. Because it is possible to promise sincerely to serve God, and yet not be convinced that Jesus freely gives eternal life to all who just believe in Him, commitment isn't an absolute indicator of saving faith. (Many cult members are radically committed.) Pledges to serve God in hopes of gaining salvation actually become a stumbling block, for to be saved one must believe in Christ *alone* for eternal life, not Christ *plus commitment.*

• *Praying.* A very popular evangelistic technique today is to ask unbelievers to pray to become Christians. However, there is not one biblical example of anyone ever praying to be saved. Jesus never led anyone in a prayer of salvation, nor did any of the apostles or evangelists mentioned in the Bible. A person is saved by *believing in Christ* for eternal life, not by praying.[10]

• *Walking an aisle.* Asking unbelievers to come forward—to walk the aisle or come to the front of the auditorium—in order to be saved is another popular evangelistic practice without biblical precedent. A person may stand before others with complete sincerity and with a strong desire to be saved and yet return to his seat not having believed in Christ for eternal life. Coming forward will not save. Only believing in Christ will save.[11]

• *Being sorry for your sins.* A popular song of years past contained the phrase, "Cry me a river." You may indeed shed many tears, be extremely sorry for your sins, and yet not believe in Christ for eternal life. No amount of anguish over sin can open the way to heaven. Only believing in Christ alone can.

Recognition of one's sinfulness shows a person that he needs a Savior, and this acknowledgment may result in tears. But the presence or absence of tears is not the point. Nowhere does the Bible say that being sorry for your sins is a condition of eternal life. There is but one requirement: believing that Jesus is the Guarantor of eternal life to all who just believe in Him.

• *Turning from your sins.*[12] Can someone undergo radical changes in his or her life without believing the gospel? Of course. Often, for example, unbelieving alcoholics give up drinking. Moral reform is certainly possible. And it is a good thing to do in the sense that it is always best to follow God's blueprint for living, whether or not you are a Christian. Yet, moral reform will not save.

In fact, if people think that turning from sins is a condition of salvation, their faith in moral reform can actually *prohibit* them from being saved. To be saved, a person must believe that Jesus guarantees eternal life to all who believe in Him.

• *Inviting Jesus into your heart.* Another very common and unfortunate evangelistic appeal is telling people to invite Jesus into their hearts in order to be saved. The problem here is that they can invite Jesus into their hearts and yet not believe in Him for eternal life.[13]

Some individuals have invited Jesus into their hearts hundreds of times. Whenever they doubt the efficacy of what they did (with good reason), they just repeat the invitation, thinking: *Maybe I didn't invite Him in sincerely enough the last time.*[14] Jesus enters the lives of people the moment they believe in Him for eternal life.

• *Believing with a special kind of faith.* Some pastors today teach that saving faith is different than everyday faith.[15] However,

11

this is just not true. All faith is the conviction of the truth of some proposition. What makes saving faith *saving* is not the uniqueness of the faith, but its object. Saving faith results instantly in eternal salvation because it believes in the right object: the guarantee of life made by Jesus Christ to every believer.

• *Doing good works.* Saving faith should not be confused with doing good works. In their zeal to call people to godliness, some pastors and theologians today mingle the two.[16]

A desire for godliness is admirable. However, it is simply not true that in order to believe in Christ for eternal life you must also do good works and forsake bad works. Works have no place in saving faith. Saving faith is based solely on what the Lord Jesus has already done and promises to do for us. It is not based even in part on what we might do for Him.

The thief on the cross was a terrible sinner who was at death's door. He had only hours left to live. He couldn't offer Jesus any good works, any service, any moral reform. He could only believe in Him, and that he did. Even though Jesus' own disciples were disheartened and had lost faith in His return to set up the kingdom, the thief boldly said, "Lord, remember me when You come into Your kingdom" (Luke 23:42). Jesus' response shows the freeness of the gospel for all who believe in Him: "Assuredly, I say to you, today you will be with Me in Paradise" (Luke 23:43).

Head Faith, Heart Faith, and Mind Games

How do you convince someone that saving faith is not just faith in the gospel, that it includes commitment, turning from sins, perseverance in obedience, and the like? Since there is no verse in Scripture that identifies saving faith as anything other than believing the gospel, you'd have a hard time proving your view from the Bible. However, there is an easier way.

The best way to sell the idea that saving faith includes the kitchen sink is through the use of pejorative terms like *intellectual faith* or *head faith*. Some preachers and teachers tell people that just believing the facts of the gospel is *intellectual faith* or *head faith*. Then they espouse the idea that the Bible teaches that the faith that truly saves is *heart faith*.[17]

Heart faith can include almost anything. However, heart faith raises potential problems. *How much* commitment, turning from sins, obedience, and the like is enough? The biblical evidence demonstrates that this supposed distinction between head faith and heart faith is really a mind game.

First, the Scriptures never refer to the *head* as the source of thinking and feeling. In addition, the word *head* is never associated with faith in the Bible.[18]

Second, of the two remaining words, *heart* and *mind*, the Scriptures often use them interchangeably.[19] Both refer to the inner self where one thinks and believes[20] and feels.

Third, the mind is not viewed as being inferior to the heart in Scripture. In one of the most famous verses on sanctification in the Bible, Paul exhorted the believers in Rome, "Be transformed by the renewing of your *mind*" (Romans 12:2). Similarly, he exhorted the Ephesian believers, "Be renewed in the spirit of your *mind*" (Ephesians 4:23). Paul spoke to the Corinthian believers of having "the *mind* of Christ" (1 Corinthians 2:16). Luke said that the Lord "opened [the disciples'] understanding [literally *mind* in Greek], that they might comprehend the Scriptures," that is, the Old Testament Scriptures, concerning His resurrection (Luke 24:45).

Fourth, while the words *believe* and *faith* occur approximately 450 times in the Bible, only a few passages specify where belief takes place.[21] They speak of believing as though the reader of Scripture knows what that means and where it occurs.

Believing in Christ is the sole condition of eternal life. There is no such thing as special types of faith called *heart faith* and *head faith*. Saving faith doesn't include commitment, obedience, or turning from sins. It is merely the conviction that Jesus is speaking

13

the truth when He says, "He who believes in Me has everlasting life" (John 6:47).

There Is No Additional Step

Many well-meaning people unintentionally introduce a lot of confusion when they say something like this, "Do you believe that Jesus, by His death and resurrection, freely gives eternal life to all who believe in Him? Great! Now would you like to *trust* Him?"

This two-step approach to saving faith is confusing. How does a person who already believes something choose to trust it? Say, for example, that you believe that Jesus is God. Do you also need to choose to *trust* His deity in order to really believe it? Of course not. You believe in Jesus' deity if the evidence convinces you that He is indeed the Second Person of the Trinity. What you believe, you trust to be true.

The same is true with the gospel. If you believe it, you are saved. Jesus guarantees it.

Sometimes this supposed distinction is illustrated by means of a chair and belief in its ability to hold one up. The illustration goes as follows.

"Do you believe that this chair will hold you up if you sit in it?"

"Yes, I believe it will."

"Okay, then have a seat."

"No, I won't do that."

"Then you don't *really believe* the chair will hold you up, for to truly believe it, you must trust that it will hold you up. And you only trust it when you take a seat."

The illustration is patently false. Only a masochist would sit in a chair he didn't "really believe" would hold him up. You sit in a chair *because* you already believe it is dependable, not *in order to* believe it is.

The only condition of eternal life is belief in Him for it. Once you do that, you have eternal life. There is no additional step involved.

14

Yes, Believing the Gospel Is Enough!

Saving faith means believing the gospel, believing in Christ alone for eternal life. Nothing else is saving faith. Not only is believing the gospel enough, but it is the only way to salvation. Jesus guarantees eternal life to all who believe in Him for it. Do you believe this?

CHAPTER 2

THE ORIGINAL NIC AT NITE
John 3:16

YOU MAY HAVE memorized John 3:16 as a child. It has only twenty-five words, but is one of the most beautiful sentences in the English language.

> For God so loved the world that He gave His only
> begotten Son, that whoever believes in Him should
> not perish but have everlasting life.

This wonderfully simple verse of good news tells how sinful people can gain a relationship with God that is secure for eternity. Simple though it may be, however, many fail to grasp its meaning. While working on my Master's thesis, I ran across an article in which an author cited a pastor who said he never preached on John 3:16 because it was such a difficult verse! [1] John 3:16 *is* a difficult verse if you think, as that pastor did, that it takes more than faith in Christ to gain eternal life.

Nicodemus was a ruler of the Jews (John 3:1), a member of the Sanhedrin, which was somewhat of a cross between our Senate and Supreme Court. He came to Jesus by night—the original Nic at nite. Every time the apostle John mentioned Nicodemus, he reminded the reader that he came to Jesus by night (John 3:2; 7:50; 19:39).

In his Gospel, John loves to stress opposites like love and hate, life and death, light and darkness, night and day, belief and unbelief. For John, night and darkness often have ominous overtones as the realm of evil where people hide their evil deeds. While his coming to Jesus was not an evil deed, Nicodemus was cloaking his inquiry with the dark of night. He didn't want his fellow rulers to know that he was seeking an audience with Jesus for fear of their negative reaction. Nicodemus knew that he might face expulsion from the Sanhedrin as a result of this visit (John 12:42-43). He came to Jesus in spite of the danger because he wanted to know more.

Nicodemus was a learned man. Jesus refers to him not merely as "a teacher," but as "the teacher of Israel" (John 3:10). He was the Albert Einstein of theology in his day, yet he came to Jesus seeking a primer on salvation.

Nicodemus was open to the truth. That is a wonderful attitude to have. So many people are close-minded, unwilling to be influenced. "Don't confuse me with the facts," they say.

In spite of the attitude of his fellow rulers, Nicodemus came to Jesus and said, "Rabbi, we know that You are a teacher come from God; for no one can do these signs that You do unless God is with Him" (John 3:2). The use of the first person plural, *we*, by Nicodemus was hyperbole, since most of the rulers did not share that view.

Born Again

Before Nicodemus could even voice a question, Jesus responded, "Most assuredly, I say to you, unless one is born again, he cannot see the kingdom of God" (John 3:3). In His wisdom Jesus realized that Nicodemus wanted to know what he needed to do to enter the kingdom of God.

The concept of being born again was new to Nicodemus: "How can a man be born when he is old? Can he enter a second time into his mother's womb and be born?" (John 3:4). Thinking of a second physical birth, this brilliant man asked a ridiculous question— because he didn't have a clue what Jesus was talking about.

Jesus expanded on His earlier statement, "Unless one is born of water and the Spirit, he cannot enter the kingdom of God. That which is born of the flesh is flesh, and that which is born of the Spirit is spirit" (John 3:5-6). The new birth of which Jesus spoke was spiritual. Physical birth is "of water." Spiritual birth is "of the Spirit."

Birth is a beginning of life. Spiritual birth is thus the start of spiritual life. All people begin this life alive physically, yet dead spiritually. Until a person experiences spiritual birth, regeneration, he is cut off from God's life and kingdom. Once a person is born again, he is secure forever since he has *eternal* life, which is God's kind of life.

Nicodemus didn't get this. Since he was a teacher, he knew that the only truly dumb question is the one left unasked. Therefore, he unashamedly revealed his lack of understanding, "How can these things be?" (John 3:9).

We would all do well to learn from Nicodemus. He responded to what he had heard by seeking more information. When he received that information and didn't understand it, he asked for clarification. None of us would ever seek God if left purely to our own initiative (Romans 3:11); but since God is seeking each and every one of us, we are free to respond to the light God gives us.

Jesus began His final response to Nicodemus with mild rebuke, "Are you the teacher of Israel, and do not know these things?" (John 3:10). The Old Testament offered sufficient background so that all the rulers of Israel, and all who diligently studied the Scriptures, should have understood about the new birth. However, Nicodemus, like his contemporaries, was caught up in "tradition." Rather than asking God to show them what the Old Testament meant, they read it through the lens of rabbinical thought. They accepted traditional views without challenging them in light of prayer and meditation upon the Word of God.

The rabbis taught that good Jews, and also good proselytes, would get into the kingdom (Luke 18:9-12). However, if a Jew soiled his life with major sin, he would forfeit the right to the kingdom. Harlots and tax collectors were held up as examples of those who would never make it.

There really is nothing new under the sun. The notion of gaining salvation by works has been with us since the beginning. All religions, including Judaism and Christianity, are filled with people who believe that if their good deeds outweigh their bad, they will make it to heaven.

The Serpent in the Wilderness

Until this point in the interview, Jesus had not stated the condition for the new birth. He now turned to that vital truth:

> And as Moses lifted up the serpent in the wilderness, even so must the Son of Man be lifted up, that whoever believes in Him should not perish but have eternal life. For God so loved the world that He gave His only begotten Son, that whoever believes in Him should not perish but have everlasting life. For God did not send His Son into the world to condemn the world, but that the world through Him might be saved. He who believes in Him is not condemned; but he who does not believe is condemned already, because he has not believed in the name of the only begotten Son of God.
>
> —John 3:14-18

Jesus began with an Old Testament incident which Nicodemus would have known very well, the lifting up of a bronze serpent in the wilderness to save the nation from a deadly plague (Numbers 21:4-9). This bronze serpent on a wooden pole is the source of the American Medical Society's symbol, an uplifted serpent that healed all who looked upon it.

The bronze serpent was a *type*, that is, a divinely intended picture, of Christ. God told Moses to lift up the bronze serpent on the pole specifically to foreshadow the death of the Messiah on the cross for the spiritual healing of all who would look to Him in faith. Jesus expected that Nicodemus, and all students of the Old Testament, would understand this.

The condition is simple: believe in Jesus, the Son of Man: "Whoever believes in Him should not perish but have eternal life" (John 3:15).[2]

In John 3:16 Jesus summarized the lesson of the bronze serpent. Salvation begins with God's love: *For God so loved the world.* That love motivated Him to give His Son, the Lord Jesus, to die on the cross in our place: *that He gave His only begotten Son*. The intended result is that all might believe in Him for eternal life: *that whoever believes in Him should not perish, but have everlasting life*. Eternal life does not begin at death. It begins at the point of faith! The believer has already passed from death into life (John 5:24). And, since that life is everlasting, it never ends.

Jesus paid the complete penalty for our sins by His death on the cross. It made us *savable*. Yet, it doesn't automatically result in salvation. To *actually* be saved, to receive eternal life, we must "believe in Him."

Saving faith is the conviction that "whoever believes in Him should not perish but have everlasting life" (John 3:16), and that "he who believes in Him is not condemned" (3:18). Jesus promises to give eternal life to all who merely believe in Him for it.

Some stumble over what it means to "believe in Him." They realize that there are multitudes who believe that He was a good man, yet give no evidence of being children of God. As we saw in chapter 1, to believe in Jesus is not merely to acknowledge that He was a good man, or even that He is God and died on the cross for us. It is to accept that He is the Guarantor of eternal life to all who come to Him (John 11:25-27; 20:30-31).

The gospel simply stated is this: by virtue of His death, burial, and resurrection, Jesus Christ gives eternal life to anyone who just believes in Him for it. If you are convinced of this, you have believed the gospel. This message is hard for people to believe because it seems too simple. How could it be so uncomplicated? How could so many people be so wrong? What about turning from sins, commitment of life, and doing good works?

Whether it seems too simple or not, that is the gospel. No matter how many people reject it, that is the gospel. Though it doesn't include turning from sins, commitment of life, and doing good works, that is the gospel. Whether that is the way we would have done it or not, that is the gospel. God is God and He is perfectly within His rights to determine what we must do to escape eternal condemnation and to have eternal life.

John doesn't tell us how Nicodemus responded. In light of the openness he displayed to this point in the dialogue, it is extremely likely that Nicodemus was born again that very night. When John next tells us of Nicodemus, he is standing up for Jesus before his colleagues in the Sanhedrin (John 7:48-52). At that time Nicodemus implies that he believes in Jesus, yet he is still unwilling to come completely out in the light. It isn't until the death of Jesus that he comes forward to claim the body for burial, along with Joseph of Arimathea, a fellow ruler of Israel and another secret disciple of Jesus (John 19:38-39).

The reason why so many people stumble over the simplicity of John 3:16 is that it contradicts their traditions—the teachings of their church or denomination.

Jesus has the answer, and is the answer, to the question of what is required. If we are open, the Spirit of God will show us that there is but one condition: believing in Jesus for eternal life.

I have found a question, one popularized by Pastor James Kennedy, to be helpful in getting people to reflect on why they think they should go to heaven. It goes like this: "If you were to die tonight and stand before God and He asked, 'Why should I let you into My heaven?' what would you say?" I have asked that question to scores of people. Far and away most people point to their good deeds and to the effort they are putting in. Very few say that whoever believes in Jesus will not perish but has everlasting life. Their tradition causes them to stumble over the simple beauty of the good news.

Nicodemus learned the good news that night two thousand years ago. Jesus guarantees eternal life to all who believe in Him. Nothing else is added. Faith is the sole condition. If you add any other condition, you don't believe Jesus' guarantee. A friend in Florida, Pastor Tim Kelley, likes to tell his congregation, "There's no bill in the mail." That's right. Eternal life is free, free to all who merely believe in Jesus for it. There's nothing left for us to pay because the Lord Jesus paid it all when He died on the cross in our place.

While knowing you are secure forever won't eliminate all of life's problems, it will solve the biggest one. What joy and peace there is in knowing that you will spend eternity with God in His kingdom! And all it takes is to believe what Jesus said. It's really that simple.

"For God so loved the world that He gave His only begotten Son, that whoever believes in Him should not perish but have everlasting life" (John 3:16). *Whoever* includes everyone. Only believe in Jesus for eternal life and you will have it, for He is completely trustworthy. He does what He promises.

CHAPTER 3

FAITH ON THE ROCKS
Luke 8:11-13

L INDA WAS DRIVING down the freeway with her radio tuned to a Christian station. She heard the gospel clearly proclaimed and joyfully received the message, believing in Christ for eternal life. Tragically, one minute later a drunk driver crossed the median and hit her. She died instantly.

Most would agree that Linda went to heaven, since she had believed in Christ. Eternal life is granted to a person *at the very moment of faith*. It isn't bestowed after you have believed for a certain length of time. When you place your faith in Christ for eternal life, you are born again right then.

What if instead of dying in that car accident, Linda had been badly hurt and subsequently became very depressed? Eventually, she even began to doubt that Christianity was true. How could it be true, when God had let this happen to her? If she had died in this state of unbelief and bitterness, where would she go—to heaven or hell?

Some say that under those conditions (since she stopped believing in Christ) she would go to hell. Yet, this is odd, since Linda would have gone to heaven if she had died in that crash. Did surviving the crash turn out to be an eternal disaster for her? If she lived long enough for her faith to falter, was she in danger of failing to make it to heaven?[1]

Have you ever experienced hardship that shook your faith? Even if you haven't, you probably realize this as a possibility. None of us can be sure that our experience of faith will remain intact until we go to be with the Lord. Thus, it is vital that we know what the Bible declares about believers whose faith falters.

Jesus' Parable of the Sower is the perfect place to consider the issue of faith on the rocks.

The Sower, the Seed, and the Soil

.In the Parable of the Sower, Jesus told of a man who sowed seed in his field. Some of the seed fell on the footpaths between the rows. It never germinated because the birds ate it.

Of the seed sown in the rows, some fell on very shallow soil with a layer of rock only inches below the surface. Some of this seed germinated and began to grow. However, because it had an insufficient root system, the growth was stunted, and the plants withered away (Luke 8:6).

Some of the seed fell in soil filled with weeds. The seed germinated and began to grow. However, the weeds grew even faster and stunted the growth of the plants. They, too, did not come to maturity.

Finally, some of the seed fell in good soil with no rocks or weeds. The seed germinated, grew to maturity, and brought forth a good crop.

When Jesus explained the parable, He indicated that the seed falling on rocky soil represented those who "believe for a while and in time of temptation fall away." Note Jesus' explanation of the meaning of the parable in regard to the first two soils:

> "...The seed is the word of God. Those by the way-side are the ones who hear; then the devil comes and takes away the word out of their hearts, lest they should believe and be saved. But the ones on the rock are those who, when they hear, receive the word with joy; and these have no root, who believe for a while and in time of temptation fall away."
>
> —Luke 8:11-13

The seed sown by the wayside represents those who hear the gospel but don't believe it and hence remain unsaved. The seed sown on the rocky soil represents those who hear the gospel and believe it, yet only for a time. Eventually they fall away. That heaven is the spiritual destiny of those who fall away is clear when we carefully consider Jesus' words.

Even *Temporary* Faith Results in *Eternal* Salvation

The question raised by this passage is whether a true believer would ever stop believing. Many Bible teachers mistakenly reason that since the faith that is mentioned in Luke 8:13 does not endure, it is not genuine. John Martin, for example, writes:

> The second group are those who listen and rejoice but then do not stick with the truth of the message for they have no root (verse 13). The fact that they believe for a while but...fall away means that they only accept the facts of the Word mentally and then reject it when "the going gets rough." It does not mean that they lose their salvation, for they had none to lose.[2]

According to this view, a person proves that he was never really saved in the first place if he stops believing in Christ.

There are many problems, however, with this reasoning. It is contradicted by the words of Jesus in this very passage! In the first place, the Lord Jesus clearly said that the people represented by the rocky soil *believed*. How can we conclude that they didn't believe, when Jesus said that they did? To say that they believed "mentally" is to skirt the clear meaning of the text.

What these people believed is nothing other than the saving message, the gospel. When Jesus said that the devil takes away the word "lest they should believe *and be saved*" (verse 12), He was talking about *saving faith*. He said that whoever believes in Him is saved the very moment he believes. There is no minimum time requirement on saving faith.[3] Thus, when Jesus said that these rocky-soil people believed, we have no choice but to conclude that they were saved, since according to verse 12 all who believe are saved.

In the second place, in verse 13 the Lord indicated that the rocky-soil people *received the word*. Luke used the same expression[4] twice in Acts to refer to the growth of the church: "Now when the apostles who were at Jerusalem heard that Samaria had *received the word* of God, they sent Peter and John to them" (Acts 8:14). "Now the apostles and brethren who were in Judea heard that the Gentiles had also *received the word* of God" (Acts 11:1). Those who *receive the word* are born again.

In the third place, Jesus said that the seed sown on the rocky soil *sprang up:* "Some fell on rock; and as soon as it sprang up, it withered away because it lacked moisture" (Luke 8:6). Springing up refers to initial growth. Only a seed that has germinated can spring up. Germination and growth are proof that life has begun.

The people represented by the rocky soil exercised saving faith. Whether they believed for a second or for a century, they were born again at the very moment they believed in Christ for everlasting life.

In the fourth place, when Jesus said that "the devil comes and takes away the word out of their hearts, *lest they should believe and be saved*" (verse 12), He was talking about *eternal salvation*. He wasn't talking about some type of temporary salvation that could be lost.[5] He was speaking of a *fait accompli.* Satan wouldn't have such a sense of urgency if he could snatch the word away later and still keep people from heaven. Once the word germinates, eternal life has begun, and since it is eternal, nothing—not even Satan—can destroy . that life.

Believers are held by the promise of God, not by their own faithfulness or by the endurance of their faith. If Satan can't stop someone from believing the gospel, he loses the battle for that soul. Eternal salvation occurs the moment that a person believes the promise of the gospel. Thus it cannot and does not depend on continuing to believe the gospel.

Called to Be Productive

Clearly the main point of this parable is that every believer in Christ is called to be productive. We should give attention to the quality of the "soil" in which our lives are growing. That soil must be cultivated, fertilized, weeded, and watered. We do this by reading, studying, and meditating on the Bible, praying, having fellowship with other believers, and developing a spiritual mind-set and worldview.

However, this parable also shows that our eternal salvation is not dependent on *our* faithfulness. It is rooted in *God's* faithfulness. The moment we believe, we are saved forever. Our faith may fail, but God will never turn His back on His promise to us: "If we are faithless, He remains faithful; He cannot deny Himself" (2 Timothy 2:13).

What *is* at stake are our eternal *rewards*: "If we endure, we shall also reign with Him" (2 Timothy 2:12). Enduring in our confession of faith in Christ[6] until the end of our lives is the condition for ruling with Christ and for having the other rewards which only persevering saints shall receive.[7]

Just as ships sometimes crash into rocks near the coastline, so the faith of some Christians fractures against the rocks of temptation and hardship that line the shores of their lives. Not all believers successfully navigate their way through this life. Yet God guarantees all believers eternal life, even those who suffer shipwreck concerning the faith (1 Timothy 1:19).[8] There is no time requirement on saving faith. At the moment of faith the believer receives eternal life once and for all—whether he dies shortly thereafter or whether he lives for 100 more years. Even if a person believes only for a while, he still has eternal life.

You don't need to wait until you die to discover your eternal destination. Jesus gives eternal life to all who believe in Him for it. And He gives this gift at the very moment of faith.

CHAPTER 4

WILL THE REAL BELIEVER PLEASE STAND UP?
John 12:42-43

I N THE OLD television show "To Tell the Truth," celebrity panelists would quiz three contestants who all professed to be the same renowned person (an inventor, a son or daughter of a famous individual, etc.). One of the three individuals really was this person. The panelists would ask the contestants questions to determine which one really was who he or she professed to be.

Many people think that faith in Christ is similar. There are lots of professors, they say, but few are the real thing.[1] They believe that a key (or *the* key) to discerning the true from the false is whether a person regularly confesses his faith in the Lord Jesus both in word and deed, regardless of the persecution which he must endure for doing this.

Have you ever heard a pastor or evangelist say that in order to be saved you need to come forward and publicly confess Christ? "The buses will wait" has become part of the gospel message for some evangelists! They view walking the aisle as the start of a life of confessing Christ. However, adherents to this belief have a problem when they come to a passage such as this:

> Nevertheless even among the rulers many believed in Him, but because of the Pharisees they did not confess Him, lest they should be put out of the synagogue; for they loved the praise of men more than the praise of God.
>
> —John 12:42-43

On the one hand, they see that inspired Scripture says that these rulers "believed in Him." Based on John 3:16, *whoever* does that has everlasting life and shall not perish. This leads them to conclude that there were genuine believers even among the rulers of Israel.

On the other hand, they see that these believers were not confessing Christ because of their fear of persecution. If all true believers confess Christ, these professing believers couldn't be genuine. This is a sticky problem. Were these rulers true believers or not?

There are three options regarding believers who fail to confess Him: 1) they lose their salvation; 2) they prove that they didn't *really* believe in the first place; or, 3) they remain eternally secure, since believing in Christ is the only condition of salvation.

The first option is impossible. Eternal life cannot be lost. If it could, it would not be *eternal* life.[2]

The second option is advanced by a number of Reformed pastors and theologians. For example, D. A. Carson, a seminary professor and Bible scholar, writes:

> The leaders themselves (same word as in 3:1) seem at this point to fit the pattern of inadequate, irresolute, even spurious faith that John repeatedly describes in this Gospel (e.g., 2:23-25; 6:60; 8:30ff.). Nicodemus was willing to stand up for Jesus in the Sanhedrin (7:50-52); he and Joseph of Arimathea publicly identified themselves with Jesus' cause by providing decent burial for him. Doubtless there were other leaders, less courageous even than this, who maintained some distant attachment to Jesus, who believed in Him in some sense, of whose faith the Pharisees knew nothing (7:48). Sadly, their faith was still so weak that they would not take any step that would threaten their position in the synagogue; *they loved praise from men more than praise from God,* and therefore fell under Jesus' searing indictment (5:44), here repeated by the Evangelist (cf. Mt. 6:1-21; Rom. 2:29). They still knew nothing of the powerful new birth that could make them children of God and enable them to enter the messianic kingdom (3:3, 5; 1:12, 13; cf. 12:26).[3]

Many Believed in Him

Let's evaluate this second position. Is it true that the faith of the believers of John 12:42-43 was "inadequate, irresolute, even spurious"?[4] Scripture tells us that these rulers believed in Christ. No qualifying word or phrase is employed. John doesn't indicate that they "believed in Him *in a sense.*" He makes a direct and unequivocal statement: They believed in Him.

The same expression is used in the preceding paragraph. Writing about the vast majority of Israel in Jesus' day, John says, "But although He had done so many signs before them, *they did not believe in Him*" (verse 37). This explains the first word in verse 42, *nevertheless.* That is a contrast word. Most of the nation did not believe in Him. "*Nevertheless* even among the rulers *many believed in Him.*"

The contrast between the unbelievers of verse 37 and the believers of verse 42 reminds us of the pinnacle of the prologue of John's Gospel, "He came to His own, and His own did not receive Him. But as many as received Him, to them He gave the right to become children of God, to those who believe in His name" (John 1:11-12). Although the nation was filled with unbelievers, many of its leaders were believers, even though they were secret ones.

It is possible, of course, to believe facts about Christ and yet not be saved. If John had said that many of the rulers "believed that Jesus was a good man" or "believed that He was from God," we wouldn't know if they were saved.

However, John said that many of the rulers "believed in Him" (*pisteuō eis auton*). In John's Gospel, the expression *pisteuō eis auton* is used only to refer to those who believed savingly (see John 2:11; 3:16, 18; 4:39; 6:29, 40; 7:31, 39; 11:45).[5] Since the rulers "believed in Him," then they must have received eternal life just as Jesus promised in John 3:16[6] and elsewhere in the Fourth Gospel.

John even gave two specific examples of rulers who believed in Jesus, yet were not confessing Him. Immediately after Jesus died on the cross, Joseph of Arimathea came to Pilate and asked him for the body of Jesus so that he might give Him a proper burial before Passover began. John indicates that Joseph was "*a disciple of Jesus, but secretly, for fear of the Jews*" (John 19:38, italics added).[7] Also along was another member of the Sanhedrin, Nicodemus. Referring to the private conversation between Nicodemus and Jesus (John ?:1ff.), John now wrote, "And Nicodemus, who at first came to Jesus by night, also came..." (John 19:39).[8]

The notion that John was speaking of some special kind of faith in Christ, which was less than saving, is contradicted by the text. While some people might falsely profess to believe in Christ,[9] Scripture never makes a false profession!

But They Did Not Confess Him

The third view, that true believers are eternally secure, whether they confess Christ or not, is the simplest and most obvious understanding of the text. After all, John told us that many of the rulers "believed in Him" and that "they did not confess Him." The obvious conclusion is that it is possible to believe in Christ and yet not confess Him. In fact, to suggest any other option is to distort the plain sense of the words.

Nowhere in John's Gospel, or anywhere else in the Bible,[10] is confessing Christ given as a requirement of eternal salvation. According to John's Gospel there is but one condition of eternal life: believing in Christ and Him alone for it (see John 1:12; 3:16; 5:24; 6:47; 11:25-27; 20:30-31).

John clearly shows that eternal life is a completely free gift. In John 4:10 he cites Jesus' claim that eternal life is "the gift of God." John speaks of the same idea also in Revelation 22:17: "Let him who thirsts come. Whoever desires, let him take the water of life *freely*" (emphasis added).

If a person has to confess Christ in order to have eternal life, then faith is not the sole condition of eternal salvation, and salvation is not really a gift. It does not come to us simply by grace through faith (Ephesians 2:8). And thus Paul was wrong, salvation really is of works and there is room for boasting (contra Ephesians 2:9).

The good news collapses if any condition other than child-like faith is added to it. Yes, this does leave room for failure in the Christian life. Believers may abuse grace. However, the gospel of grace does not need our help, and we dare not change the gospel in a well-intentioned effort to make it impossible for anyone to abuse grace. God is perfectly willing and able to discipline disobedient believers.

For They Loved the Praise of Men
More Than the Praise of God

Sadly, these believing rulers were more concerned with their social standing than with God's praise. Some today have no room in their theology for Christians like this. John, however, did.[11] These verses are a challenge for all believers to confess their faith in Christ, regardless of the cost. God's praise is much more important than man's, and His rewards are far more lasting.

Every Christian will one day appear before the Judgment Seat of Christ (2 Corinthians 5:9-10), where our works will be evaluated and we will be recompensed. Some believers will be praised and some will be rebuked (see Luke 19:11-26; 1 Corinthians 3:10-15; 1 John 2:28). Those believers who have confessed Christ in word and deed will be praised (see Matthew 10:32-33; 2 Timothy 2:12).

Wouldn't you love to have your epitaph read, "This person loved the praise of God more than the praise of men"? That should be our aim in life (2 Corinthians 5:9).

Will the Real Believer Please Stand Up?

Since the apostle John was not constrained by some modern theological construct, he was free to write about believers who did not confess Christ, since they valued the praise of men more than the

35

praise of God. While that doesn't fit some forms of theology, it does fit the theology of the Fourth Gospel and of the New Testament as a whole (Galatians 2:11-21; 2 Timothy 2:12-13). That is the theology of the cross. The sole condition of eternal salvation is to believe the Lord Jesus for it.

Confessing Christ is both a wonderful privilege and an awesome responsibility. All Christians are ambassadors for Christ (2 Corinthians 5:20). How well we do in our role as His representatives is determined by how well we heed the warning in John 12:42-43. If we love the Lord Jesus and desire His praise, then we will confess Him in word and in deed.

Don't be a secret disciple. Be a beacon for the grace of God and someday you will hear the Lord Jesus say to you, "Well done, good and faithful servant."[12]

CHAPTER 5

FREE AT LAST!
John 8:30-32

OWARD THE END of my doctoral work at Dallas Seminary, after I had completed my course work, I faced the dreaded *written exams*. Like all doctoral students at DTS, I was required to take six different three-hour written examinations within two weeks. The tests for doctoral students in the New Testament department covered Greek grammar, translation, exegesis in the Gospels, exegesis in Paul's epistles, exegesis in the rest of the New Testament, and the history of New Testament interpretation.

One of my questions on the exam covering the Gospels concerned John 8:30-32:

> As He spoke these words, many believed in Him.
> Then Jesus said to those Jews who believed Him,
> "If you abide in My word, you are My disciples
> indeed. And you shall know the truth, and the truth
> shall make you free."

The following is my recollection of that question:

> The expression *pisteuō eis auton* is used by John
> to refer to saving faith in passages like John 3:16-
> 18, 36, and 6:47. Thus we might be inclined to think
> that when John uses the same expression in 8:30,
> he was referring to true believers who had ever-
> lasting life. However, in the verses which follow,
> Jesus came into conflict with the audience and said,
> "You are of your father the devil" (John 8:44) and
> "You do not believe Me" (John 8:45). This would
> lead us to conclude that these weren't true
> believers and that they didn't have everlasting life.
> Which is it? Were these true believers or not?
> Defend your answer.

One way to interpret John 8:30-32 is that those mentioned believed in Christ, but not with the right kind of faith. I call this understanding of the passage the False Professor view. Let's begin by seeing why that view is inconsistent with the context.

Inspired Scripture Says These Aren't False Professors

Ed Sullivan used to start his variety shows with the line, "Tonight we have a *really big show* for you." Some people view saving faith that way. They believe there is standard everyday faith and then there is saving faith. Saving faith is *really big faith*. It is persevering and obedient.

Many pastors and theologians suggest that the belief mentioned here by John is not saving faith. However, this is impossible for two reasons. In the first place, saving faith is not some special kind of faith. What makes saving faith saving is its object, not the faith itself. The object of saving faith is Jesus Christ as the Guarantor of eternal life to everyone who just believes in Him. Anyone who believes that has eternal life, whether or not they persevere.

In the second place, if inspired Scripture tells us that someone has exercised saving faith, we are bound to agree with that assessment. And that is exactly the case here: "As He spoke these words, many believed in Him" (John 8:30).

But why, then, did Jesus call His listeners "children of the devil"?

Jesus Called the Unbelievers in the Crowd "Children of the Devil"

A heated exchange between Jesus and the crowd (John 8:33-43) gave rise to His searing indictment, "You are of your father the devil" (verse 44). What a charge to be leveled against someone!

While we might imagine that He was merely indicating that their words truly came from Satan, as when He rebuked Peter saying, "Get behind Me, Satan!" (Matthew 16:23), Jesus was saying more than that here. He was saying that these people had Satan as their spiritual father, that they were unsaved. Twice Jesus declared, "You do not believe Me" (John 8:45-46). Jesus' antagonists in verses 33 and following were clearly *not* believers. However, this in no way intimates that the people He spoke to in verses 30 to 32 were false professors. Actually, it suggests the opposite.

In verses 30 and 31 John twice indicated that some of the Jews in the crowd believed in Christ. In contrast, twice in verses 45 and 46, Jesus told some gathered there that they did *not* believe Him. How do we harmonize these facts? The obvious solution is that the group referred to in verses 30 to 32 was different from the one referred to in verses 33 and following.

Jesus was speaking to a large crowd made up primarily of Jews who rejected Him and His message (see John 8:3, 13, 21-22, 37, 40, 44-47, 48, 52, 59). Verses 30 to 32 are a digression from the main flow of the chapter. In the midst of a sea of people who rejected Jesus was a small pool of people who came to believe in Him.

To illustrate this, picture a presidential candidate in New Hampshire campaigning for his party's nomination. During a speech before a rather large crowd in an outdoor meeting, he spots a small group of people wearing T-shirts and carrying placards that display pro-life slogans. Being strongly pro-life himself, the candidate turns to this group and encourages them to remain true to the cause. Suddenly some pro-choice advocates in the larger audience begin to challenge him. A heated verbal exchange ensues during which the candidate chides them for their pro-choice stand.

Would anyone recounting this event later conclude that the pro-life group at the rally was not really pro-life at all? Of course not.

Because of the care taken in audience selection, politicians almost never face a crowd that is largely adversarial. However, Jesus wasn't a candidate running for office or looking for votes. The Lord was never intimidated by speaking before a crowd comprised largely of those who vigorously opposed Him and even sought His death (e.g., John 5:16; 8:59).

But two other questions yet remain about verses 30 through 32. The first question concerns the relationship between eternal salvation and discipleship.

It Takes More than Saving Faith
to Be a Disciple of the Lord Jesus

Jesus invited the new believers of John 8:30 to follow Him in discipleship: "Then Jesus said to those Jews who believed Him, 'If you abide in My word, you are My disciples indeed'" (John 8:31). Some feel that this is additional evidence that the believers of verse 30 were not yet true believers. After all, if all true believers are Jesus' disciples and these believers are not yet His disciples, then they must not be true believers, right?

Wrong! The premise is absolutely wrong and this very passage proves it. More than belief in Jesus is required to be His disciple. Jesus said so here.

Believing in Christ for eternal life occurs at a point in time and results in instantaneous and irreversible spiritual life. Being a disciple is an ongoing experience and is conditioned on abiding in Jesus' word (studying it, meditating on it, and applying it).

To read these verses in such a way that implies one is not saved until he is abiding in Christ's teachings is to tragically misunderstand and garble the gospel.

If a believer doesn't abide in the teachings of Christ, then he is not truly following Christ—no matter how religious he may seem. Though he has eternal life, he isn't living as he should.

It is vitally important to realize that there is a difference between eternal salvation and discipleship. One who thinks that he must follow Christ to be saved, to stay saved, or even to prove he is saved does not believe the biblical gospel. Jesus promises eternal life to all who merely believe in Him.

The second question concerns the relationship between discipleship and freedom from sin.

To Experience Freedom from Bondage to Sin Requires More Than Faith in Christ[1]

In verse 32 Jesus asserts that only the believer who is abiding in His word knows the truth and shall be set free from bondage to sin—the freedom spoken of here (compare verse 34). Some feel that this too shows that the believers of verse 30 were not yet true believers. The reasoning goes like this:

Major premise:	All true believers are free from sin.
Minor premise:	The people in question are not yet free from sin.
Conclusion:	The people in question are not yet true believers.

Again, the major premise is wrong and this passage proves it. More than belief in Jesus is required to know the truth and to be set free from sin. An experiential knowledge of the truth of God's Word does not happen at the moment of regeneration. And an experience of deliverance from bondage may not occur overnight. There really is no surprise here. Habits that took years or decades to develop don't often disappear with one session of Bible study and prayer. It takes time before a new believer is so grounded in God's Word that he becomes spiritually minded (Romans 8:6) and experiences freedom from bondage to sin.

God didn't stop pointing out wrong attitudes in my life the moment I was born again. Quite the opposite. Decades later, to my chagrin, I am regularly discovering wrong attitudes toward money, possessions, time, etc. For example, I only recently realized that I am sinning when I embrace thoughts like "I can't take this" or "This shouldn't be happening to me" or "This is more than I can bear." God says that we can do all things through Christ who strengthens us

41

(Philippians 4:13). He says that with every temptation He also gives the way of escape (1 Corinthians 10:13). When I am bombarded by such thoughts, my response should be to reject them, meditate on Scripture, and pray. I am reminded of Luther's remark—you can't stop the birds from flying overhead, but you can keep them from making a nest in your hair!

The apostle Paul urged *believers* to transform their thinking and behavior by abiding in God's Word. He wrote, "All Scripture is given by inspiration of God, and is profitable for doctrine, for reproof, for correction, for instruction in righteousness, that the man of God may be complete, thoroughly equipped for every good work" (2 Timothy 3:16-17). He admonished *believers*, "Be transformed by the renewing of your mind, that you may prove what is that good and acceptable and perfect will of God" (Romans 12:2). To the Corinthian *Christians* he wrote, "But we all, with unveiled face, beholding as in a mirror the glory of the Lord, are being transformed into the same image from glory to glory, just as by the Spirit of the Lord" (2 Corinthians 3:18).

Regular intake of the Word of God is just as vital for believers as eating food. Indeed, it *is* their spiritual food. While it is true that all believers are *positionally* free from bondage to sin, they *experience* that freedom only if they are abiding in Christ's teachings. Following Christ in obedience is the only way to be truly free of the bonds of sin and to experience life as God meant for it to be. The believer who fails to abide in Christ's word is enslaved to various sins. His is not the abundant life that God wants him to enjoy.

Free at Last!

A person who is saved by believing in Christ should then follow Christ in discipleship by abiding in His teachings. To confuse or combine these points is to distort the gospel. Good news loses its goodness if you change the message. With only the elimination of a space, "God is now here" becomes "God is nowhere." Likewise, remove the space between salvation and discipleship and the good news becomes bad news.

There is no such thing as a faith in Christ, in the biblical sense, which will not save from eternal condemnation (John 3:16). If you have believed in Christ for eternal life, then you are a believer and you have eternal life.

Positionally every believer is already free from sin. Ultimately one day soon when the Lord returns or when we go to be with Him, we will have a total experience of freedom. However, we can experience a measure of that freedom right now. While we cannot attain sinlessness yet, we can and should experience freedom from bondage to sin.

The freedom of discipleship is the wonderful privilege of every believer. Won't you take advantage of that privilege? It makes no sense to be enslaved by sin when God is ever ready to set you free: "If you abide in My word, you are my disciples indeed. And you shall know the truth, and the truth shall make you free."

Assurance

CHAPTER 6

ASSURANCE IN FOCUS

"EVERYBODY TALKIN' ABOUT heaven ain't goin' there." While the lyrics of this old spiritual may be true, it's equally true that many that *are* going there aren't talking as if they know it.

You may wonder how anyone can know for sure. Perhaps you come from a family or church background where no one had assurance of salvation. Or, maybe you think it sounds presumptuous to talk of being certain that you're bound for heaven.

As part of my mid-life crisis, I have taken up distance running and Master's Track. Early one Saturday morning I headed out for a 10-kilometer race in a small town west of Fort Worth, Texas. Halfway there, my car engine went "kaboom." That was it for driving—and for racing—that day.

Sometimes circumstances intervene and things don't work out the way we expect. We come to realize that nothing is 100 percent sure in this world—other than death and taxes! However, when people apply this way of thinking to God's promises, certainty of heaven goes "kaboom."

Faulty Views of Salvation and Assurance

• *Tomorrow I might lose it.* Some people believe that while you can be reasonably confident you're saved now,[1] you may lose your salvation in the future, and hence your assurance, by falling into major sin.

Arminians, named for theologian Jacob Arminius, consider claims of eternal security to be arrogant boasting. They view it as inconceivable that anyone whose works are not good enough to satisfy God could go to heaven.

• *Tomorrow I might discover I never had it.* Others maintain that while you can't lose your salvation, if you fall into major sin, you may prove that you were never really saved in the first place. This group, often called Calvinists, after theologian John Calvin, believes that heaven is denied to anyone who fails to persevere in good works.

According to Calvinists[2] there are saved and unsaved believers. Saved believers are those who truly believe in Christ and hence are eternally secure. Unsaved believers are those who believe in Christ *intellectually*, but in reality have never *really* believed *from the heart*. Therefore, the person who falls away never possessed salvation in the first place.

Unfortunately, for the Calvinist there is no way to be sure if you are a true believer.[3] No one can be sure that he won't blow it tomorrow.

• *The bottom line: certainty is impossible.* Which fear is less daunting, that you might spend eternity in hell because you might lose your salvation, or because you might discover when you die that you were never really saved? There really is no difference, is there? Neither permits you to rest in the certain knowledge that you are a child of God.

I call such qualified "assurance" *daisy theology*. You know the story of the young girl thinking about a boy that she admires as she contemplates a daisy. Plucking off one petal at a time she recites, "He loves me; he loves me not. He loves me; he loves me not. He loves me…" hoping that the last petal pulled will confirm that "He loves me." Of course, regardless of how the petals turn out, there is no real confirmation of the young man's love for her.

So, too, people who believe that they could lose their salvation, or that they may never have truly been saved in the first place, can only hope against hope that they end their lives accepted by God. But they can't be sure. And, as long as they look to their works or faithfulness for assurance, they won't be certain until they die.

48

Assurance: The Real Thing

There is a third view of assurance that rests solely on the wonderful, objective promises in God's Word—that whoever believes in Christ has eternal life that can never be lost.

When government officials train agents to recognize counterfeit currency, they begin by making the trainees experts on authentic bills. Once they can recognize the genuine article, they find it easier to spot the counterfeit.

Therefore, before we examine texts that seem to deal with assurance but really don't (chapters 7 to 10), let's take a look at five passages that are indisputably clear on this doctrine. Once we understand what to look for, we will be able to discern when a text deals with assurance and when it doesn't.

• *John 5:24.*

> "Most assuredly, I say to you, he who hears My word and believes in Him who sent Me has everlasting life, and shall not come into judgment, but has passed from death into life."

Jesus' promise here involves the past, present, and future. The one who believes in Jesus is guaranteed that he *has passed* from death into life (past), that he *has* everlasting life (present), and that he *shall not come* into judgment regarding his eternal destiny (future).

D. L. Moody was a very gifted preacher and evangelist. His vibrant personality and clever wit came into play even when he was evangelizing people. One of the verses he liked to use was John 5:24. J. Wilbur Chapman tells the following true story about how Moody used that verse to help him gain assurance of salvation.

> I was studying for the ministry, and I heard that D. L. Moody was to preach in Chicago. I went down to hear him. Finally I got into his aftermeeting. I shall never forget the thrill that went

through me when he came and sat down beside me as an inquirer. He asked me if I was a Christian. I said, "Mr. Moody, I am not sure whether I am a Christian or not."

He very kindly took his Bible and opened it at the fifth chapter of John, and the twenty-fourth verse, which reads as follows: "Verily, verily, I say unto you, he that heareth My word, and believeth on Him that sent Me, hath everlasting life, and shall not come into condemnation; but is passed from death unto life."

Suppose you had read it through for the first time, wouldn't you think it was wonderful? I read it through, and he said, "Do you believe it?"

I said, "Yes."

"Do you accept it?"

I said, "Yes."

"Well, are you a Christian?"

"Mr. Moody, I sometimes think I am, and sometimes I am afraid I am not."

He very kindly said, "Read it again."

So I read it again: "Verily, verily, I say unto you, he that heareth My word, and believeth on Him that sent me, hath everlasting life, and shall not come into condemnation; but is passed from death unto life."

Then he said, "Do you believe it?"

I said, "Yes."

"Do you receive Him?"

I said, "Yes."

"Well," he said, "are you a Christian?"

I just started to say over again that sometimes I was afraid I was not, when the only time in all the years I knew him and loved him, he was sharp with me. He turned on me with his eyes flashing and said, "See here, whom are you doubting?"

Then I saw it for the first time, that when I was afraid I was not a Christian I was doubting God's Word. I read it again with my eyes overflowing with tears.

Since that day I have had many sorrows and

many joys, but never have I doubted for a moment
that I was a Christian, because God said it.[4]

Moody helped Chapman to see that if he wasn't sure he was
a Christian, then he didn't believe Jesus' words. When the truth of
Jesus' promise became clear to him, he believed it and knew eternal
life was his present possession, that he would never come into judgment, and that he had already passed from death into life.

I enjoy singing the old hymn, "Whosoever Surely Meaneth
Me." Based on John 3:16, its premise is that "whosoever believeth in
Him should not perish, but have everlasting life" (KJV). The
"whosoever" of John 3:16 indeed applies to all. Even to you and to
me! We don't need to achieve or maintain some level of goodness
for it to apply. Simply believe and you know you have eternal life—
because God said it.

- *1 John 5:9-13.*

> If we receive the witness of men, the witness of
> God is greater; for this is the witness of God which
> He has testified of His Son. He who believes in the
> Son of God has the witness in himself; he who does
> not believe God has made Him a liar, because he
> has not believed the testimony that God has given
> of His Son. And this is the testimony: that God has
> given us eternal life, and this life is in His Son. He
> who has the Son has life; he who does not have the
> Son of God does not have life. These things I have
> written to you who believe in the name of the Son
> of God, that you may know that you have eternal
> life, and that you may continue to believe in the
> name of the Son of God.

Have you ever served on a jury? As a juror, you hear
witnesses for the prosecution and for the defense. Some witnesses
give testimony that shows that a defendant is guilty as charged.
Others testify to his innocence. In each trial, the jury has to decide

which testimony is reliable and which is not, since not everyone is a credible witness.

There is only one witness in the universe whose credentials are completely trustworthy—God Himself. His testimony is *always* true; God cannot lie. He testifies concerning eternal life, "He who has the Son has life; he who does not have the Son of God does not have life" (verse 12). Whoever believes in Jesus Christ has eternal life.

The phrase, "these things I have written," refers to verses 9 through 12. (Compare 2:1 and 2:26 where the same expression occurs, again referring to the immediately preceding words.) Why did John remind his readers of the testimony of God? "That you may *know* that you have eternal life." Notice the words "that you may *know*." Assurance is not "hope so," "maybe so," "think so." Assurance is "know so." Anyone who accepts God's testimony knows that he has eternal life.

- *Ephesians 2:8-9.*

> For by grace you have been saved through faith,
> and that not of yourselves; it is the gift of God, not
> of works, lest anyone should boast.

Here the apostle Paul reminds the Ephesian Christians about their salvation. How had they been saved? By grace through faith. What part did their works play? None. Salvation is "the gift of God, not of works, lest anyone should boast."

If good works were necessary to obtain salvation, then why would Paul say that salvation is "not of works, lest anyone should boast"? And why would he speak of the salvation of the Ephesians as an already accomplished fact, "You have been saved"? The answers are simple. Good works are not a condition. Faith is the only condition and salvation occurs at the moment of faith. No subsequent sins can change this. Salvation is a done deal the moment one believes in Christ for eternal life.

The apostle's words unmistakably verify that faith in Christ is the basis of assurance. If I have faith in Christ alone for eternal life, then I know that I "have been saved." Nothing else is required. Salvation and assurance are *sola fide*, by faith alone.

- *1 Corinthians 3:10-15.*

> According to the grace of God which was given to me, as a wise master builder I have laid the foundation, and another builds on it. But let each one take heed how he builds on it. For no other foundation can anyone lay than that which is laid, which is Jesus Christ. Now if anyone builds on this foundation with gold, silver, precious stones, wood, hay, straw, each one's work will become clear; for the Day will declare it, because it will be revealed by fire; and the fire will test each one's work, of what sort it is. If anyone's work which he has built on it endures, he will receive a reward. If anyone's work is burned, he will suffer loss; but he himself will be saved, yet so as through fire.

The foundation of the Christian faith is Jesus Christ. The apostle Paul laid this groundwork by leading people in Corinth to faith in Christ—"It pleased God through the foolishness of the message preached to save those who believe" (1 Corinthians 1:21).

The bricks of the Christian life are the good works that we do in the power of the Holy Spirit.[5] Every Christian's life/building will be tested at the Judgment Seat of Christ. Some Christians will suffer loss of rewards they could have had if their works had stood the test of enduring quality. However, even in such cases, the believer "will be saved, yet so as through fire." There is no possibility here of loss of salvation or even of proving by one's works that one is not saved. Anyone who is a believer is saved, regardless of the quality or quantity of his works.

Assurance of salvation is grounded on faith in the objective promises of God, not on works that may well not stand the test.

• *Romans 4:4-5.*

> Now to him who works, the wages are not counted
> as grace but as debt. But to him who does not work
> but believes on Him who justifies the ungodly, his
> faith is accounted for righteousness.

The "ungodly" are the ones whom God justifies or declares righteous, not the godly, since no one is godly apart from faith in Christ: "There is none righteous, no, not one" (Romans 3:10). Salvation is a gift of God's grace received by faith. It is not dependent on works that we do, before or after the new birth.

A brand new believer, even though "ungodly" in his behavior, is absolutely sure that he has eternal life because he believes Jesus' guarantee.

Assurance Is of the Essence of Saving Faith

John Calvin held that assurance is "of the essence" of saving faith.[6] He meant by this that when anyone believes the gospel he is sure he has eternal life. In other words, it is impossible for someone to believe the gospel and not simultaneously be sure that he is eternally secure in Christ. If a person lacks assurance, he does not believe the biblical gospel. Unfortunately, some of Calvin's followers abandoned this view of assurance.

Most people today have never considered whether or not assurance of salvation is of the essence of saving faith. In fact, most gospel tracts don't get to the issue of assurance until *after* a person has supposedly been born again. I call this the two-step approach to evangelism. Step one is to believe the gospel. Step two is to gain assurance. The problem with this two-step approach is that it contradicts the gospel. Note Jesus' promise to Martha and her response:

> "I am the resurrection and the life. He who believes
> in Me, though he may die, he shall live. And who-
> ever lives and believes in Me shall never die. Do
> you believe this?" She said to Him, "Yes, Lord, I

54

believe that You are the Christ, the Son of God, who is to come into the world."

—John 11:25-27

When Jesus asked Martha, "Do you believe this?" she did not hesitate to say yes. She believed and hence she knew that she would never die spiritually because Jesus guaranteed it.

An inevitable by-product of believing the gospel is assurance, because the gospel guarantees the eternal destiny of everyone who believes it. Jesus guarantees *everlasting* life to all who just believe in Him. If I believe that, I know that I have everlasting life.

It is impossible for someone to believe in Christ for eternal life and yet to doubt he has it, since those are contradictory ideas. It is like believing that the U. S. government will never let the Social Security system fail and yet being unsure that the Social Security system will still exist when you reach retirement age. If someone believes in Christ for eternal life, what does he believe in Him for? Obviously he believes in Him for eternal life. How ridiculous, then, for someone to say he believes in Christ for eternal life, and yet to say he isn't sure if he has eternal life.

But how can we be sure that we have *really* believed? Therein lies a problem created by traditions, not by the Word of God. That question is foreign to the biblical gospel. There is no such thing as true faith as opposed to false faith. All faith is faith. If we believe in Christ for eternal life, then we have eternal life and we know we have it, because He guarantees it, "He who believes in Me has everlasting life" (John 6:47). To doubt that we *really* believe is to disbelieve Jesus' promise.

Jesus' promise is to the one who believes, not to the one who *really* believes. The "really big faith" way of thinking—what I call "Ed Sullivan faith" based on his famous variety show introduction, "We have a *really big show* for you tonight"—transforms the gospel from "He who believes in Me has everlasting life" to "He who *really* believes in Me—with his heart and not just his head, with faith that

55

never ends, and with faith which produces perseverance in good works—has everlasting life." This redefinition of faith eviscerates the gospel.

If justification is by faith alone, and it is, then it is absolutely essential that people come to faith in Christ. Yet, the redefining of saving faith makes this impossible (unless one rejects the redefinition) and reduces people to hoping that they persevere in good works to the end of their lives so as to prove they are really saved. That's a bit late to find out. No one in hell is going to get a second chance.

I'm not suggesting that those who are born again are guaranteed to always remain sure they are eternally secure. The Scriptures teach that those who believe the gospel are sure they have eternal life the moment they exercise saving faith. However, while eternal life can't be lost, assurance can be. Even a luminary such as John the Baptist, arguably one of the greatest men who ever lived, doubted Jesus Christ when he was prison. He sent messengers to Him with this question, "Are You the Coming One, or do we look for another?" (Luke 7:19). This question came from someone who had earlier confidently said of Jesus, "Behold! The Lamb of God who takes away the sin of the world!" (John 1:29). Clearly John the Baptist temporarily ceased to believe in Jesus while in prison.

In all probability John the Baptist was confused by circumstances. He didn't believe that the Messiah, once on the scene, would let him go to prison. Thus he concluded that Jesus must not really be the Messiah, and he ceased believing in Him. However, after Jesus sent His reply back to John, it is likely that his doubts were eliminated and his faith restored.

We too can become confused by circumstances if we aren't careful. We might think that no believer should ever experience depression, marital problems, financial problems, etc. When we have those problems, we may doubt our salvation. Yet, we have no such promise. Jesus' promise to the believer is eternal life, not freedom from problems in this life. If we take our eyes off His promise, and try to make it something other than what it truly is, we lose assurance of eternal life.

As we have already seen, another way we can lose assurance is by hearing faulty teaching on faith and assurance, like the idea that no one can be sure whether or not he *really* believes. If anyone stops believing Jesus' promise, he loses assurance.

Thus a person who doesn't have assurance may or may not be born again. He is born again if he ever believed the gospel. We are not saved by eternal faith. We are saved eternally the moment we exercise faith. However, if a person has *never* been sure that he is eternally secure in Christ, then he has never believed the gospel. For assurance that I have what He promises, eternal life, is the necessary by-product of faith in Him and His promise.

Of course, for those who lack assurance, there is no comfort in the fact that they might really be saved since they might have believed the gospel in the past. To be sure today we must believe Christ's promise today. Assurance is never based on looking back to some past event. Assurance is always based on what we believe right now. Even if we can't remember precisely when we first believed, we are sure we have eternal life if we believe the promise now.

An Amazing Testimony of God's Grace

Years ago I came across a young man stretched out on a bench at 11 A.M. in a city park in downtown Dallas. He had a bottle of wine at his side. I was a bit surprised when he agreed to talk with me about his views concerning Christianity.

My next surprise came when he indicated that he was sure he had eternal life. However, his explanation of *why* he was sure was even more remarkable:

> A few years ago in a small church in Oklahoma I heard that Jesus died on the cross for all my sins and that He saves anyone who just believes in Him. Well, I know I don't deserve it. I'm not living the

way I should. But I know that I have eternal life
because I believe in Jesus and He promised that all
who believe in Him have eternal life.

That was a clear testimony of one who was trusting in Christ
alone for eternal life. That he was a wino, a vagrant, and had deserted
his wife and small children did not alter the reality that he had placed
his faith in Christ alone for eternal life. Whoever believes in Jesus
Christ has eternal life—whoever.

This may not seem fair. How is it that a sinful person,
without turning from his sinful ways, can die and yet still go to heaven?
Doesn't such a one deserve to go to hell?

Yes, he does, but based on our own merit, so do we all. "All
have sinned and fall short of the glory of God" (Romans 3:23). However, Jesus' death on the cross completely paid for all of our sins—
past, present, and future, giving Him the exclusive right to grant eternal
life freely to all who believe in Him.

It is just as fair for a backslidden believer to go to heaven as
it is for the godliest saint. Both are sinners. Both have been born
again by grace through faith plus nothing. Grace is *unmerited favor.*
If people had to lead a good life to stay saved, or to prove that they
really were saved, then salvation would not be a gift of God, but
something they had partly earned.

Are You Sure?

We all like testimonies of down-and-outers whose lives are
dramatically transformed after they come to faith in Christ.
Overcomer stories are encouraging. However, if our view of the
gospel doesn't have room for failure in the Christian life, then we
don't believe the gospel of Scripture. The gospel is good news
because God has done all the work for us. All we do to receive the
gift of eternal life is to believe God's promise in Christ. Attach any
other condition and the gospel ceases to be the good news.

God desires that all of His children continue to be sure of

their eternal security. They begin the Christian life by being sure they are alive, and it is tragic if they ever lose that certainty. When they are keenly aware of their secure relationship with God, they experience a profound gratitude and love and are spurred by a desire to obey the Lord.

Combat pilots can't be sure that they will make it through the war—or even a single mission—without injury. However, they can be sure that no matter what happens, they will remain citizens of their country. So, too, we can't be sure we will come through the war against the world, the flesh, and the devil unscathed. We may fail in the Christian life. However, we can and should know that no matter what happens in the war, we are citizens of heaven. We can be sure that we will spend eternity with God in His kingdom—regardless of how we fare in our spiritual warfare! And we will be sure and remain sure as long as we believe the simple yet glorious gospel of Jesus Christ.

CHAPTER 7

ASSURANCE AND GOD'S APPROVAL
2 Corinthians 13:5

I N 1994 THE Texas Rangers called up a young infielder named Benji Gil. Needing a shortstop on the big league team, the Rangers promoted him directly from AA to the majors, something rarely done. But Benji had a hard time, especially at bat, and after a while the Rangers sent him back down to the minors.

In 1995 Benji was invited back to the major league spring training camp where he performed superbly. Not wanting him to worry that a few bad games might send him back to the minors, manager Johnny Oates assured Benji that the shortstop position was his for the entire season.

Starting well, Benji had an excellent year. While he experienced a few slumps at the plate, his batting ranged from adequate to good and his fielding was very good. The assurance Benji received—that he was the Rangers' shortstop, no matter what—had a powerful influence on the way he played.

As Christians we have a much greater and more permanent promise than Benji Gil did. His manager, Johnny Oates, promised Benji that he would be the starting shortstop for the Rangers in the 1995 season, and he fulfilled that promise. In 1996, Kevin Elster, who had had fantastic spring training and a tremendous year, replaced Benji in the starting lineup.

Unlike Benji, we don't need to worry about *ever* being cut from God's team. Our divine Manager has promised that once we believe in the crucified and risen Lord for eternal life, we are secure forever in our relationship with God. He guarantees it.[1] And God will never change His mind.

Like Benji, however, we *should* be concerned about our

service. We should check our stats regularly to see what needs improving and then to ask, "Am I really doing what God wants me to do? Am I pleasing Him?" The apostle Paul admonished the believers at the church of Corinth to do this when he wrote:

> Examine yourselves as to whether you are in the faith. Test yourselves. Do you not know yourselves, that Jesus Christ is in you?—unless indeed you are disqualified.
>
> —2 Corinthians 13:5

Some well-meaning pastors and theologians suggest that Paul was concerned that his readers might not truly be Christians. One such pastor recently wrote, "Periodic doubts about one's salvation are not necessarily wrong. Such doubts must be confronted and dealt with honestly and biblically. Scripture encourages spiritual self-examination."[2] Then, after quoting 2 Corinthians 13:5, he commented on our need for self-examination:

> That admonition is largely ignored—and often explained away—in the contemporary church.
>
> It has become quite popular to teach professing Christians that they can enjoy assurance of salvation no matter what their lives are like. After all, some argue, if salvation is a gift to people who simply believe gospel facts, what does practical living have to do with assurance? That teaching is nothing but practical antinomianism. It encourages people living in hypocrisy, disobedience, and sin by offering them false assurance. It discourages self-examination. And that clearly violates Scripture. We are *commanded* to examine ourselves at least as often as we celebrate the Lord's Supper (1 Cor. 11:28).[3]

The New Geneva Study Bible also suggests that self-examination of our works to see if we are regenerate is appropriate:

> Paul's words help clarify the doctrine of assurance of faith. Paul asks the Corinthians to examine their

own lives for evidence of salvation. Such evidence
would include trust in Christ (Heb. 3:6), obedience
to God (Matt. 7:21), growth in holiness (Heb.
12:14; 1 John 3:3), the fruit of the Spirit (Gal. 5:22,
23), love for other Christians (1 John 3:14), positive influence on others (Matt. 5:16), adhering to
the apostolic teaching (1 John 4:2), and the testimony of the Holy Spirit within them.[4]

Such an understanding of 2 Corinthians 13:5 and of
assurance is inconsistent with the gospel[5] and also with the
immediate and broader context in Second Corinthians. I certainly
agree that Christians are to examine themselves. That *is* commanded
in Scripture. However, Paul's readers already knew that they were
genuine believers. Paul had a different purpose in mind for this
self-examination.

Paul Affirmed Assurance apart from Works

Paul was writing to believers, a fact he repeatedly asserted
throughout both First and Second Corinthians. Nine times in these
two epistles he referred to the fact that his readers had faith in Christ
(1 Corinthians 2:5; 3:5; 15:2, 11, 14, 17; 16:13; 2 Corinthians 1:24;
10:15). He affirmed this in spite of the fact that the believers in Corinth
were guilty of a number of significant moral failings. They had been
plagued with divisions, strife, envy, drunkenness, and immorality
(1 Corinthians 1:11; 3:1-3; 5:9–6:20; 11:21, 30). Their works
certainly didn't prove they were saved. In fact, according to Paul,
they were "behaving like mere men," that is, like the unsaved
(1 Corinthians 3:3).

In addition, Paul made a number of other statements which
give evidence that they were regenerate, "To the church of God which
is at Corinth, to those who are sanctified in Christ Jesus"
(1 Corinthians 1:2). "But you were washed, but you were sanctified,
but you were justified in the name of the Lord Jesus and by the Spirit
of our God" (1 Corinthians 6:11). "Now He who establishes us with

63

you in Christ and has anointed us is God, who also has sealed us and given us the Spirit in our hearts as a guarantee" (2 Corinthians 1:21-22). "Do not be unequally yoked together with unbelievers" (2 Corinthians 6:14). "You know the grace of our Lord Jesus Christ" (2 Corinthians 8:9).

In 1 Corinthians 3:1-3 and 6:19-20, Paul referred to the carnal behavior of the believers at Corinth, and yet he called them "babes in Christ" (3:1) whose "body is the temple of the Holy Spirit who is in you" (6:19).

Paul didn't want his readers to doubt their salvation, but to live in light of the fact that they were secure children of God. His appeals to live righteously were built upon their assurance that they were born again. To understand 2 Corinthians 13:5, we must take into account that Paul did not link assurance to their works but to their faith in Christ.

Putting the Puzzle Together

• *The meaning of "in the faith."* Being "in the faith" could be considered a reference to being regenerate. In answer to the question, "Are you a born again Christian?" we might say, "Yes, I'm in the faith." However, that isn't a normal way of speaking today. Nor was it a normal way to speak in the first century.

Paul used the expression *in the faith (en tē pistei)* four times.[6] These all refer to the believer's experience not his position. Paul always used this expression in conjunction with imperatives. In the three uses outside of 2 Corinthians 13:5, he commanded believers to "stand fast in the faith" (1 Corinthians 16:13), to "be sound in the faith" (Titus 1:13), and to be "established in the faith"[7] (Colossians 2:7). "The faith" is the body of truth that has been delivered to us from God. Thus Paul was exhorting his spiritual charges to obey in their experience that teaching which they had received. Dave Lowery comments:

Paul's question is usually construed with regard to positional justification: were they Christians or not? But it more likely concerned practical sanctification: did they *demonstrate* that they were in the faith (cf. 1 Cor 16:13) and that Christ was in them by their obeying His will? To stand the test was to do what was right. To fail was to be disobedient and therefore subject to God's discipline.[8]

• *The meaning of "Christ in you."* This phrase could refer to salvation since Christ lives in all believers. However, "Christ in you" is associated in Scripture with progressive sanctification. For example, after saying, "You are already clean because of the word which I have spoken to you" (John 15:3), Jesus commanded the apostles, "Abide in Me, and I in you" (John 15:4). In order for Christ to abide in the believer, the believer must abide in Christ. Christ is at home in the lives of believers only if they openly and honestly obey Him. Paul was imploring the Corinthian believers to examine their works to see if Christ was abiding in them, in their experience.

• *The meaning of "disqualified."* The term "disqualified" (Greek: *adokimos*) occurs three times in verses 5 to 7. All of its other New Testament uses refer exclusively to believers who fail to gain Christ's approval. *Adokimos* means "disapproved." Its antonym, *dokimos*, occurs in 2 Timothy 2:15, "Be diligent to present yourself *approved* to God, a worker who does not need to be ashamed, rightly dividing the word of truth."[9] Approval and disapproval are terms related to the Judgment Seat of Christ. Believers whose lives have been pleasing to Christ will be approved, while the believers whose lives have displeased Christ will be disapproved. Rewards will be given to those who receive the Lord's approval, His "Well done."

Acceptance and approval are two different things. God accepts all believers solely on the basis of their faith in Christ. Once they come to faith in Christ, they are forever accepted. Approval requires more than faith. It is conditioned upon spiritual maturity and is not a once-for-all event. A believer who is approved today is

65

not guaranteed approval this time next year. Remaining in a state of Christ's approval is contingent upon continuing to confess Christ in word and deed (2 Timothy 2:12; Hebrews 10:23-25).

Paul used *adokimos* in only one other place in First and Second Corinthians. There he indicated his fear that *he himself* might be disapproved by Christ at His Judgment Seat, "But I discipline my body and bring it into subjection, lest, when I have preached to others, I myself should become *disqualified*" (1 Corinthians 9:27, italics added). Paul knew that he was saved. What he feared was God's disapproval.[10]

In verse 5 Paul challenged the believers at Corinth to examine themselves to see if they were approved or disapproved. In verse 6 he reminded them that he and his fellow missionaries were not disapproved, although he acknowledged in verse 7 that they might seem disapproved to some in the Corinthian church. In other words, Paul knew that he was currently living in such a way as to merit Christ's approval. This he could not affirm of the believers at Corinth, for there was plenty of evidence to suggest otherwise.

Examination of your works to see if you can rightfully expect Christ's approval at His Judgment Seat is completely consistent with Paul's teachings elsewhere in First and Second Corinthians (see 1 Corinthians 3:10-15; 9:24-27; 2 Corinthians 5:9-10), and in his other letters as well (see Romans 14:10-13; Galatians 5:19-21; 6:7-9; Ephesians 5:5-7; Philippians 3:11-14; Colossians 1:21-23; 2 Timothy 2:12, 15). We should always be living in light of the fact that Jesus might come back today. According to Paul, approval or disapproval by Christ will be based on how we live. Self-examination is an important discipline that helps us be prepared to receive Christ's approval.

• *The meaning of "proof."* A related noun and verb of the just-cited term further support this understanding. In verse 3 Paul indicated that some of the Corinthians were seeking "a proof" (Greek: *dokimēn*) that Christ was speaking through *him*. Turning the tables on them in verse 5, Paul challenged the congregation "to test [or to prove] *yourselves*" (Greek: *dokimazō*).

What was it that some of the Corinthians were questioning about Paul (verse 3)? Certainly it was not his *salvation*. No, they questioned whether Christ was speaking through him. Therefore, when Paul turned the tables on them and asked them to test or prove themselves, he was questioning their experience in Christ, not their position.

Does God Approve of You?

To return to our baseball analogy, if you believe in Christ for eternal life, you are on the team and in the game. But that doesn't mean that you will hit a home run or even get a base hit every time you're up at the plate. Your batting average may slump. If so, you may need to examine your swing to correct the problem.

Similarly, the Scriptures challenge us as Christians to examine ourselves to determine how we are doing in our individual walk with Christ. Are we delighting Him by our lives? Does He approve of us? Or, are we living for the praise and approval of others? Is our mind conformed to God's Word or to the world?

Self-examination can help us prepare for the Judgment Seat of Christ. If we are ready, we will hear those words of approval, "Well done, good servant" (Luke 19:17).

We're never told to examine our performance (works) to see if we are born again. That has already been settled. We're under contract—an eternal contract!

CHAPTER 8

THE PLACE OF FEELINGS IN ASSURANCE
Romans 8:15-16

D O ALL SAVED people have some special inner feeling that assures them that they are children of God? If they do, how can they identify this feeling?

One gospel tract uses a train diagram as an illustration of the place of feelings in assurance. The diagram consists of a locomotive called *facts* and two cars, called *faith* and *feelings*. The tract says that we should put our faith in the facts of the gospel, not in our feelings. Feelings change; facts don't. By focusing on the facts of the gospel, we can be assured and remain assured of our salvation.

That sounds good, since we all know that feelings are unreliable. One day we may feel on top of the world. The next day we may sense that the world is on top of us. Whole books are devoted to the subject of emotions. Even born again people experience fluctuations in their feelings. However, Romans 8:15-16 is thought by many to suggest that all truly born again people possess a special inner feeling which assures them that they are saved:

> For you did not receive the spirit of bondage again to fear, but you received the Spirit of adoption by whom we cry out, "Abba, Father." The Spirit Himself bears witness with our spirit that we are children of God.
> —Romans 8:15-16

Based on this passage the Westminster Confession of Faith states that the inner witness of the Holy Spirit is one of three grounds of assurance of salvation, the others being the promises of God's Word regarding salvation and evidences of saving grace manifested in the works that believers do.[1]

However, when we ask some questions about Romans 8:15-16,

we discover that it isn't talking about personal assurance of salvation at all.

A Closer Look

• *Witnessing with our spirit?* The first question we must ask is what Paul meant by the little preposition *with*: "The Spirit Himself bears witness *with* our spirit that we are children of God." If he was referring to some witness of the Holy Spirit *to* us that we are saved, why didn't Paul say that the Spirit Himself bears witness *to* our spirit?

The Greek verb *symmartureō* conveys the meaning of "bears witness with." It is a compound verb with a preposition prefixed to it. The preposition means "with" or "along with," not "to."[2]

Romans 8:16 speaks of two witnesses, the Holy Spirit and our human spirit. They both bear witness. This is in keeping with the Old Testament principle that all matters need to be verified by at least two witnesses.

• *To whom do believers and the Holy Spirit bear witness?* If the Spirit is not witnessing *to us* that we are children of God, to whom is He witnessing? The answer is clear in the context.

Verse 15 indicates that we (our human spirits) cry out, "Abba, Father." Our witness is clearly to God the Father. Thus in order for the two witnesses to be to the same Person, then the Holy Spirit, too, must be bearing witness to God the Father. This conclusion is confirmed by verse 26, which asserts that whenever we pray the Holy Spirit intercedes for us. Clearly the Person to whom He is interceding for us is God the Father.

• *When does this witness take place?* The Holy Spirit's witness does not occur continually. Rather, it happens as we pray. Whenever our human spirits cry out to God saying, "Abba, Father" (Romans 8:15; Galatians 4:6; see also the Lord's Prayer, Luke 11:2, "Our Father..."), the Holy Spirit attests to God the Father that we are indeed His children.

When we pray, "Our Father," we remind God that we are His

children. Whenever that greeting is true, the Holy Spirit confirms its validity.

• *Is the Spirit's witness detectable to the believer?* While we are aware when our human spirits cry out to God in prayer, calling Him our Father, we are unable to monitor the Holy Spirit's independent witness to the Father. We cannot feel, see, hear, or tune into the witness of the Holy Spirit to God the Father that we are His children—even though in our experience of prayer we might have a general sense that the Holy Spirit is at work. The only sure way we know that He does this is because the Scriptures *tell* us that He does.

Paul doesn't share this information to help us know we're saved. He shares it because knowing of this confirming witness of the Holy Spirit spurs us on to pray all the more. God takes pleasure in this twofold testimony of our status as His children. This should motivate us to do our part—which is to pray.

What a joy it is for us to dwell on the fact that God delights in being reminded by us, and by the Holy Spirit, that we are His children. Yes, but doesn't this show that feelings do lead to assurance? No, it shows just the opposite. Dwelling on the fact that we are God's children, and that God delights in our prayers, can produce positive feelings in believers. Rather than good feelings resulting in assurance, assurance results in good feelings.[3]

God's Promises Are All We Need

My birth certificate indicates that I was born in Los Angeles in 1952. It objectively testifies to me that I am a citizen of the United States. I don't need to ask myself, "Do I feel like a U.S. citizen?" My birth certificate tells me I am, regardless of how I feel. It is all I need. Feelings play no role in assurance of our earthly citizenship.

Feelings also play no role in assurance of our heavenly citizenship. The birth certificate of believers is God's Word. It objectively testifies to us that all who simply believe in Christ for eternal life are citizens of heaven.

God's promises are all we need to be sure we have eternal life.

71

CHAPTER 9

CONFIRMING YOUR CALL AND ELECTION
2 Peter 1:10-11

D WIGHT L. MOODY used to tell the story of a man arriving at the Pearly Gates. At the entrance he saw a sign that read, "Whoever believes in Him has everlasting life." On the other side of the gate he saw the back of the sign, "He chose us in Him before the foundation of the world."

God doesn't publish a list of names of the elect. However, He does tell us that all who believe in Christ for eternal life are elect. Thus, if you believe in Christ, you can be sure you are elect.

Yet, 2 Peter 1:10-11 seems to suggest that certainty about being numbered among the elect requires more than believing in Christ. In context, these verses appear to add perseverance in good works as a condition of assurance of election, and hence of salvation as well:

> Therefore, brethren, be even more diligent to make your call and election sure, for if you do these things you will never stumble; for so an entrance will be supplied to you abundantly into the everlasting kingdom of our Lord and Savior Jesus Christ.
> —2 Peter 1:10-11

Those who espouse Lordship Salvation have claimed this passage as proof of their position. As one such author wrote:

> It would seem that words could not be clearer that one is to make sure of his election by using the means, and Peter has just listed several character qualities that we must cultivate in our lives by the power of the Spirit (vv 5-7)...If we make it sure, what is this but assurance?[1]

Also commenting on verse 10, another Lordship Salvation

writer said, "We are commanded to *cultivate* assurance, not take it for granted."[2]

Many pastors and theologians understand this passage as teaching that as we grow in holiness, we gain more and more confidence that we are truly elect.[3] Yet, as we shall see, there is strong evidence that these verses do not concern personal assurance of salvation, or even election *to eternal salvation*, at all.

What Is Our Part and What Is God's Part?

Verses 10 and 11 are built on verses 5 through 9. Peter uses the verb *epichorēgeō*, "to add" or "to supply," once in each section to tie them together. *If we add* to our faith certain character qualities, *then God will add* to our eternal experience by giving us a rich entrance to the eternal kingdom. Most English translations unintentionally obscure the fact that the same verb is used in both places:

Version	Translation of *epichorēgeō* in verse 5	Translation of *epichorēgeō* in verse 11
KJV	add	shall be ministered
NKJV	add	will be supplied
NIV	add	you will receive
NASB	supply	will be supplied
RSV	supplement	will be provided
NEB	supplement	you will be afforded

As you can see, only in the NASB is the same verb used in both cases. Even so, all of these versions show that more than faith is necessary to acquire the rich entrance to the kingdom spoken of in verse 11. It is impossible to conclude that Peter is promising an abundant entrance to the kingdom merely on the basis of faith in Christ! God will only supply this bountiful kingdom entrance to believers who "add to [their] faith."

Occurring at the beginning and end of verses 5 through 11, the two usages of *epichorēgeō*, serve as bookends. The first is in the active voice and relates our part: we are to add to our faith a number of character qualities. The second is in the passive voice and proclaims God's part: He will provide a rich entrance to the eternal kingdom to those who have added these character qualities to their faith. Let's now give closer attention to our part and to God's part.

• *Our part: adding to our faith... (verses 5-9).* Peter specifies seven character qualities we are to add to our faith: virtue, knowledge, self-control, perseverance, godliness, brotherly kindness, and love. Developing and maintaining these qualities is a lifelong pursuit and we never "arrive." "Please be patient; God is not finished with me yet!" is true of the holiest believer.

One result of cultivating these qualities is that we "will be neither barren nor unfruitful in the knowledge of our Lord Jesus Christ" (verse 8). A believer who fails to do so, however, "is shortsighted, even to blindness, and has forgotten that he was cleansed from his old sins" (verse 9).[4]

Were it not for the verses that follow, this passage would not be difficult to understand at all. Peter is urging believers to grow in the faith, to be fruitful. We have similar exhortations throughout the whole New Testament (Ephesians 4:17-34; Hebrews 13:1-17; James 4:7-10; 3 John 11). The problem is, if salvation is a free gift whose only condition is faith in Christ alone, how is it possible that we must add character qualities to our faith to gain a rich entrance to the eternal kingdom?

• *God's part: supplying a rich kingdom entrance (verses 10-11).* God promises a glorious future to the believer who adds to his faith the qualities listed in verses 5 to 8: "For so an entrance will be supplied to you abundantly into the everlasting kingdom of our Lord and Savior Jesus Christ" (verse 11).

The adverb translated "abundantly" (*plousiōs*) literally means "richly," and is similarly translated in two of its other three New Testament uses.[5] It is related to the noun *plousios* referring to material riches or earthly possessions, or to spiritual wealth, such as one who is "rich in faith" (James 2:5) or "rich in mercy" (Ephesians 2:4, referring to God Himself).[6]

A friend who now pastors a church in the Detroit area, Tom Lewellen, made a startling discovery while preparing to preach on this passage during our seminary days. He noted the repetition of the verb *epichorēgeō* in verses 5 and 11. As he meditated on the significance of this, it suddenly dawned on him that this rich entrance to the kingdom could not be talking about something all believers receive.

Tom realized that Peter didn't say that all who exercise saving faith would have this rich entrance. Just the opposite. Peter said that believers must "*add* to [their] faith" (verse 5) before God will supply them with this rich kingdom entrance. He concluded that Peter must be talking about eternal rewards here, since believing the gospel is the only condition of eternal salvation (e.g., John 3:16).

Riches are repeatedly associated in the New Testament with the believer's service for Christ. Jesus commanded His followers to lay up *treasure* in heaven, not on earth (Matthew 6:19-21). While you can't take treasure with you (the fallacy of the Egyptian pyramids), you can send it on ahead. Paul said that when you give to worthy causes, "fruit abounds to your account" (Philippians 4:17)[7] and that "whatever a man sows, that he will also reap" (Galatians 6:7). Elsewhere, Peter said that *a crown of glory* would be awarded to those elders who have served well (1 Peter 5:1-4).

The condition of entering the kingdom is faith in Christ. The condition of having a rich entrance to the kingdom is faith in Christ plus godly character.

Now we are in position to consider the meaning of *making our call and election sure*.

Confirming Our Call and Election

I began this chapter with what theologians call the doctrine of election. This is the biblical teaching that God elects, or chooses, those who will be saved. There is great mystery in this doctrine in terms of the relationship between God's sovereignty and human responsibility. While it is clear that God elects those who will be saved, it is also clear that the elect freely respond to God's drawing and that they indeed believe in Christ.[8] God is sovereign and yet we have responsibility.

A common understanding of verse 10 is that Peter is referring to the doctrine of election when he urges his readers, "Make your call and election sure." Before we discuss what the word translated "sure" means, let's consider the meaning of "call and election."

It is possible that *call and election* here refers to God's calling and electing of people *to eternal salvation*.[9] However, this is unlikely, for if that were the case, the order should be election and call, not call and election. Election to eternal salvation occurred in eternity past, long before any person was called to eternal salvation (see, for example, Romans 8:30, 33; Ephesians 1:4).

Both words, *call* and *election*, are used sparingly in the New Testament. In fact, this is the only place where these exact forms of the Greek words occur together. However, there are three places where related forms of these words occur in this order. Two of those occurrences are especially helpful in understanding the calling and election here since Peter's words are most likely based upon those passages.[10]

Peter twice heard the Lord Jesus teach about calling and election (or choosing)—in that order. In both the Parable of the Workers in the Vineyard and the Parable of the Marriage Supper, the Lord told Peter and the others in the audience, "Many are called, but few chosen [or elected]" (Matthew 20:16; 22:14).

Both parables concern eternal reward, not eternal salvation. The first parable is about day laborers and their *pay* (*misthos*, the word for wages or rewards). Obviously entering the kingdom cannot be in view, since that is not a reward or payment for work done! The second concerns a wedding feast to which many are called. Many of those invited make excuses and refuse the invitation. Among those who accept the invitation, there is a man who is improperly dressed. This pictures a believer who is not properly clothed in a spiritual sense. Such a believer will get into the kingdom, yet he will not be chosen for the privilege of ruling with Christ. That is to say, he will not have a *rich* entrance to the kingdom (verse 11).[11]

Calling does precede election if we are speaking of being chosen to rule with Christ. All believers are invited to rule. Yet only some of those will actually be chosen to rule. As Paul said, "If we endure, we shall also reign with Him" (2 Timothy 2:12).

Now in what sense should believers *make sure* their call and election to ruling with Christ?

The word translated "sure" (*bebaios*) occurs only one other time in Second Peter, and there with a suffix meaning "more." In that use it cannot mean "more sure," since sureness has no degrees, but must refer to *additional confirmation* of a truth already known: "So we have the prophetic word confirmed [*bebaioteros*]" (2 Peter 1:19).

In verses 16 to 18 Peter refers to the Mount of Transfiguration experience where he and James and John beheld the glory of the Lord Jesus as He "was transfigured before them. His face shown like the sun, and His clothes became as white as the light" (Matthew 17:2). Peter, James, and John already knew with certainty that the prophecies regarding the Messiah were fulfilled in Jesus. They had watched Him calm storms, cast out demons, resurrect the dead, heal the sick, restore sight to the blind, and even walk on water. They had heard His brilliant teaching and observed His sinless life. They were already *sure*. What they received, on the Mount of Transfiguration, was more *confirmation*.

Therefore, a better translation of verse 10 would be, "Therefore, brethren, be even more diligent to *confirm* your call and election" (emphasis added). That, in fact, is essentially the translation of the RSV, "Therefore, brethren, be the more zealous to confirm your call and election."

Peter was not challenging his readers to see if they were

regenerate. Rather, his appeal here is based upon the fact that the readers, "brethren," were born again. Only born again people have the opportunity to confirm that they are in position to rule with Christ. In the very first verse of Second Peter, the apostle affirmed that he was writing, "To those who have obtained like precious faith with us by the righteousness of our God and Savior Jesus Christ." Only believers fit that description. (See also 1 Peter 1:23, "having been born again, not of corruptible seed, but incorruptible.")

But to whom were Peter's readers to confirm their election to rulership? To themselves or to others?

Peter was taught by the Lord, "By this all will know that you are My disciples, if you have love for one another" (John 13:35).[12] In his first epistle Peter urged his readers to "abstain from fleshly lusts…that…*they [unbelieving Gentiles] may, by your good works which they observe*, glorify God in the day of visitation" (1 Peter 2:11-12, italics added). Clearly Peter believed in the importance of believers manifesting godly character *to others*. Thus, in the absence of any indication contextually that this confirmation was to be to oneself, it appears most likely that this was to be a corroboration to others.

Zane Hodges beautifully summarizes Peter's point in this way:

> Peter, therefore, wishes his readership to produce in their lifestyle appropriate verification that they are "royal" people, destined for high honor in the coming kingdom of God. By doing *these things* (i.e., the things Peter is talking about) their road into the glories of that kingdom will be smooth. They will not *stumble* on that path and thus run the risk of losing the rewards they are "called" to obtain (see 1 Cor 9:27). Instead they shall prove themselves "chosen" for divine reward.[13]

Laying Up Riches for the World to Come

Eternal riches are promised to believers who add godliness, brotherly kindness, perseverance, and love to their faith. You have two possibilities: stumbling and missing out on the riches you could have had[14] or persevering and receiving the riches God has invited you to receive. Even the apostle Paul feared he might fail to achieve this rich entrance (1 Corinthians 9:24-27). Yet, as his death approached he could joyfully say:

> For I am already being poured out as a drink offering, and the time of my departure [death] is at hand. I have fought the good fight, I have finished the race, I have kept the faith. Finally, there is laid up for me the crown of righteousness, which the Lord, the righteous Judge, will give to me on that Day, and not to me only but also to all who have loved His appearing.
>
> —2 Timothy 4:6-8

A rich future awaits the Christian who perseveres in loving obedience. Believer, are you ready for Christ's return? If He returns today, will you be chosen to rule with Him? You will be if you are adding godly character to your faith. Then God will add to you the wonderful rich entrance to the kingdom that He has reserved for faithful believers.

CHAPTER 10

BELIEVER, DO YOU KNOW GOD?
1 John 2:3-6

I T WAS THE night before Jesus was to be crucified. He and the disciples had shared a Passover supper together and then He offered some last words, at one point remarking, "If you had known Me, you would have known My Father also; and from now on you know Him and have seen Him" (John 14:7).

"Lord, show us the Father, and it is sufficient for us," was Philip's awkward reply (14:8).

"Have I been with you so long," Jesus rejoined, "and yet you have not known Me, Philip? He who has seen Me has seen the Father; so how can you say, 'Show us the Father'?" (John 14:9). How we long for the spectacular when so often it is right in front of us.

After three years of living, traveling, and ministering together, surely Philip and the other disciples knew Jesus. Yet in one sense, they didn't, for Jesus said, "Yet you have not known Me." As we shall see, knowing God encompasses much more than being born again by faith in Christ.

A few years ago while I was on a radio talk show, a caller asked me to explain what the apostle John meant when he wrote, "By this we know that we know Him, if we keep His commandments" (1 John 2:3). I had been saying on the program that all we need to do to be 100 percent sure of our salvation is to believe the promises of God in His Word. The caller thought that 1 John 2:3 taught that *in addition to believing God's Word* we needed to look at how obedient to God we are, in order to be sure of our salvation.[1]

> Now by this we know that we know Him, if we keep His commandments. He who says, "I know Him," and does not keep His commandments, is a

liar, and the truth is not in him. But whoever keeps
His word, truly the love of God is perfected in him.
By this we know that we are in Him. He who says
he abides in Him ought himself also to walk just
as He walked.

—1 John 2:3-6

In order to decide the meaning of 1 John 2:3, we need to
understand both the context of the verse and the purpose of John's
letter as a whole.

The Purpose of First John

• *The purpose is not to help readers determine whether they
are born again.* The view evidently held by the caller to the radio
show is that the apostle John was encouraging his readers to examine
whether or not they were believers. This is often called the Tests-of-
Life View of First John, popularized by Robert Law in his commentary by that name early in the twentieth century. It has been widely
taught ever since.[2]

According to this view, the purpose of First John is found at
the end of the book: "These things I have written to you who believe
in the name of the Son of God, that you may know that you have
eternal life" (5:13).[3] However, there are a number of problems with
embracing 1 John 5:13 as the purpose statement of the whole book.

First, the words "these things I have written" (Greek: *tauta
egrapsa*) do not refer to the content of the entire book, but only to the
immediate context (5:6-12). In those verses John indicates that
assurance is found in believing God's testimony regarding His Son.

The same Greek expression occurs two other times in the
book. In 2:26 John says, *"These things I have written to you*
concerning those who try to deceive you," and in 2:1, "My little
children, *these things I write to you,* so that you may not sin." Clearly,
neither of those is the purpose statement of the whole book, since
they both refer only to the immediately preceding verses.

Second, a central tenet of the Tests-of-Life View is that both believers and unbelievers comprised John's audience. However, in 1 John 5:13 we read, "These things I have written to you who believe in the name of the Son of God." There are no unbelievers in 5:13. John made it clear here, and throughout the book, that he was writing exclusively to *believers* (2:12-14, 25; 3:1-2; 5:19).

Third, John gives a clear-cut statement of purpose for his letter in the prologue (1:3-4), as we shall now see.

• *The purpose is to help readers determine whether they are in fellowship with God.* This second view is that John was writing to encourage his readers, all of whom were already believers, to examine their works to discern whether or not they were in fellowship with Christ. This might be called the Tests-of-Fellowship View.[4] John reveals his purpose in the prologue of his epistle:

> That which we have seen and heard we declare to you, that you also may have fellowship with us; and truly our fellowship is with the Father and with His Son Jesus Christ. And these things we write to you that your joy may be full.
>
> —1 John 1:3-4

"These things *we write* to you" is in the first person *plural.* As seen above, in three other places in the book John used the first person *singular* to refer to what he wrote in the immediate context (2:1, "these things I write to you," and 2:26 and 5:13, "these things I have written to you"). That the first person plural is used in 1:4 suggests it refers to his purpose in writing the entire letter. This is supported by the fact that purpose statements for epistles were often found in the prologue.[5]

The Tests-of-Fellowship View is further supported by the fact that much in First John is drawn from Jesus' teaching on abiding, as found in the Upper Room Discourse (John 14–16). That discourse was delivered to believers; Judas had already departed (John 13:27-30). Jesus exhorted the apostles to abide in Him so that they would continue in fellowship with Him. So too in First John, the apostle exhorted his believing audience to abide in Christ so that they might remain in fellowship with God.

If the purpose of First John is to exhort the readers to abide in fellowship with Christ, we are still left with a key question: What, then, *does* 1 John 2:3-6 mean?

Knowing Him

When John speaks of *knowing* Christ ("by this we know that we know Him"), he is using a term that can refer either to position[6] or experience.[7] In this context the latter is in view. As believers we know Jesus Christ in our experience when we obey Him. The reverse is also true: sin is never an expression of knowing Christ— "Whoever sins has never seen Him nor *known* Him"[8] (1 John 3:6).

The word *know* was as flexible in Koiné Greek as it is in English. Imagine hearing this statement about a man who had just divorced his wife of many years, "They were married for thirty years, and yet he never knew her." The man certainly knew his wife of thirty years in one sense. However, his knowledge of her was not the intimate knowledge that comes from years of close fellowship. So it is with a disobedient Christian and his knowledge of God. He lacks the intimate knowledge of God that comes from years of walking in fellowship with Him.

When I was in college ministry, we used to sing 1 John 4:7-8, "Beloved, let us love one another, for love is of God; and everyone who loves is born of God and knows God. He who does not love does not know God, for God is love." We understood that only by loving each other could we demonstrate that we knew God in our experience: "Everyone who loves is born of God and knows God." Unregenerate people cannot truly know God in their experience. Regenerate people can, and they do when they love one another.

Any believer who claims to know God and yet doesn't keep His commandments is lying (verse 4). In other words, a Christian who is not keeping God's commands does not know God *in his experience*, no matter what he might claim verbally. Zane Hodges comments:

> The truth is either *in* me as a Christian or it is not. If it is, then I will be engaged in active obedience to God's commands. If it is not, I am sadly out of touch with the transforming power of the truth of God.
>
> Thus it is altogether appropriate for each of us as born-again believers to ask ourselves, "Is the truth really *in* me? Is it working dynamically *in* my heart and life?" On the answer to questions like these depends the reality of our communion with our living Lord.[9]

In the 1988 elections, vice-presidential candidates Dan Quayle and Lloyd Bentsen debated each other. One of the criticisms used against Quayle was that he was such a young man. He countered in the debate by saying that he was then the same age as John Kennedy when he became President in 1960.

Lloyd Bentsen could hardly wait to respond. He fired back, "I *knew* Jack Kennedy. And you are no Jack Kennedy!"

It's easy to see that Quayle was implying that he was as capable to serve as President as John Kennedy had been. Bentsen picked up on this and cleverly implied that it was false.

We often use the word *know* in this way in our daily conversation. When I was a teenager, I asked my parents for a motorcycle. Their answer went something like this, "You really don't know us, do you?" Any time I asked for something which was contrary to my parents' expectations, I could expect that kind of reply.

What if a Christian asks God for something that is inconsistent with His character? God can rightly say, "You really don't know Me, do you?"

If a Christian professes to know God, yet is walking in the darkness of willful sin, then his assertion is patently false. While all Christians are saved and know God in a positional sense, only those

85

Christians who are walking in the light of openness and honesty before Him can rightly claim to know Him in their daily walk.

Think of a member of a local church who hasn't attended a church service in more than a year. Does he know the church? Well, in his position he does, since he is a member. However, in his experience he does not, since he hasn't participated in the life of the church in over a year. While the church is glad that he knows it in the first sense, it will greatly appreciate him knowing it in the second sense as well.

Knowing That We Are in Him

Verses 5 and 6 say that we know we are "in Him" when we "keep His word" and "walk just as He walked." Now when the apostle Paul spoke of being "in Christ" he was referring to being in the Body of Christ, to being in Christ in our *position* (Ephesians 1–2). While many see John's reference to knowing we are "in Him" in the same way, the context makes it clear that John was referring to being "in Him" in our *experience*.

In the Upper Room Discourse the Lord Jesus commanded the disciples, "Abide in Me, and I in you. As the branch cannot bear fruit of itself, unless it abides in the vine, neither can you, unless you abide in Me" (John 15:4). Here is mutual abiding, Christ in the believer *and the believer in Him*. This concerns the believer's daily experience, not his position.

The theme of abiding is also found in 1 John 2:3-6, immediately after the reference to knowing we are in Him. After saying, "By this we know that we are in Him," John says, "He who says *He abides in Him* ought himself also to walk just as He walked" (2:6). When John speaks of knowing that we are "in Him," he is referring to knowing that we are "abiding in Him."

We know that we are in Christ, and that we are abiding in Him, if we keep His word and walk as He walked. Love is the ultimate fulfillment of Jesus' word and it characterizes the way He walked. Therefore, as John went on to say, the believer who walks in love is abiding in Christ.[10]

Believer Do You Know God?

On the night He was betrayed, Jesus told His disciples, "You are My friends *if* you do whatever I command you" (John 15:14).[11] Only a few Old Testament giants of the faith were ever specifically referred to in Scripture as friends of God.[12] Yet, every believer in Christ has the potential of being called His friend. If we do what He has commanded us, we are His friends, not merely His servants. What a privilege! And Jesus has promised to reveal His teachings to His friends, "No longer do I call you servants, for a servant does not know what his master is doing; but I have called you friends, for all things that I heard from My Father I have made known to you" (John 15:15).

Are you open before Christ? Or are you keeping something back from Him? Are you committed to do whatever He has commanded you? Are you open to Him showing you which of your attitudes are wrong? How about your words and actions? Are you prepared to give up those things that are contrary to God's Word? Only by being open and honest before Him can you be His friend (compare 1 John 1:9 with 2:3-6).

The new birth is only the beginning of knowing God. Babes in Christ do not know God intimately in their experience. They must grow in order to move out of spiritual infancy. Maturity takes time. New believers can and should become spiritual people who have a Christian perspective on life, people who look at everything in light of eternity.[13] This is not, however, guaranteed. The apostle John exhorts all believers to enter into an intimate knowledge of God and to continue in that knowledge until Jesus returns: "And now, little children, abide in Him, that when He appears, we may have confidence and not be ashamed before Him at His coming" (1 John 2:28).

In a sense, it really is true that life is all about *who* you know. There is no one in the world whose friendship is more important than God's. Knowing the wealthiest and most powerful people is nothing compared to knowing God. Remember James's warning, "Friendship with the world is enmity with God" (James 4:4). You have a choice to make. Believer, do you want to be a friend of God, or of the world?

Eternal
Security

CHAPTER 11

ETERNAL SECURITY IN FOCUS

P ROFESSIONAL GOLFERS "make the cut" only if their scores in the first two rounds are in the top half of the field. Those who miss the cut don't get any prize money. This is true even for Tiger Woods or Jack Nicklaus.

Similarly, many think that only those Christians who make the cut, morally and ethically, go to heaven. Christians who backslide and fail to repent of their major sins before they die miss the cut. Thus, even the most moral of professing Christians is in danger of missing the ultimate cut. Doesn't this seem fair? Good Christians go to heaven. Bad Christians and nonbelievers go to hell.

God's method of determining who goes to heaven and who doesn't is fair, but it has nothing to do with "fairness" as we judge that. It has nothing to do with our morality, our good deeds, or our coming out ahead of the curve. God says that everyone who simply believes in His Son, the Lord Jesus Christ, for eternal life is eternally secure.

Eternal Security?

Eternal security is the biblical teaching that once a person receives eternal life, he is secure forever. That is, once a person is saved, he remains saved—eternally. For that reason, another expression for eternal security is *once saved, always saved.*

Many Bible passages support this doctrine, as we shall soon see. God guarantees that no born again person will ever lose his salvation. This guarantee is not dependent on anything we do. It's totally up to God to make sure that everyone who believes in Christ stays saved forever.

Almost everything in our experience tells us that nothing is free or certain, except death, which is both free and certain, and taxes, which are certain but not free. The idea that we are saved merely by faith, and that once saved we are forever secure, seems unbelievable to many. I know.

For years the idea of eternal security seemed ridiculous to me. In the fall of 1972, at the start of my senior year in college, I attended a Christian fellowship at the University of Southern California. While there, I heard one person use profanity and saw another light up a cigarette.

I remember asking John Carlson, the friend who invited me, "How can people who swear and smoke be Christians?"

John's answer stopped me cold, "Bob, maybe there is a difference between being a Christian and acting like a Christian. Isn't it possible that Christians can *grow* in their walk with the Lord?"

I didn't have an answer that night. I had to think about it. What John was saying did make sense and it helped explain many passages of Scripture that were puzzling to me.

With John's help I made contact with the same ministry at my school, the University of California at Irvine (the Anteaters!). I met with Athletes in Action staff member Warren Wilke many times, and the Lord used him to open my eyes to see that the sole condition of eternal life is to believe in Christ. Once you believe, you have eternal life that can never be lost. No sin, big or small, can separate the believer from Christ.

What an impact this had on me! For the first time in my life, I knew that I had eternal life and that I could never lose it. No matter what happened in the future, I was heaven-bound. This assurance motivated me to live for God and to devote my life to telling others this wonderful message.

When Does Eternal Security Begin?

People who do not believe in eternal security this side of the grave (everyone believes in eternal security for those who make it to heaven) are often called *Arminians* after a Dutch scholar in church history named Jacob Arminius (1560-1609). Most Arminians are not as extreme as the group which influenced me (see the Introduction). Most feel that it takes a *major* sin to cause you to lose your salvation,[1] and that you can regain salvation by confessing and repenting of the sin or sins you committed. Most Arminians believe they can be saved and lost many times. Of course, if a person dies with an unconfessed major sin on his account, they believe he would go to hell, because he didn't repent before he died.[2]

I have found that most people who don't believe in eternal security this side of the grave have never really considered a few vital questions. If God guarantees eternal security once we die, why does He not grant it once we are born again? After all, if we can't lose it *then*, why *now*? And, if we can lose it *now*, why not *then*?

God guarantees that anyone who believes in His Son for eternal life is from that moment eternally secure. The following five passages demonstrate this promise.

• *People irreversibly pass from death to life when they believe the gospel.*

> "Most assuredly, I say to you, he who hears My word and believes in Him who sent Me has [present tense] everlasting life, and shall not come [future tense] into judgment, but has passed [past tense] from death into life."
>
> —John 5:24

Eternal life doesn't begin when we die! It begins when we believe in Christ. Jesus didn't say that those who believe "will have" everlasting life in the future. He said that they have everlasting life right now.

In this context, to "hear" Jesus' word is to believe what He has to say about eternal life. Likewise, to "believe in Him who sent Me" is to believe the gospel which Jesus' Father sent Him to preach.

Jesus guarantees that those who believe in Him will never be eternally condemned—"shall not come into judgment." In other words, Jesus promises all believers eternal security because they have already passed from the sphere of death into life. That is a one-way journey.

• *Jesus doesn't lose even one believer.*

> "For I have come down from heaven, not to do My own will, but the will of Him who sent Me. This is the will of the Father who sent Me, that of all He has given Me I should lose nothing, but should raise it up at the last day. And this is the will of Him who sent Me, that everyone who sees the Son and believes in Him may have everlasting life; and I will raise Him up at the last day."
> —John 6:38-40

Jesus completely fulfills the will of His Father, including keeping every believer secure forever. Jesus has never lost a believer to Satan and He never will. Satan cannot steal even one of Jesus' sheep (John 10:1-30). Jesus will raise up each and every person who believes in Him for eternal life.

Many people mistakenly think it is up to us to stay saved. Yet Jesus clearly declares that it is up to *Him* to keep us saved. If any Christian lost his salvation, then Jesus would have failed to do the will of His Father.

• *No one is able to snatch believers out of God's hand.*

> "My sheep hear My voice, and I know them, and they follow Me. And I give them eternal life, and they shall never perish; neither shall anyone snatch them out of My hand. My Father, who has given them to Me, is greater than all; and no one is able to snatch them out of My Father's hand. I and My Father are one."
> —John 10:27-30

No one can remove us from God's hands. If we could take ourselves out of His hands, we would have to be stronger than God.

Once you are born again, you have eternal life and can never lose it. Even if you came to the point where you wanted to renounce your salvation, you couldn't. You can't do anything to reverse the new birth. God guarantees it.

• *Even the bodies of carnal believers are the temples of the Holy Spirit.*

> Or do you not know that he who is joined to a harlot is one body with her? For "the two," He says, "shall become one flesh." But he who is joined to the Lord is one spirit with Him. Flee sexual immorality. Every sin that a man does is outside the body, but he who commits sexual immorality sins against his own body. Or do you not know that *your body is the temple of the Holy Spirit who is in you,* whom you have from God, and you are not your own? For you were bought at a price; therefore glorify God in your body and in your spirit, which are God's.
> —1 Corinthians 6:16-20 (italics added)

Eternal security is so foundational that the writers of the New Testament based their instructions about the Christian life upon it. A case in point is Paul's appeal to the believers in Corinth to stop their immoral behavior. Some of them were frequenting prostitutes. Surely if salvation could be lost, that would do it. However, rather than telling his readers that they had lost their salvation, Paul reaffirmed it! He told these carnal believers, "Your body is the temple of the Holy Spirit who is in you." They weren't glorifying God with their bodies as they should have been. The apostle Paul appealed to the eternally secure standing of the Corinthian believers—and through them to all of us—to motivate them to live godly lives.

• *Whether their works are good or bad, believers will appear at the judgment exclusively reserved for the saved.*

> Therefore we make it our aim, whether present or absent, to be well pleasing to Him. For we must all appear before the judgment seat of Christ, that each one may receive the things done in the body,

according to what he has done, whether good
or bad.

—2 Corinthians 5:9-10

The Bible describes two judgments after death, one for
unbelievers, the Great White Throne Judgment (Revelation
20:11-15), and one for *believers*, the Judgment Seat of Christ (this
passage). At this judgment the Lord Jesus will determine and
announce what rewards each believer will receive, if any.

The apostle's claim in verse 10 was dependent on all
believers being eternally secure. Even the carnal Christians at Corinth
were sure to appear at the judgment of the saved.

The Results of Rejecting Eternal Security

Those who do not believe in eternal security miss out on some
of the most important things God wants us all to have. Those who
have *never* believed in eternal security miss out on *the* most important thing.

• *Missing the new birth.* As the five passages cited above
illustrate, we do not believe the gospel of Jesus Christ until we are
sure that we personally are eternally secure because we have
believed in Christ (see chapter 6, especially the section "Assurance
Is of the Essence of Saving Faith"). The promise of the gospel is that
all who simply believe in Christ for eternal life are eternally secure
from that point onward. And, since believing the gospel is necessary
to be born again and to go to heaven, a person who has *never* had
assurance that he is eternally secure has not yet been born again.

Jesus gave but one condition for eternal life: believing in Him
for it. Thus the person who thinks that faith in Christ is necessary,
but not enough, doesn't believe what Jesus said.

• *Missing freedom from the fear of hell.* People who don't
believe in eternal security are obviously afraid they might end up in
hell.[3] This fear can be so intense that some can't stand it anymore
and drop out of church to join groups like Fundamentalists
Anonymous.

Those who manage to keep their fear in check may even feel a sense of pride that they aren't obsessed with concern. However, if they slow down enough to think about the possibility that they might spend eternity in hell, their fear builds. Many devout persons, including pastors and missionaries, have agonized on their deathbeds over the possibility that they were doomed. They realized their life and their works were far from perfect. Did they really do enough?

Even born again persons can lose their assurance and fear that they aren't saved. Being born again is no guarantee that they will continue to believe in eternal security. If they stop believing it, they remain saved, for eternal security is true, but they miss out on the joy of knowing they are secure in Christ forever. They feel a terrible fear that God never intended for His children to have.

Does this mean that if you don't believe in eternal security, you aren't saved? That depends. If you have *never* believed in eternal security, then you aren't saved, because eternal security is the promise Jesus makes in the gospel.[4] However, if you at one time believed it, you remain saved even if you have stopped believing it.

• *Missing the ability to please God.* When our works come out of a desire to earn or to keep salvation, then we are truly *self-righteous*. Only by relying on Jesus' promise can we be *Christ-righteous*: "He made Him who knew no sin to be sin for us, that we might become the righteousness of God in Him" (2 Corinthians 5:21). The believer who forgets this and tries to work to get to heaven, though still secure, has fallen from grace in his Christian experience and no longer pleases God with the works he does (see chapter 14).

The apostle John said, "He who believes in the Son of God has the witness in Himself; he who does not believe God has made Him a liar, because he has not believed the testimony that God has given of His Son" (1 John 5:10). God doesn't like anyone calling Him a liar! The believer who ceases to believe God's testimony is doing just that.

97

Jesus told the apostles, "Without Me, you can do nothing" (John 15:5). Even the apostles were unable to do anything pleasing to God apart from abiding in Christ. And in order to abide in Christ, we must continue to believe the gospel.

The gospel is foundational to a successful Christian life (1 Corinthians 3:5-15; the Book of Galatians).

• *Missing the powerful motivation of gratitude.* When a sinful woman whom Jesus had forgiven washed His feet with her tears and wiped His feet with her hair, some of the bystanders objected that He was permitting a sinful woman to touch Him. Jesus explained that she loved Him much because He had forgiven her much (Luke 7:36-50). Of course, anyone who is born again has been forgiven much. Thus, we all should love much: "We love Him because He first loved us" (1 John 4:19).

A common objection to eternal security is that if someone believed that they would be motivated to go out and live like the devil. That is, however, a straw man. While eternal security makes abuses of grace *possible*, it does not *promote* such abuses. In fact, eternal security promotes holiness. Gratitude is one of the most powerful motivators.[5]

The believer who ceases to believe in eternal security loses sight of the fact that all his sins are forgiven and that he is secure forever. Therefore, he cannot be motivated out of gratitude for these things, since he isn't sure they are true of him.

A Personal Invitation

If you don't believe in eternal security, I invite you to prayerfully and thoughtfully consider what the Bible has to say.[6] The Scriptures show that eternal security is true.

Jesus Christ guarantees eternal life to all who believe in Him for it. Once you come to faith in Him and Him alone, you are secure forever.

Eternal security is an apt description for the life that Jesus gives. Eternal life is eternal.

CHAPTER 12

A PUNISHMENT WORSE THAN DEATH
Hebrews 10:26-31

HAVE YOU EVER noticed the difference between horror films—or even advertisements for them—in decades past and now? The original Frankenstein has become almost a comic, friendly figure, and *The Blob*, which created nightmares for thousands, looks insultingly tame next to the latest Hollywood aliens. Because we have become desensitized, it takes a lot to frighten us.

Although the Bible offers the believer many passages of love, peace, and joy, it also contains some frighteningly stern passages concerning judgment. In the verses we'll now consider, we'll see one of the strongest warnings in Scripture and, consequently, a valid reason for fear. Hebrews 10:26-31 is filled with ominous terms such as "judgment," "fiery indignation," "devouring the adversaries," "vengeance," and "worse punishment."

Though it may take a lot to scare people today, this passage has plenty of firepower. However we understand it, we know that it is certainly talking about something dreadful:

> For if we sin willfully after we have received the knowledge of the truth, there no longer remains a sacrifice for sins, but a certain fearful expectation of judgment, and fiery indignation which will devour the adversaries. Anyone who has rejected Moses' law dies without mercy on the testimony of two or three witnesses. Of how much worse punishment, do you suppose, will he be thought worthy who has trampled the Son of God underfoot, counted the blood of the covenant by which he was sanctified a common thing, and insulted the Spirit of grace? For we know Him who said, "Vengeance is Mine, I will repay," says the Lord. And again, "The Lord will

judge His people." It is a fearful thing to fall
into the hands of the living God.
—Hebrews 10:26-31

Why This Isn't about Hell

How do we know that eternal condemnation is not being
threatened in this passage? Let's look at two reasons.

• *No believer will go to hell.* The Book of Hebrews is
addressed to believers. See, for example, 3:1, "Therefore, *holy
brethren, partakers of the heavenly calling...*" (italics added).
Compare also 6:4-6 which says that those in danger of falling away
were once enlightened, partakers of the Holy Spirit, and had tasted
the good word of God and the heavenly gift.

In the verses preceding Hebrews 10:26-31, the author speaks
of being made perfect (verses 1, 10, 14) and of the forgiveness of
sins (verses 4, 17-18). In verses 19 to 20 he calls the readers
"brethren," people who have "boldness to enter the Holiest by the
blood of Jesus" and who have Jesus Christ as their High Priest. The
immediate context of this passage says that those being addressed
have *already* been sanctified (verse 29)! Only *believers* have been
sanctified (see 10:10, 14). In addition, they are called "His people"
(verse 30)—something true only of believers.

No believer will ever go to hell (John 3:16-18; 5:24; 6:38-40;
1 Thessalonians 5:9-10; Hebrews 10:10). Since this passage is
addressed to believers, we can be sure that whatever this punishment
is, it is not hell.

• *Hell isn't even mentioned.* There is no reference to "the lake
of fire," "Gehenna," "hell," "unquenchable fire," "eternal torment,"
or any terms commonly associated with eternal condemnation. Take
a moment and reread the passage and you will see what I mean.

Why This Is about Temporal Punishment

Born again people experience only two types of judgment
from God: a judgment after this life, the Judgment Seat of Christ,

when Jesus will judge their works and announce their eternal rewards, and a judgment during this life, temporal judgment, when God disciplines them for disobedience. Thus, this judgment must refer to one of those two judgments.

There is nothing in the context to indicate that the Judgment Seat of Christ is in view. Therefore, this passage must be talking about temporal judgment that falls upon disobedient believers. That is supported by references in the context.

• *Capital punishment is a temporal judgment.* The author of the Book of Hebrews compares this fearful judgment with the death penalty under the Law of Moses: "Anyone who has rejected Moses' law dies without mercy on the testimony of two or three witnesses. Of how much worse punishment, do you suppose, will he be thought worthy…" (verses 28-29).

Like our legal system today, the laws of the nation of Israel had a number of crimes that allowed for the death penalty (for example, adultery and murder). The death penalty applied to both believers and unbelievers in ancient Israel, just as it does in most countries today. For example, after Aaron's sons, Nᵣdab and Abihu, offered up strange fire during the dedication of the tabernacle, evidently because they were drunk (Leviticus 10:9-11), God sent fire from heaven and took their lives (10:1-2). They were saved men, yet they died for violating God's commands.

Similarly, during the start of the church age, God took the lives of two believers who lied to the apostle Peter, and ultimately to God Himself. Ananias and his wife, Sapphira, were dramatically struck dead in front of the church for their sin (Acts 5:1-11).

Now a comparison is valid only if you are comparing similar things. Comparing one apple with another apple is fine. But comparing an apple with an orange does not offer sufficient likeness. So, too, this comparison is valid only if the two judgments are of the same general type. Physical death is a type of temporal punishment. Eternal death is not.

If the author of Hebrews had been talking about eternal condemnation, he would have offered a comparison dealing with eternal punishment, such as the rich man Jesus spoke of in Luke 16:19-31, or of the final judgment of the moral unbelievers of Matthew 7:21-23.

Since a temporal judgment was used as the point of comparison, this "worse punishment" must refer to some type of temporal judgment that is worse than immediate physical death.

• *Many temporal judgments are worse than immediate death.* Lingering and unabated emotional, spiritual, and physical pain can be much worse than immediate death. As Zane Hodges writes:

> The writer was not thinking of hell. Many forms of divine retribution can fall on a human life which are worse than immediate death. In fact, Jeremiah made just such a complaint about the punishment inflicted on Jerusalem (Lam 4:6, 9). One might think also of King Saul, whose last days were burdened with such mental and emotional turmoil that death itself was a kind of release.[1]

We might also think of King David. After his immorality with Bathsheba and murder of her husband, he suffered through one loss and calamity after another (see Second Samuel 12–24). The fact that God spared David from immediate death (2 Samuel 12:13) doesn't necessarily mean he received a lesser punishment. After one of those losses, the death of his beloved son Absalom, David said, "O my son Absalom—my son, my son Absalom—if only I had died in your place!" (2 Samuel 18:33).

Don't Be Fooled about Apostasy

It's possible for a believer who is living an outward life of godliness and morality to have little concern about the fact that he is becoming attracted to a different view of the gospel.[2] However, outward morality is not the sole measure of discipleship. Holding fast our confession of the true gospel is also vitally important. If we fall away from the true gospel, we are in serious trouble. The following comment by Philip Edgcumbe Hughes is a powerful warning on the danger of apostasy:

> The apostate falls into the hands of the living God: *he abandons God as his Savior only to meet Him as his Judge.*[3]

CHAPTER 13

THE BURNED BRANCHES
John 15:6

A S I WRITE, the NFL pre-season has begun. Sportscasters describe the action using colorful imagery such as blitzes, sweeps, air strikes, sacks, knockdowns, and pancake blocks. One such expression often heard is "being burned." Often a cornerback, the loneliest position on any football team, will have to cover the other team's fastest man all by himself. A cornerback is "burned" on a play if a wide receiver gets past him and catches a ball for a long gain.

Burning is also used figuratively in the Bible. The Lord Jesus spoke of the burning of believers in Christ who do not abide in Him:

> "If anyone does not abide in Me, he is cast out as a branch and is withered; and they gather them and throw them into the fire, and they are burned."
> —John 15:6

What did the Lord mean? How could a believer ever be "burned"? Let's begin by considering the setting for these words.

The Setting

Jesus was talking to His disciples about bearing fruit. When He spoke of the vine and the branches, He was using something the disciples knew well to illustrate the demands of discipleship. In order for a branch to bear grapes, it must remain attached to the grapevine. If any branch is detached from the vine, no fruit will grow on it, and it is useless for its intended purpose. A common practice of viticulture is the burning of unproductive branches.

So, too, remaining connected with "the true vine" (15:1), the Lord Jesus, is vital in order for believers to produce good works.

Believers can do nothing apart from active connection with the Lord Jesus, "Without Me you can do nothing" (15:5).

This Doesn't Refer to Burning in Hell

• *Jesus was talking about believers.* Jesus' audience that day was eleven of the most important men in the history of the church. There were no unbelievers present since Judas, the unbelieving traitor, had already left to betray Jesus (John 13:30). He specifically had just told the remaining eleven, "You are already clean because of the word which I have spoken to you" (15:3; compare 13:10).

We know from other references in John's Gospel that no believer will ever burn in hell. Jesus said that the believer, "shall not come into judgment" (John 5:24), "shall never perish" (10:28), and, "shall never die" (11:26). Therefore, Jesus wasn't speaking of eternal condemnation here.

• *Fire often refers to temporal judgment.* When used figuratively in Scripture, fire (Greek: *pur*)[1] is often symbolic of temporal judgment. Paul spoke of heaping coals of fire on the head of one's enemy by dealing lovingly with him (Romans 12:20). Paul's point was that it would upset an enemy if you treated him in a loving manner. That has to do with the here and now, not with eternal condemnation.

James wrote, "The tongue is a fire...and is set on fire by hell" (3:6). He was saying that the tongue can be very destructive.

Jude spoke of pulling believers from the fire of impending temporal judgment (verse 23).

Peter and Paul said that fire tests the works of believers (1 Corinthians 3:10-15; 1 Peter 1:7).

Only when qualifiers like "eternal" or "unquenchable" are used does fire in Scripture refer to eternal judgment.[2] Boice writes:

> Burning is not always used of hell, as the passage in 1 Corinthians about works [1 Corinthians 3:10-15] proves. And it is its association with the

destruction of useless works rather than with the loss of salvation that is most appropriate in this passage.[3]

• *The illustration suggests temporal judgment.* There is nothing in the illustration or in the context to suggest eternal condemnation. Rather, the burning of unproductive branches suggests temporal judgment.

Some think that because the branches were "burned up" and done away with that eternal judgment is meant.[4] However, whether this refers to branches being *burned,* or being *burned up* (see the discussion below), temporal judgment is meant. God can and does judge believers in this life, sometimes even taking them home prematurely (1 Corinthians 11:30; James 5:19-20). A believer can experience temporal judgment, but not eternal condemnation.

• *Only believers can abide in Christ.* Urging an unbeliever to abide in Christ and bear fruit would be like urging an oak branch to abide in a grapevine and bear grapes. Unbelievers can't "abide" in a place that is foreign to them.

Abiding is the theme of John's first epistle: "And now, little children, abide in Him, that when He appears, we may have confidence and not be ashamed before Him at His coming" (1 John 2:28). First John is written to believers to urge them to be in fellowship with God (1:3) so that they might hear the Lord's "Well done" when He returns. It is believers, not unbelievers, who need to take this warning seriously. No matter how gifted we are, if we cease to stay in God's Word and in fellowship with God, we can do nothing that will draw God's praise. Instead, we will elicit something we don't want. Let's now consider the nature of this judgment.

Difficulties Here and Now Are in View

It is probably wrong to conclude that the expression "they are burned" refers specifically to physical death. That expression is a translation of the last word in the Greek sentence, *kaietai.* Had the

Lord meant that unfruitful believers unequivocally experience premature physical death, John could have easily used the related Greek verb *katakaietai*, meaning, "they are burned up." John's choice of the softer verb indicates that the Lord was referring generally to various types of temporal judgment. This judgment could include guilt, illness, financial losses, accidents, depression, family problems, difficulties at work, reproof from a fellow believer, etc.

We must remember, of course, that not all suffering is a result of God's chastening hand.[5] There are many other reasons, including persecution (as in the case of our Lord and the apostles), character formation (James 1:2-12), testimony to the unsaved (Acts 26:1-29), and the revelation of the glory of God (John 9:1-2ff.).

How can we know if we are under God's chastening hand? There is no biblical formula, but a good guideline to follow is this: If you are suffering, and you are aware of unconfessed sin in your life, then confess and forsake it immediately (James 5:16; 1 John 1:9). On the other hand, if you are unaware of any such sin, and to the best of your knowledge you are walking with Christ, then pray and ask the Lord to show you if you are overlooking something.[6] If nothing comes to your attention, you can reasonably conclude that your difficulties are not due to sin in your life.

The key is to avoid the two extremes. On the one hand, don't view all your problems as judgment from God. On the other hand, don't go the other way and conclude that God *never* judges His children. If you've just robbed a bank and bullets are whizzing by your head as you attempt to flee, it would be reasonable to conclude that God is trying to get your attention!

Believers Who Play with Fire Get Burned

We began with the illustration of a cornerback being "burned" in an NFL football game in order to point out that all burning is not literal. That cornerback—and his coach—would undoubtedly take that play very seriously. Football players tend to be intense about playing their best and winning. To them (and to many armchair quarterbacks) football is far more than a game.

Being burned in a football game is mild compared to being burned as a believer. Tragically, many Christians often fail to take seriously enough the call to abide in Christ and produce fruit. They play with their faith and responsibilities as if this were a game.

Verses such as John 15:6 can help us all to remember what we are about. God's grace abounds, but the grace of God is not a license to sin. Rather, it provides a powerful motivation to please God by bearing much fruit. Those who do will be greatly rewarded. But believers who choose to play with fire will get burned.

CHAPTER 14

FALLING FROM GRACE
Galatians 5:4

THOMAS F. TORRANCE wrote an insightful book called *The Doctrine of Grace in the Apostolic Fathers*.[1] He showed that the apostolic fathers, who were "Christian" writers of the second century,[2] to a man distorted the concept of grace. They replaced justification by faith alone with justification by faith plus works.

Baptism was one of the first major areas of confusion. The apostles taught that baptism was not a part of the gospel (1 Corinthians 1:17), but that it was the first step every believer should take in following Christ, publicly identifying oneself as a believer in Him (Matthew 28:19-20; Acts 8:12-13; 10:47-48; 16:15; 18:8). The apostolic fathers, however, said that baptism was necessary for eternal salvation, and that at the point of baptism one's former sins were forgiven. There are two problems with this. First, water baptism is not a condition of eternal salvation. Second, the forgiveness received when a person is born again—by faith, not baptism—is total, covering all sins, past, present, and future.

What would you do if you were told that a clean slate was necessary to go to heaven and that baptism gave you a clean slate, but that the slate would not stay clean long? You would probably do what many in the second-century did, wait until you were on your deathbed to be baptized!

The leaders of the early church had to do something since this situation wasn't good. After several ecclesiastical huddles, a new and improved gospel emerged. Now baptism gave you a clean slate; repentance was a way of recleaning your slate; and you could have an unlimited number of opportunities to repent in your lifetime.[3] The doctrine of penance was born.

All of this resulted because the apostolic fathers and their disciples departed from the gospel of grace. Baptism and turning from sins, both important aspects of following Christ in discipleship, became parts of the gospel itself. Tragically, multitudes went to their graves without Christ, because their tradition told them that all baptized and repentant church people went to heaven.

Things didn't improve much until the sixteenth century and the Reformation led by Calvin and Luther. Sadly, however, many people rejected their teachings. More tragic still, many of the followers of Calvin and Luther departed from them on key points, and by doing so garbled the gospel.

Only a small segment of Christendom in any era of church history has believed in the gospel of grace. Of course, this should be no surprise to those familiar with the teachings of Jesus. He said, "Enter by the narrow gate; for wide is the gate and broad is the way that leads to destruction, and there are many who go by it. Because narrow is the gate and difficult is the way which leads to life, and there are few who find it" (Matthew 7:13-14). The narrow way goes against the flow. In order to believe the gospel, you must believe something that the vast majority of people not only do not believe, but consider foolishness (1 Corinthians 1:18).

Years ago I came across a tract based on Galatians 5:4 entitled, "Can a Saved Man Fall from Grace?" According to that tract, "Once he has been saved from his past sins, the newborn child of God must maintain his saved state by walking in the light." After quoting 1 John 1:7, it continued, "This is how a child of God stays saved. It is by walking in the light! One walks in the light by daily obedience to the truth—by regular worship, purity of life, love of the brethren, etc."

That is not my idea of "blessed assurance."

Many people believe that if a professing Christian falls from grace, he either loses his salvation[4] or proves he was never truly saved in the first place.[5] According to Lordship Salvation, the idea that one can be saved simply by believing in Christ for eternal life is *easy believism, cheap grace,* or *fire insurance.* They maintain that commitment, obedience, and perseverance in good works and sound doctrine must accompany faith in order to make it to heaven.

This way of thinking, though well intentioned, is misguided. By failing to see the distinction between eternal life, which is absolutely free, and eternal rewards, which are very costly, this view confuses the call of discipleship with the invitation of the gospel. Heaven is no longer for all who believe, but only for those who believe and persist in faithful service.

Falling from grace is painful. It is something we should strive to avoid. However, it does not close heaven's gates, as the context of Galatians 5:4 makes clear. Sadly, those who believe that it does do not believe the gospel of grace.[6]

Only Christians Can Fall from Grace

That the Galatian readers were born again is unmistakably clear. Paul indicates that they had received his gospel (1:9) and the Holy Spirit (3:2). He repeatedly calls them "brethren" (e.g., 1:11; 3:15; 4:12, 28; 5:11, 13; 6:1, 18)—a term that he reserved in his epistles for Christians.

Additionally, Galatians 5:4 itself makes it clear that Christians are being addressed. Paul said,

> You have become estranged from Christ,[7] you who attempt to be justified by law; you have fallen from grace.

Only a person who has received the grace of God can fall from that grace. An unregenerate person can't fall from grace because he has never received it.

This is consistent with our experience. A person can only fall from a place where he is. A person can't fall from one of the seats of a Ferris wheel, for example, unless he is in one of the seats. Likewise, a person can't fall from the sphere of grace unless he is in the sphere of grace.

Falling from Grace Is Not a Loss of Eternal Life

Paul taught that it was impossible for Christians to lose their salvation. For example, he encouraged the believers at Thessalonica by telling them that Christ "died for us, that *whether we wake or sleep*, we should live together with Him" (1 Thessalonians 5:10, emphasis added). In that context, waking and sleeping are used figuratively for being morally watchful and sober and morally blind and drunk (verse 6). Yet, Paul says that even believers who are walking in the darkness will be raptured and will "live together with Him." Once a person is saved, he is guaranteed to live with Christ forever.

Paul also said, "If we are faithless, He remains faithful; He cannot deny Himself" (2 Timothy 2:13). What great news! Even if we are faithless (and who hasn't been occasionally?) the Lord will remain faithful. He guarantees eternal life to everyone who comes to faith in Him.

Paul reminded all believers that we "were sealed with the Holy Spirit of promise, who is the guarantee of our inheritance until the redemption of the purchased possession, to the praise of His glory" (Ephesians 1:13-14). That seal is God's guarantee. Our eternal salvation is signed, sealed, and delivered. God couldn't revoke our salvation even if He wanted to, because He has bound Himself with a promise and it is impossible for Him to break a promise. His nature will not allow it.

Paul beautifully affirmed that *nothing* can separate the believer from God's love in Christ:

> For I am persuaded that neither death nor life, nor angels nor principalities nor powers, nor things present nor things to come, nor height nor depth, nor any other created thing, shall be able to separate us from the love of God which is in Christ Jesus our Lord.
>
> —Romans 8:38-39

114

In those two verses Paul employs a figure of speech called *merism*. In a merism two extremes are stated and everything in between is implied. For example, "nor height nor depth" refers to everything between the highest and lowest places in the universe. "Nor things present nor things to come" contemplates anything that could ever happen from now through all of eternity. And, just in case a person might wonder if Paul left anything out, he includes a general reference that nothing created can separate us either.[8]

Falling from Grace Is the Loss of an Experience of Grace in Your Daily Life

The Greek verb *ekpiptō* is translated "you have fallen." While its basic meaning is "to fall" (as in withered flowers that *fall* to the ground), in this context it is used figuratively and refers to the loss of one's grip on grace as a principle to live by. Donald Campbell writes:

> The issue here is not loss of salvation, for "grace" is referred to not as salvation itself but as a method of salvation (cf. 2:21 where "a Law" route is mentioned as an unacceptable way to come to Christ). If the Galatians accepted circumcision as necessary for salvation, they would be leaving the grace system for the Mosaic Law system. The same error is repeated today when a believer leaves a church that emphasizes salvation by grace through faith and joins one which teaches that salvation depends on repentance, confession, faith, baptism, and church membership.[9]

The Galatian Christians were being told by legalistic teachers, often referred to as Judaizers, that while salvation begins by faith in Christ, final salvation would be achieved only through ongoing obedience to the Law of Moses, including circumcision (Galatians 3:1-5; 5:1-4). Believers lose their grip on grace by falling prey to the teachings of legalism. If a Christian leaves a church that is clear on the gospel and joins one that is not, he is in great danger of losing his

115

grip on grace. If a well-grounded young person goes to a high school, college, or seminary that promotes a "faith-plus" view of the gospel, that student is, like Humpty Dumpty of old, a candidate for a great fall.

That's why Paul told the Galatians to run, not walk, away from the legalists. His advice is as relevant today as it was then.

You will lose your grip on God's grace if you ever start thinking that believing is not enough to be eternally secure. Once you fall back to a faith-plus view of salvation, you have fallen from grace, for you regard your salvation as partly dependent on your performance.

Since assurance of salvation is central to the gospel itself, a faith-plus view of assurance also results in falling from grace. Many churches today teach that works are indispensable for assurance of salvation. However, a believer who accepts that teaching has fallen from grace and is no longer looking to Christ alone for assurance. He begins to think that in order to go to heaven he must do good works. That is not salvation by grace.

Quite a few Lordship Salvation pastors and theologians testify that at one time they believed in the Free Grace gospel! Respected scholar Dr. J. I. Packer writes:

> I was just such a Gospel hypocrite for two years before God mercifully made me aware of my unconverted state. If I seem harsh in my critique of [Zane] Hodges' redefinition of faith as barren intellectual formalism,[10] you must remember that *once I almost lost my soul through assuming what Hodges teaches*, and a burned child always thereafter dreads the fire.[11]

If the Free Grace view of the gospel is correct—and it is, then by his own admission Dr. Packer has fallen from grace.[12] Though born again and heaven bound, he is missing out on a present experience of God's grace.[13] The following table compares Lordship Salvation with the biblical gospel, or what I call *Free Grace Salvation*:

	Lordship Salvation	Free Grace Salvation
Will simply believing in Christ for eternal life save?	No	Yes
Is perseverance required for final salvation?	Yes	No
Do those who fall from grace go to heaven?	No	Yes
Should fear of hell motivate Christians to live holy lives?	Yes	No

Any believer in Jesus Christ, no matter how well educated or how dedicated, is in danger of falling from grace. It is vital that we stay in God's Word and fellowship at a church that is clear on the gospel.

Stand Against the Tide

Professing Christendom is like an ocean whose tide flows away from the shore of grace. Watch out for the undertow. It will take you right out to sea. To continue in your experience of God's grace, you must resist the tide. Don't let anything pull you away from God's glorious gospel of grace.

CHAPTER 15

ERASERS IN HEAVEN?
Revelation 3:5

A READER OF our free bimonthly newsletter, *Grace in Focus,*[1] sent me this question:

> Revelation 3:5 is one passage that has been very hard for me to understand and clarify. My question is, can a believer lose his salvation or be erased from the Book of Life if he does not overcome? This seems to contradict John 5:24 and Ephesians 2:8-9 that appear to view everlasting life as a free and secure gift. Or, does it mean that a believer who is truly saved will automatically produce good works and overcome? This seems to contradict Romans 6–7 which views the Christian walk as a struggle and a choice that every believer must make for himself.

The writer is correct. Neither of the two interpretations he has suggested can be harmonized with the clear teaching of other Scripture. In Revelation 3:5 we find three promises from the Lord Jesus:

> "He who overcomes shall be clothed in white garments, and I will not blot out his name from the Book of Life; but I will confess his name before My Father and before His angels."

Jesus Isn't Warning Believers
They Might Lose Their Salvation

Some think that Revelation 3:5 implies that believers who don't overcome in their experience in this life lose their salvation. The problem with this understanding is that it makes the Lord Jesus Christ a liar! "He who believes in the Son of God has the witness in himself; he who does not believe God *has made Him a liar*, because

119

he has not believed the testimony that God has given of His Son. And this is the testimony: that God has given us *eternal* life, and this life is in His Son" (1 John 5:10-11, italics added).

Jesus promised that once a person comes to faith in Him he is secure forever. "The one who comes to Me I will by no means cast out" (John 6:37). "This is the will of the Father who sent Me, that of all He has given Me I should lose nothing, but should raise it up at the last day" (John 6:39). "He who believes in Me *has* everlasting life" (John 6:47, italics added).[2]

For a believer to lose his salvation, Jesus would have to fail to keep His promise. Many wrongly reason we can lose our salvation since *we* might fail to persevere in good works. Yet we are not the ones who made the promise that all who believe in Jesus have eternal life. He is the One who made that promise. Thus for a believer to lose his salvation, Jesus would have to fail to do what He said He would do. That will never happen. Therefore, Jesus is definitely not warning believers that if they fail to live an overcoming life that they will lose their salvation.

Jesus Isn't Warning Believers
They Might Not Be Saved

Some think that this verse is implying that believers who don't overcome in their experience prove that they were never saved in the first place. John MacArthur writes: "John was so confident of the ultimate triumph of faith over sin that he had a special name for the believer: 'the one who overcomes' (1 John 5:5; Rev. 2:7, 11, 26; 3:5, 12, 21; 21:7)."[3] He interprets overcoming as "the ultimate triumph of faith over sin."[4] One might argue that MacArthur meant merely that believers will live holy lives once they go to be with the Lord (1 John 3:2). However, based on the context of his remarks, it is clear that the ultimate triumph to which he refers occurs in this life, prior to going to be with the Lord.[5]

According to the Reformed doctrine of the perseverance of

the saints, all true believers persevere in a life of godliness. While there may be temporary setbacks and bouts with sin, believers are people who live victorious, holy lives. People who hold this interpretation of Revelation 3:5 understand it in light of that doctrine.

However, the Bible does *not* promise that all believers will live victorious, holy lives.[6] They may have more than temporary setbacks and bouts with sin, and may even backslide terribly and die in that state. The Corinthian believers had abused the Lord's Supper to the extent that many of them were weak and sick and some had even died (1 Corinthians 11:30). Earlier in his letter Paul had criticized the Corinthians for being carnal and having envy, strife, and divisions among them (1 Corinthians 3:3). This is hardly a picture of believers experiencing ultimate victory over sin in their lives! Compare also Galatians 6:1-5, James 5:19-20, and 1 John 5:16.

In the second and third chapters of Revelation, we find letters addressed to seven churches. While a church building can contain some non-believers, the true church, which is precisely Jesus' audience here, consists only of believers.

Each of the seven letters refers to rewards which overcoming believers will receive. In every letter we also find the phrase, "I know your works." Works, not faith. There is a clear correspondence between overcoming, rewards, and works in each of the letters.

In this context, overcoming is not something all believers are guaranteed to do. Just the opposite. Believers are being exhorted to overcome with the clear possibility that they may not. Consider, for example, these statements from Revelation 2–3:

> "Be faithful until death, and I will give you the crown of life" (2:10).

> "And he who overcomes, and keeps My works until the end, to him I will give power over the nations" (2:26).

"You have a few names even in Sardis who have not defiled their garments; and they shall walk with Me in white, for they are worthy. He who overcomes shall be clothed in white garments" (3:4-5).

"Hold fast what you have, that no one may take your crown" (3:11).

"To him who overcomes I will grant to sit with Me on My throne, as I also overcame and sat down with My Father on His throne" (3:21).

Jesus Is Speaking about the Possibility of Eternal Rewards

• *Watchfulness is tied to eternal rewards, not to eternal salvation.* The Lord warned the church at Sardis, "If you will not *watch*, I will come upon you as a thief, and you will not know the hour I will come upon you" (3:3, italics added). Calls to watchfulness in light of the Lord's imminent return as a thief are found in several other places in the New Testament. Eternal reward, not eternal salvation, is in view in each of those places.[7]

In 1 Thessalonians 5:10, a context dealing with Christ's return "as a thief in the night" (5:2), Paul wrote, "[Christ] died for us, that whether we wake or sleep, we should live together with Him." In this context "waking"[8] means to walk in the light, or to be sober, faithful, and loving, and "sleeping" means to walk in the darkness, or to be drunk, unfaithful, and unloving (1 Thessalonians 5:4-8). All believers, even those who are morally asleep—that is, those who don't overcome—will be raptured when Christ returns for them.

If watchfulness concerns eternal salvation, then Jesus is teaching salvation by works. Yet He and His apostles directly deny that (Luke 18:9-14; John 4:10; 6:28-29; Romans 4:4-5; Ephesians 2:8-9; James 1:17-18; Revelation 22:17).

• *Worthiness is linked with eternal rewards, not eternal salvation.* The Lord indicated that some of the believers in Sardis were "worthy" to walk with Him in white (3:4) because they had not "defiled their garments," that is, because they had not walked in disobedience.

If walking with Christ in white garments is not seen as a reward, then Christ is teaching salvation by personal worthiness here! We know from Jesus' teachings and from the entire Bible that *no one* is worthy to be in God's kingdom because of his deeds. We can be worthy to enter God's kingdom only because we have trusted in the Worthy One. This is compelling proof that the issue here is reward, not salvation.

• *Walking with Christ in white garments deals with eternal rewards, not eternal salvation.* Some understand white garments to refer to the clothing that all believers will have forever. However, if all believers wear these garments, then all must be overcomers.

It is incorrect to draw the conclusion that these garments represent the clothing that all believers will wear in the kingdom. A comparison with Revelation 16:15 makes this evident, "Behold, I am coming as a thief. Blessed is he who watches, and keeps his garments, lest he walk naked and they see his shame." This verse contains all of the same elements, the coming of the Lord as a thief, the need for watchfulness, the need to keep one's spiritual garments clean, the prospect of walking with Christ in white garments or no garments, and the prospect of joy versus shame. Only the believer who is watchful will walk in white. A distracted believer will "walk naked" and others will "see his shame." He doesn't have the good works necessary to provide adequate spiritual clothing. The result is shame at the Judgment Seat of Christ.

The Lord Jesus appeared in glorious white garments when He was transfigured: "His face shone like the sun, and His clothes became as white as the light" (Matthew 17:2). So, too, believers who persevere will be clothed in glorious white garments: "They will walk with Me in white, for they are worthy," (verse 4), and "He who overcomes shall be clothed in white garments" (verse 5).

123

• *Having one's name confessed by Christ concerns eternal rewards, not eternal salvation.* God the Father on several occasions, including the Mount of Transfiguration, publicly praised the Lord Jesus: "This is My beloved Son in whom I am well pleased" (Matthew 17:5). Similarly, the Lord Jesus will publicly praise the overcomer: "I will confess his name before My Father and before His angels."

At the Judgment Seat of Christ, the Lord Jesus will acknowledge faithful believers before the Father and before His angels. Compare Matthew 10:32-33 and Luke 19:11-19. His "Well done, good servant" (Luke 19:17) is a reward that faithful believers will receive, not a condition of entrance into the kingdom.

Therefore, it is evident that Revelation 3:5 concerns eternal rewards, not eternal salvation. We now turn to the meaning of the expression in question.

Jesus Promises to Exalt the Name of the Overcomer

This passage is difficult because it is the only reference in the Bible that speaks of the blotting out[9] of one's name from the Book of Life.[10]

There are five[11] other references to the Book of Life in Revelation: 13:8; 17:8; 20:12, 15; and 21:27. Those texts suggest that the Book of Life contains the names, and possibly the deeds, of all those who have eternal life. If your name is not in that book, then you are not saved.[12] This might seem to suggest that to have your name blotted out of the Book of Life would be to lose your salvation.

• *No one's name will be blotted out.* Since we know, as John's readers did, that the gospel is a promise of eternal security, we know that Jesus was not threatening to take anyone's name from the Book of Life.[13] His promise to the overcomer is not a threat to the non-overcomer.

But how, then, are we to understand this promise? We must realize that Jesus is using a figure of speech known as understatement.

• *Understatement is a common figure of speech in Scripture.* Whether or not we realize it, we all use understatement. When we say, "He is an architect of no small stature," we mean, "He is an outstanding architect." There are many examples of understatement in Scripture:

> *"And we were like grasshoppers in our own sight, and so we were in their sight" (Numbers 13:33).*

Ten of the twelve Jewish men sent to spy out the land understated their own size in order to emphasize the size of the Anakim. In comparison to such giants, they were small indeed, but clearly not the size of grasshoppers.

> *"It is not good to take the children's bread and throw it to the little dogs" (Matthew 15:26).*

Not only is it not good, but it is extremely bad to deprive children of food they need in order to feed a dog instead.

> *I appeal to you for my son Onesimus...who once was unprofitable to you (Philemon 10–11).*

Onesimus had not only been unprofitable to Philemon, he had stolen from him by running away and hence shirking his responsibilities.

> *And they brought the young man in alive, and they were not a little comforted (Acts 20:12).*

Paul restored Eutychus to life after his deadly fall. "Not a little comforted" is clearly understatement. They were greatly encouraged.

> *"The one who comes to Me I will by no means cast out" (John 6:37).*

What the Lord means, via understatement, is that He will keep forever all who come to Him. Not only won't He cast them out, He will keep them secure in His hands (John 10:27-28). They will never perish (John 3:16).

• *The understatement here refers to exalting the overcomer's name in the Book of Life.*[14] There is a particular type of understatement called litotes "in which an affirmative is expressed by the negation of its opposite."[15] For example, the expression, "This is no small problem," means, "this is a big problem." So too, the promise, "If you mow the yard today, I won't forget you," means "If you mow the yard today, I will repay you."

One of the keys to understatement in general and litotes in particular is that the understatement is reasonably obvious. For example, in the above example of a promise not to forget someone, no one would take either the stated negative statement or the implied positive affirmation literally. The person asked to mow would not think that if he mowed the yard the speaker would merely continue to remember him. Nor would he think that if he failed to mow the yard the speaker would lose all memory of him. Clearly a reward is being promised.

The promise in Revelation 3:5 not to blot the name of the overcomer out of the Book of Life is also obviously understatement. None of the original readers of Revelation would have thought that the Lord Jesus was merely promising not to remove the names of overcoming believers from the Book of Life. Nor would they have thought that He was threatening to remove the names of believers who failed to overcome. They knew that Jesus promised eternal life to all who simply believe in Him (see chapter 11).

But what is suggested by the pledge not to blot the overcomer's name out of the Book of Life? The opposite of blotting out a name is exalting it. The Lord is promising to exalt the name of the overcoming believer.

While it is possible that the Lord meant to be no more specific than that,[16] I believe that He is promising to exalt the overcomer's name *in the Book of Life.* That book includes the names of all who have eternal life (compare Revelation 20:15). Yet it is far from certain that all the names are listed in exactly the same way.

The Book of Life may be like a phone book.[17] While all believers are listed, the names of some may receive special attention. Maybe there will be a little crown in front of the names of all overcomers, to signify that these rule with Christ. Possibly the names of overcomers will be in bold print, italicized, in a special color, or in a larger size of type. In any case, the overcomer's name will be set apart in the Book of Life, indicating that this person is an exemplary saint.[18]

This view harmonizes well with the context. All three promises in Revelation 3:5 refer to special honor that the overcomer will receive. The overcomer will wear special white garments. His name will be highlighted in the Book of Life. And he will hear the Lord Jesus publicly praise his name at the Judgment Seat of Christ.[19]

Be a Nike Christian!

William Fuller writes these insightful words regarding Revelation 3:5, "A command that everyone keeps is superfluous, and a reward that everyone receives for a virtue that everyone has is nonsense."[20] The eternal rewards interpretation takes the command seriously and views the reward as something which only some receive, making it a powerful motivation to obedience—while, at the same time, not distorting the gospel in the process.

The Greek word for overcoming used in this verse is *nikaō*. The noun form of that same word is *nikē*. Yes, Nike means victor, overcomer. God wants you to be a Nike Christian, to be a victor in your Christian life. "Let us not grow weary while doing good, for in due season we shall reap if we do not lose heart" (Galatians 6:9).[21] Just do it.

Perseverance

CHAPTER 16

PERSEVERANCE IN FOCUS

I WAS LITERALLY moved to tears when I saw the finish of the 1997 Ironman Triathalon from Hawaii. This is a grueling competition that involves swimming, biking, and running over a hundred miles in one day. The *fastest* athletes take nearly nine hours to finish. Imagine swimming, biking, and running at a near world-class pace for that many hours!

The competition ends with a marathon, a 26.2-mile run. With only a few hundred yards to go, two women battled for fourth and fifth place. Separated by just a few yards, both were struggling, walking like drunken sailors, staggering across the road. Each fell, got up, staggered forwards a short way, and fell again.

When they were about twenty feet from the finish line, both fell yet again. Neither woman had the strength to get up one more time. Even though they were so close to the finish, it seemed that they wouldn't be able to finish the race. But no! Suddenly one of the women realized there was another way. She rocked onto her hands and knees and *crawled* past the finish line. The other woman, seeing that this might be her answer as well, managed to crawl the last few feet, collapsing onto the finish line. What persistence! They gave that competition their all.

As Christians, are we that committed to pleasing God and running the Christian race well? Are we ready to give our best, even if the going becomes extremely tough?

Of course, we should be much *more* committed than anyone competing in a sports event. Paul said, "Bodily exercise profits a little, but godliness is profitable for all things, having promise of the life that now is and of that which is to come" (1 Timothy 4:8). However, the key to perseverance is motivation. What should motivate believers to persevere in discipleship? According to Paul it is a desire for God's blessing on "the life that now is and of that which is to come." God rewards those who obey Him, both now and eternally. While all believers have life, persevering believers have it more abundantly (John 10:10).

All religions proclaim the importance of perseverance in good works. Unfortunately, most religions, including most branches of Christendom, confuse the motivation. Rather than speaking of the profit that comes to the believer now and in the life to come, they speak of the necessity of perseverance in good works in order to go to heaven. In their zeal to motivate perseverance, they destroy the gospel of grace and replace it with a gospel of works.

This is not a new way of thinking. The rabbis of Jesus' day taught that only Jews who persevered in good works would enter God's kingdom (Luke 18:9-14).

The apostles also encountered this type of thinking (Acts 15:1, 5; Galatians 1:6-9). People called Judaizers taught that while faith in Christ was necessary, it wasn't enough for one to go to heaven. The Judaizers insisted that perseverance in good works was necessary to perfect one's salvation (Galatians 3:1-5). Failure to persevere in good works, they argued, would result in a failure to enter God's kingdom.

Calvinism is typically remembered by the acrostic TULIP, with each letter standing for one of the five points of Calvinism. The *P* stands for perseverance.[1] According to those who came after Calvin, all truly born again people persevere in good works.[2] Thus, those who fail to persevere prove they never really believed in Christ in the first place. This allows Calvinists to maintain a formal belief in eternal security[3] while holding to the idea that perseverance in good works is a condition of final salvation.

According to the Bible, however, perseverance is not a condition of getting into God's kingdom, and believers have no guarantee that they will persevere.

What the Bible Says about Perseverance

• *Perseverance is not a condition of eternal salvation.* As we have seen many times in this book, there is but one condition of eternal salvation, believing in Christ. The moment one believes, he has eternal life. Nothing can reverse that, since eternal life is eternal. Therefore, even if a believer fails to persevere, everlasting life remains.

If faith is the only condition, then perseverance could be a condition only if it were a synonym for faith, which it is not. Whereas saving faith is the passive acceptance of God's promise to the believer, perseverance is the active ongoing obedience of the believer.

Those who condition eternal salvation on perseverance, however well intentioned they are, replace grace with works. Yet, Paul said that eternal salvation is "not of works, lest anyone should boast" (Ephesians 2:9).

Let's say Phil and Bill are both believers. Phil perseveres and goes to heaven. Bill doesn't and goes to hell. Whether we say that Bill lost his salvation, or that he proved to be a false professor, he doesn't make it because he didn't persevere. This would, however, give Phil a ground for boasting. He could legitimately say that he got into heaven because he persevered in good works.[4]

Paul's words in Romans 4:4-5 apply specifically to the question of perseverance and salvation, "Now to him who works, the wages are not counted as grace but as debt. But to him who does not work but believes on Him who justifies the ungodly, his faith is accounted for righteousness."

• *Believers are not guaranteed that they will persevere.* Other than the apostles (Matthew 19:28; Mark 10:36-40; John 21:18-19), Jesus never guaranteed that any believer would persevere.[5] There is no biblical promise that says, "You will serve Me faithfully all your lives. You will persevere in sound doctrine and in godly behavior until death." The Scriptures repeatedly *command* perseverance, but they never *promise* it.

• *Believers who persevere will rule with Christ.* The apostle
Paul actually acknowledged his own uncertainty as to whether or not
he would persevere, "Therefore I run thus: not with uncertainty. Thus
I fight: not as one who beats the air. But I discipline my body and
bring it into subjection, *lest, when I have preached to others, I myself
should become disqualified"* (1 Corinthians 9:26-27, emphasis
added). Disqualification or disapproval (*adokimos*) here refers to
ruling with Christ. While Paul knew he was eternally secure
(Romans 8:38-39; 2 Timothy 1:12), he didn't know whether or not
he would reign with Christ (2 Timothy 2:12).[6]

It would be presumptuous of anyone to say, "I'm sure I'll
never fall away. I'm sure I will persevere." While a person can be
sure he will go to be with the Lord, he cannot be sure, prior to death,
that he will rule with Christ, because he can't be sure that he will
persevere.

Fear of Hell Is Not a Biblical Motivation
for Perseverance

What should motivate a Christian to persevere? Many
pastors and theologians claim that fear of hell should motivate
believers, either to *stay* saved or to keep proving to themselves that
they *are* saved. However, that is not what the Bible teaches.

If you are a believer in Jesus Christ, what did you believe in
Him for? What are you trusting Him to do for you? To give you
eternal life and keep you out of hell, right? The apostle Paul spoke of
himself as a paradigm for all believers, "However, for this reason I
obtained mercy, that in me first Jesus Christ might show all
longsuffering, as a pattern to those who are going *to believe on Him
for everlasting life"* (1 Timothy 1:16, italics added). If He
guarantees eternal life to all who believe in Him, and you have
believed in Him for eternal life, what do you *know* you have? Eternal
life! You know you won't ever "perish" since Jesus guarantees it
(John 3:16; 5:24). If you don't know that, then you don't believe that

Jesus truly guarantees eternal life to all who merely believe in Him. You think that something more is required.

It is precisely at this point that many object. "That is just fire insurance. You can't be saved simply by believing in Jesus for fire insurance without any commitment of life and desire to live for Him." Well, believing in Jesus is not fire insurance. It is *non*-fire assurance. The one who believes is sure he won't spend eternity in the lake of fire. Living for Christ is not a condition of eternal life. While believers have many reasons to live for God (see below), fear of hell is not one of them.

Fear of hell should motivate people to respond to the Lord's drawing by seeking Him. They should be motivated to pray, read the Bible, go to church, ask a Christian friend to explain what they must do to be saved, read Christian books, etc. While none of those things can save them, they can result in God opening their eyes to the gospel so that they might believe it and be saved (Acts 16:14).

But, once you're saved, fear of hell should be a thing of the past. Jesus has taken care of that once and for all.

Biblical Motivations for Perseverance: Gratitude, Blessings, and Rewards

Some people criticize those of us who believe in the free gift of salvation by suggesting that we don't call believers to perseverance and holiness. While this may be true in isolated cases, it is certainly *not* true of the vast majority of Free Grace people. In any case, we are not free to change the gospel in order to motivate people to live godly lives. We can't raise the entrance requirements to improve the caliber of people in the church. The gospel is not subject to alteration. If we change it, then we no longer have good news.

The importance of continuing to live wholeheartedly for Christ until we die or are raptured cannot be overemphasized. There are several biblical answers to the question, "If I believed I was going to heaven no matter what, why wouldn't I go out and live like the devil?"

135

These answers constitute the proper biblical motivations for perseverance.

• *Gratitude.* Do you remember the story of the lion that had a thorn in his paw until a little boy removed it? The lion was so grateful that he became the little boy's protector.

Gratitude is a powerful motivator. The one who knows he is forgiven much loves much (Luke 7:36-50). "We love Him because He first loved us" (1 John 4:19; see also 2 Corinthians 5:14). Assurance of salvation produces gratitude that motivates perseverance.

Of course, you can't be grateful for something you aren't sure you have. The tragedy of a theology that says you must persevere to stay saved, or to prove you are really saved, is that it destroys one of the most powerful motivations to obey God, gratitude. We should never underestimate the power of gratitude or the debilitating effects of lack of assurance.

• *Blessings here and now.* Our temporal well being is directly related to our walk with Christ. The Christian who perseveres experiences joy, fulfillment, and contentment. That person is characterized by the wonderful fruit of the Spirit (Galatians 5:22-23). By contrast, the believer who walks away from the Lord lacks love, joy, peace, and the rest of the fruit of the Spirit.

God doesn't promise that persevering Christians will be healthy or wealthy. What He promises is that He will meet our basic needs: "Seek first the kingdom of God and His righteousness, and all these things shall be added to you" (Matthew 6:33).

In fact, one of the keys to perseverance is contentment with what we have: "Godliness with contentment is great gain" (1 Timothy 6:6). We are called to be content, whether we have very little or very much. Paul said, "I know how to be abased, and I know how to abound" (Philippians 4:12).

God blesses those who obey Him with things that really matter: joy, peace, and contentment. Whether they are rich or poor materially, they are rich spiritually.

The Christian who falls away misses out on more than the blessings he could have had. He will also experience God's discipline which may include guilt, discontentment, heartache, rebuke by others, church discipline, arrest, trial, jail time, illness, financial setbacks, and premature physical death. It makes no sense to fall away from the Lord. The passing pleasures of sin are far outweighed by the ongoing pain they bring.

And these blessings are not limited to the faithful believer; they overflow and bless the lives of those around him. His family, co-workers, neighbors, and friends all benefit from his presence in their lives. And this in turn blesses him even more, since it brings joy and fulfillment to be a blessing to others.[7]

• *Eternal rewards.* Our eternal well being also hinges on persevering in our walk with Christ. This life is a testing ground for the Christian. Once we come to faith in Christ, we begin an adventure that will determine our role in His kingdom.

> If we endure, we shall also reign with Him.
> —2 Timothy 2:12

> And let us not grow weary while doing good, for in due season we shall reap if we do not lose heart.
> —Galatians 6:9

> If anyone's work is burned, he will suffer loss; but he himself will be saved, yet so as through fire.
> —1 Corinthians 3:15

> Do you not know that those who run in a race all run, but one receives the prize? Run in such a way that you may obtain it...But I discipline my body and bring it into subjection, lest, when I have preached to others, I myself should become disqualified.
> —1 Corinthians 9:24, 27

> I have fought the good fight, I have finished the race, I have kept the faith. Finally, there is laid up for me the crown of righteousness, which the Lord, the

137

righteous Judge, will give to me on that Day, and not to me only but also to all who have loved His appearing.

—2 Timothy 4:7-8

I have a North Carolina friend, Sandy Rudolph, whose father passed away and left him an inheritance in the form of a trust fund. Sandy receives a set amount of money each month, and he will continue to receive that same amount for life.

The kingdom of God is something like that. There will be some minimum level that all will have. However, those who have made many deposits in their eternal IRA will have much larger trusts. This will allow them to be more generous with others, to serve others more, to invest more in God's work. That in turn will provide greater fulfillment for them.

Additionally, some believers will rule with Christ and some will not. Only those who are in fellowship with God when this life ends will rule with Him forever. And there are certain privileges in the kingdom which only ruling saints will have, such as eating of the fruits of the Tree of Life, wearing special white garments, eating of the hidden manna, having a stone with a special nickname that the Lord will give you, and being able to enter the New Jerusalem through the gates.

While all believers will have joy forever, it is naive to think that all will have the same measure of joy. Some will have a much more abundant experience than others. And this life is the only opportunity we have to determine how full our eternal experience will be.

Gratitude, temporal blessings, and eternal rewards—that's a powerful package of motivations. We owe the Lord a debt we can never repay. Our gratitude moves us to persevere. The fact that life is better now if we persevere also motivates us to do so. And, knowing that our eternal experience will be directly related to our perseverance is a compelling influence in the way we live.

How to Persevere: Continue in the Faith
with a Spiritual Mind-Set

The Bible warns us against falling away and commands us to persevere. But perseverance depends on our gaining and maintaining a spiritual mind-set. The key to living as a Christian is to have God's view of things. Paul said, "For those who live according to the flesh set their minds on the things of the flesh, but those who live according to the Spirit, the things of the Spirit. For to be carnally minded is death, but to be spiritually minded is life and peace" (Romans 8:5-6). A fleshly, worldly mind-set ("If it feels good, do it") is "death." That is, it leads to sin and to death. The more we sin, the more we invite our own death (compare James 1:15, 21). As one of my seminary professors, Zane Hodges, liked to quip, "Sin is death-dealing."

To be spiritually minded is to have our minds set on the things of the Spirit; that is, to have our minds in agreement with the Word of God which the Holy Spirit inspired. "Prophecy never came by the will of man, but holy men of God spoke as they were moved by the Holy Spirit" (2 Peter 1:21). If we have a spiritual mind-set, then we experience "life and peace."

Living for Christ is, in a real sense, a battle for the mind. Will our minds be controlled by the world or by the Word? Paul admonished the Romans, "Do not be conformed to this world, but be transformed by the renewing of your mind, that you may prove what is that good and acceptable and perfect will of God" (Romans 12:2).

But how do we develop and maintain a spiritual mind-set?

• *Partake of God's Word.* Paul said, "But we all, with unveiled face, beholding as in a mirror [God's Word] the glory of the Lord, are being transformed into the same image from glory to glory, just as by the Spirit of the Lord" (2 Corinthians 3:18). God uses reading, hearing, memorizing, studying, meditating, and applying His Word to renew our minds. All areas of our lives come under God's light as we submit ourselves to Him and His Word. The Psalmist said, "Your word is a lamp to my feet and a light to my path" (Psalm 119:105).

• *Pray.* Prayer is another way we gain and maintain a spiritual mind-set. We humbly ask God to open His Word to us whenever we read and study it. When He reveals sin in our lives, we confess it (1 John 1:9). By doing so we can remain in fellowship with God moment by moment, ever ready for Christ's return (1 John 1:9; 2:28).

• *Fellowship with other Christians in a local church.* We cultivate a spiritual mind-set by fellowshipping with other Christians. The author of Hebrews tells us that such fellowship will "stir up love and good works" which are the outgrowth of a spiritual mind-set (Hebrews 10:24-25). We assemble with other Christians in local churches for worship, instruction, baptism, the Lord's Supper, accountability, and mutual ministry together.

• *Flee hindrances to perseverance.* There are many hindrances to perseverance. The apostle Paul commanded Timothy to "flee also youthful lusts" (2 Timothy 2:22). It is naive to think that because we are committed believers that we can remain true when putting ourselves in harm's way. God tells us to flee.

Addiction to alcohol and other drugs is a sure way to fall away from the Lord. We read in Ephesians 5:18, "Do not be drunk with wine, in which is dissipation, but be filled with the Spirit." Some people are predisposed because of their genes or their early environment at home to become addicted to alcohol and other drugs. A simple solution is not to use these substances at all. Don't even have them in your house or spend time in places where people use them. Why fool with something so dangerous? And, why be a potential stumbling block to weaker brothers and sisters in Christ?

Pornography is the gateway to immorality and perversion. It also is highly addicting to many.

While there are some decent programs on television, many shows are perverse and hurtful. Worse still, the tube has a powerful narcotic effect. It is very easy to become addicted to the images and the adrenaline rush we feel during a chase scene, a fight, or a verbal battle. In a society where the average person watches TV seven hours a day, taming the tube is a vital element in Christian perseverance. You won't have time to read the Bible, pray, or fellowship with other Christians if you are addicted to the set.

Improper attitudes such as haughtiness and pride can lead us away from God and a spiritual mind-set. "God resists the proud, but gives grace to the humble" (James 4:6). Humility and openness before God are vital if we are to persevere. If we are open to God and have a humble attitude toward ourselves and our role in the Body of Christ, then we will keep on keeping on. God can do just fine without our help, but we need to serve Him to be fulfilled and contented in life—"To be spiritually minded is life and peace" (Romans 8:6). We cultivate humility and openness by confessing our pride and asking God to make us humble and open before Him. Smug saints are on the slippery slope that quickly leads to downfall.

When I was ordained in the summer of 1982, one of my seminary professors, Dr. Charles Ryrie, performed the service. I still vividly remember his charge to me. I had told him how much I loved preaching each week—I'd been at it for all of four months! He told me, "Bob, it's great that you've loved proclaiming God's Word these past four months. But the key is, will you still be faithfully proclaiming the Word of God forty years from now?" That was a great question that I have kept before me ever since. I'm in this for the long haul. I'm committed to persevering to the finish line, which I could reach today or not for many years. The Christian life is the ultimate contest because we don't know when it will end.

How about you? If you are walking in obedience now, that's super. But the key is, will you still be walking in obedience forty years from now?

ARE BELIEVERS FREE OF ALL BAD HABITS?
2 Corinthians 5:17

I BECAME A Christian during my college daze. I remember being told that I was now a new person and that all my old ways had passed away. Christian friends quoted 2 Corinthians 5:17 to me,

> Therefore, if anyone is in Christ, he is a new creation; old things have passed away; behold, all things have become new.

I was a bit confused because my friends failed to explain to me why I sinned at all, if this verse meant that all of my sinful ways were a thing of the past. That understanding of the verse certainly didn't match my experience since I still struggled with worry, jealousy, anger, and other sinful ways.[1]

Since then I have discovered that this verse is understood by many to mean that all Christians lead transformed lives. They claim, "If your behavior isn't radically different than before you came to faith, then you aren't really saved. If you are truly in Christ, you are a new creation, and that means you can't help but live like a new creation."[2]

Is that really what the apostle Paul meant? Was he telling the Corinthians that all born again people live in a radically different way than before they were saved? That certainly wasn't the case with many of the believers in Corinth (see 1 Corinthians 3:1-3; 6:12-20; 11:23-34).

Luis C. Rodriguez, a long time friend and one of the pastors of my church in Dallas, tells of his early days as a believer when the old habits in his life were still very much active in his experience:

> It was a Saturday morning, but it could have been any morning. A night out drinking, smoking, shooting pool, laughing. Now a terrible hangover.

I hurt inside. And I could see that I was hurting the people I loved and the God who had saved me. This was painful—to think that though I was a Christian I was doing this.

My friends didn't know that I was a Christian. When they looked at me all they saw was a drinking buddy. Keeping my mouth shut was the easiest thing to do. I just couldn't tell my friends that I had accepted the gift of eternal life. I wanted to tell them; yet I was afraid how they'd react...

It would be a long time before I would walk with Christ. Eventually I learned that when I would stop grieving God (Ephesians 4:30) I would also stop hurting inside (Galatians 5:22-23). And that would sure make a big difference on Saturday mornings.[3]

Believers Are Part of a New World

Second Corinthians 5:17 is speaking of "anyone who is in Christ." Only those who are born again are "in Christ." Paul is telling us something about regenerate people and their relationship to "a new creation."

• *Ellipsis.* In Greek, as in English, material is sometimes left out and the reader has to fill in the blanks. This is called *ellipsis.* For example, in answer to the question, "Where did he go?" the answer, "Out" clearly means, "*He went* out." We don't need to say the words *he went* for the meaning to be clear. The same is true in Greek.

In 2 Corinthians 5:17, the Greek leaves off the subject, *he,* and the verb, *is,* in the phrase, "*He is* a new creation." Literally it says, "If anyone [is][4] in Christ, a new creation."[5] The reader is left to decide what Paul means.

• *Who or what is a new creation?* One possibility is that Paul means that the new creation is the born again person. In that case Paul is saying that to be in Christ is to be a new creation. This is certainly biblical. Anyone who is born again has life which he never had before ("He who has the Son has life; he who does not have the

Son of God does not have life," 1 John 5:12). This new life means that, in a sense, believers are new creatures.[6]

Another possibility is that the new creation is the new world in which the believer finds himself. In this case the focus is on the world in which he lives, not on the new nature of the believer. *The New Geneva Study Bible* accordingly suggests that this phrase should be translated, "There is a new creation," saying that "The believer's spiritual union with Christ is nothing less than participation in the 'new creation.'"[7]

While this may seem to be a small difference, it is very significant. Once a person comes to Christ, he is a citizen of heaven (Philippians 3:20) and an ambassador for Christ (2 Corinthians 5:20); he realizes that he and all believers are saved and that all unbelievers are lost (verses 16-21), and that God is his Father (John 1:12; Romans 8:15). The believer is even now part of a new creation, though he will not experience it fully until the Second Coming of the Lord Jesus to establish His eternal kingdom. "Beloved, now we are children of God; and it has not yet been revealed what we shall be, but we know that when He is revealed, we shall be like Him, for we shall see Him as He is" (1 John 3:2).

If Paul meant that the new creation was the believer himself, we would expect to see references to the new life believers have (1 John 5:12), to the new man (Ephesians 4:24), and to similar expressions. Instead, we find references to the way we view believers and unbelievers (verses 16-21) and to the fact that we are ambassadors for Christ (verse 20).

Colossians 1:16-20 confirms that the new creation of 2 Corinthians 5:17 is the new world in which the believer finds himself. The expression *all things* is found in both passages.[8] The six references to "all things" in the Colossians passage refer to all people, saved and lost. The Father has made all people reconcilable through Christ's death on the cross.[9] Thus when Paul says in the Second Corinthians passage, "all things have become new," he means that

145

the believer lives in a new environment. Our world and universe are different. A whole new realm opens before our eyes.

Old Things Have Passed Away

The moment a person becomes a Christian, the world he lived in until then has become old. It has passed away. He is no longer dead in his trespasses and sins (Ephesians 2:1-10), no longer a condemned person bound for hell (John 3:18). He has been transferred from the kingdom of darkness into the kingdom of light (Ephesians 5:8-11; Colossians 1:13; 1 Thessalonians 5:4-11). He lives in a new world with different citizenship, kinship, and eternal destiny.

Though this is true, the believer still lives in this dark world which is passing away. He still lives around people and temptations which are not of the new creation. This, of course, leads to conflict. While it might be the title of a science fiction novel, *When Worlds Collide* is also a description of the Christian's struggle with the sinful world in which he lives.

What about Sin?

There is no support here for the idea that all believers automatically persevere in a godly life. There is nothing in the context about changes in behavior. Even the reference to believers being ambassadors for Christ is not a guarantee that all Christians will share their faith often or at all. Some ambassadors do a wonderful job representing their country, while others enjoy the perks without putting forth any significant effort. The same is true in the Christian realm. We are citizens of another world and God has put us in this one as His ambassadors. We have the opportunity to be good ambassadors, but our job performance is not under consideration here.

Even a casual reading of the first letter of Paul to the Corinthians shows that at least some regenerate people do not experience a radical change in behavior. Some of the believers at Corinth were not good ambassadors for their heavenly country. Paul took them to task for having strife, divisions, immorality, taking one another to court, and being drunk—even at the Lord's Supper! (1 Corinthians 3:1-3; 6:1-20; 11:20-32). Yet in the very passages where he rebuked them, Paul reminded them that they were "in Christ" (1 Corinthians 3:1) and that the Holy Spirit was in them (1 Corinthians 6:19).

Elsewhere Paul commanded that believers not let sin control and dominate them (Romans 6:12-13; Ephesians 4:17-31; Colossians 3:9). Such a command would not be necessary unless it were possible to be controlled and dominated by sin.

Paul did not promise here or elsewhere that when an alcoholic came to faith in Christ he would lose all desire for alcohol. The same is true with other sins. There is no assurance that Christians will never have besetting sins. As is sadly evident today, even some Christian leaders have been guilty of ongoing sins of immorality, fraud, and theft.

Recently I spoke to a discipleship group on the questions of saving faith, assurance of salvation, and perseverance. Someone brought up 2 Corinthians 5:17 and asked, "Doesn't being new creatures in Christ, where old things have passed away and all things have become new, mean that all of your past sinfulness and desire to sin are gone?" This really hit a nerve with a man who was a recovering alcoholic. He said something like this:

> I still have a craving for liquor. I have to fight it daily. I've heard a number of preachers say that if you still crave liquor, you aren't saved. That really makes me mad. Here I am fighting the craving for liquor, and someone tells me that this means I am unsaved! That is crazy. Being a Christian doesn't mean we aren't tempted anymore. It also doesn't mean that all of our bad habits instantly vanish when we are born again.

If Paul's point is that believers can't be dominated by sin, then all sins—not just major sins—would be included. There could be no such thing as a believer, even a new Christian, who was dominated by jealously, hatred, covetousness, materialism, greed, selfishness, pride, etc. In fact, if the old things that passed away were our sinful ways, no believer would commit even one sin.

The apostle doesn't say, "If anyone is in Christ, he is a new creation *most of the time*, old things have *more or less* passed away, all things have *basically* become new." He is using absolute language here. If anyone is in Christ he is a part of a new creation all of the time; old things have completely passed away, all things have become completely new.

Paul is *not* saying that once a person comes to faith in Christ his struggles with sin are over and victory is assured. Rather, he is saying that once a person becomes a Christian, his world and his worldview have radically changed. Of course, this certainly has implications for how believers *should* live:

> You are sons of light and sons of the day. We are not of the night nor of darkness. Therefore, let us not sleep, as others do, but let us watch and be sober.[10]
> —1 Thessalonians 5:5-6

> For you were once darkness, but now you are light in the Lord. Walk as children of light...And have no fellowship with the unfruitful works of darkness, but rather expose them...See then that you walk circumspectly, not as fools but as wise, redeeming the time, because the days are evil.
> —Ephesians 5:8, 11, 15-16

Christians should live in a manner consistent with their status as children of God who are part of the new creation. All commands to godliness are predicated upon this wonderful status. Whether a believer lives up to his calling, however, is a matter of personal responsiveness to God.[11] It is not something all believers automatically do. And it is certainly not something that any believer will do perfectly this side of glory.

Ambassadors for Christ

Before government officials are sent overseas to represent the United States, they are trained in the customs, language, and culture of the country to which they are bound. The government wants them to be the best ambassadors for America they can be in a foreign land.

Unfortunately, new Christians often don't receive much training as they enter a new world of faith, foreign to all their previous thoughts and ways. They need to be taught the truth of 2 Corinthians 5:16-21 and helped to establish a reconciliation worldview that they can communicate to those around them. As they grasp this truth, they can teach it to their children, to people they lead to faith in Christ, and to other believers.

As Christians we are a part of a new world. Politicians often speak of a "new world order," but this world system can never produce an abiding new world order. Only the Lord Jesus Christ will usher that in. While the new world order is not with us physically, it is here spiritually. Every believer is a part, a citizen, an ambassador, of the new world to come! Understanding this simple truth can revolutionize our witness. Talk about self-concept! What could be more important than being an ambassador for the King of kings and Lord of lords?

Do you remember how each episode of the old TV show "Mission Impossible" began? An unseen voice would come out of a tape recorder that was programmed to self-destruct: "Your mission, should you choose to accept it, is..."

Similarly in the faith realm, the Lord is saying to believers, "Your mission, should you choose to accept it, is to represent your divine Sovereign and His new world order of which you are now a part." God won't force you to represent Him, but He will give you the opportunity to distinguish yourself in service in a world where people of faith are strangers and pilgrims. It's your mission. Do you choose to accept it?

149

CHAPTER 18

THE DANGER OF FALLING AWAY
Hebrews 6:4-8

IN THE FAMOUS story *The Emperor's New Clothes*, two men dupe an emperor into believing that they can make him beautiful garments out of magic cloth. They tell the emperor that only those people who are intelligent and worthy of their positions will be able to see the cloth. On the appointed day, the ruler puts on his new clothes. He compliments the tailors and pretends that he can see the garments, because he doesn't want to be thought unworthy of his position. As he parades through the city streets, the people ooh and ah (they too don't want to be thought unworthy). But suddenly a small child speaks up: "The emperor has no clothes." He said what everyone knew to be true, but had tried hard to overlook.

Sometimes in a Bible study, one person may point out an objection so powerful that those who hold a different interpretation realize their understanding couldn't be correct. It was through such a humbling experience that I realized that my interpretation of the following passage was incorrect:

> For it is impossible for those who were once enlightened, and have tasted the heavenly gift, and have become partakers of the Holy Spirit, and have tasted the good word of God and the powers of the age to come, if they fall away, to renew them again to repentance, since they crucify again for themselves the Son of God, and put Him to an open shame. For the earth which drinks in the rain that often comes upon it, and bears herbs useful for those by whom it is cultivated, receives blessing from God; but if it bears thorns and briers, it is rejected and near to being cursed, whose end is to be burned.
> —Hebrews 6:4-8

Before I went to seminary, I believed that this passage referred to unbelievers who fell away and ended up in hell. And then, one of my seminary professors showed me that it is clearly born again believers who are in danger of falling away. I realized that my understanding of this passage wouldn't stand up under close scrutiny.

What did the author of the Book of Hebrews mean when he wrote of the impossibility of renewing apostates to repentance and of the fiery curse that awaited them? The interpretation is rather easy to explain if your theology allows the possibility of genuine believers falling away from the Lord, and if you don't see all references to fire as concerning eternal condemnation in hell.

Only Believers Can Fall Away

There can be no reasonable doubt that believers are in view here. Only believers can be said (1) to have been enlightened, (2) to have tasted[1] the heavenly gift, (3) to have become partakers of the Holy Spirit, (4) to have tasted the good word of God, and (5) to have tasted the powers of the age to come. As I. Howard Marshall states, "The conclusion is irresistible that real Christians are meant."[2] Likewise, Homer Kent writes, "The normal understanding of these descriptive terms, in light of the author's own use elsewhere in the epistle, is to those who are regenerated."[3]

Verse 6 concerns falling away from the faith. The Hebrew Christians being addressed were considering a return to animal sacrifices for the forgiveness of their sins (2:1-18; 3:12; 7:11-28; 10:1-18). Until the death and resurrection of Christ, believers were commanded to offer animal sacrifices that looked ahead to the coming death of the Messiah (Hebrews 10:1-10ff.). Jewish Christians were now being influenced to return to the old sacrificial system and to give up the belief that the death of Jesus was enough to pay the penalty for their sins.

Apostasy is a doctrinal defection from one or more of the

fundamentals of the faith. These Jewish Christians were close to apostasy in regard to the doctrine of substitutionary atonement—that Christ died on the cross in our place, as our substitute, paying the full and complete penalty for our sins. They were in danger of ceasing to believe the gospel.

The only person who can fall is one who is in a position to fall. It is impossible to fall off the top of a ten-story building if one isn't on the top of the building. It is impossible for a person to fall from an orthodox view of the gospel unless he *has* an orthodox belief in the gospel. Only believers can fall away.

It Is Humanly Impossible to Renew
Apostate Believers to Repentance

Once a believer apostatizes, it becomes humanly impossible to renew him or her to "repentance." The word *repentance* (Greek: *metanoia*) means *a decision to turn from sins.*[4] It is a condition for fellowship with God and for escaping temporal judgment (2 Corinthians 7:8-10; 1 John 1:9).[5] *Metonymy* is a common figure of speech in which a word or phrase associated with some other word or phrase is used to refer to it. For example, "the White House said today..." is not comical to us, for we know that *the White House* stands for *the President who resides there.* Here *repentance* stands for *fellowship with God that results from it.*[6] No human being can renew *to fellowship with God* a believer who has fallen away from the faith.[7]

Many interpreters err here because they assume that the author is saying that such a person cannot be renewed *to eternal salvation.* Actually the text doesn't say anything even approaching that. All it says is that it is humanly impossible to renew to *repentance* the believer who falls away from the faith. This passage in no way questions eternal security. A person who has eternal life will always have it. Eternal life is eternal. However, as the illustration of the burned weeds of verses 7 and 8 clearly shows, an eternally secure person who falls away and is out of fellowship with God will have a fiery and inescapable experience of chastening here and now!

Productive Believers Receive Blessing from God

Like any good preacher or teacher, the author of Hebrews gives a practical illustration to clarify his point. Verses 7 and 8 speak of works which believers do and the consequences of those works.

Some believers are like good soil that produces "herbs useful for those by whom it is cultivated." The consequence of a believer being productive is that he "receives blessing from God." Clearly this does not refer to eternal salvation. Eternal salvation is not a result of works done (Ephesians 2:8-9).

This could refer to blessings here and now, or to eternal blessings and rewards. Since, as we shall soon see, the corresponding cursing is temporal, most likely the blessings are temporal also. God blesses the believer who bears much fruit. This does not mean that all faithful believers will be rich and in robust health. Rather, it means that they will have joy, peace, and contentment, and that God will meet their basic needs of food, clothing, and shelter.

Thorns and Briers Represent Sinful Words and Deeds

Other believers produce bad works, here illustrated as "thorns and briers." Thorns and briers—or thorns and thistles—are a common Old Testament motif going back to the Garden of Eden. As a result of Adam's sin, God cursed the ground declaring that it would yield thorns and thistles (Genesis 3:18). So if a believer is like ground that yields a bad harvest, fiery judgment is in his near future.

The Burning of Thorns and Briers Illustrates Temporal, Not Eternal, Judgment

The believer who is producing thorns and briers is "near to being cursed, whose end is to be burned." Burning is seen by some commentators to refer here to hell.[8] However, there is no compelling reason to draw such a conclusion. Except where qualified by modifiers like *eternal* or *unquenchable*, fire and burning in Scripture picture temporal judgment (Genesis 19:24; Leviticus 10:2; Joshua 7:15; 2 Samuel 22:9; 2 Kings 1:10ff.; Daniel 3:22ff.; Amos 1:4, 7, 10, 12, 14; 2:2, 5; Luke 9:54; John 15:6; 1 Corinthians 3:13-15; Hebrews 11:34; Jude 23). The absence of those modifiers here suggests that the believer who falls away faces fiery *temporal*, not *eternal*, judgment.

It was a common agricultural practice of that day, and our own, to burn the worthless overgrowth of a field so that the land might be restored to productivity.[9] The burning did not, of course, destroy the field. This illustration clearly shows that eternal salvation remains, though the evil works, represented by the weeds, are burned up.

In fact, the illustration suggests the possibility that God might restore the apostate through chastisement. The impossibility of renewing apostates to repentance concerns a *human* impossibility, prior to God's chastising work, for nothing is impossible with God. Fiery chastisement will certainly fall on the apostate. However, once this fire has done its work, it is conceivable that the apostate might come back to the faith (see 1 Timothy 1:19-20).

This view harmonizes with other Scriptures that deal with the judgment of believers. On the one hand, we know that believers are forever secure in Christ from the moment of faith onward (see John 3:16-18; 5:24; 6:38-40, 47; 11:25-27; Romans 8:38-39). On the other hand, other Scriptures indicate that believers are not secure from temporal judgment until they go to be with the Lord[10] (see Ezekiel 18; 1 Corinthians 11:30; Hebrews 12:3-11; James 1:21; 5:19-20). Believers who play with fire get burned (see chapter 13).

Barren Believers

Unfortunately, not all believers glorify God with their lives. Some believers "bear thorns and briers" and are "rejected" (*adokimos*).

The word translated *rejected* might be thought to suggest that the people in question are unsaved. However, the opposite is the case. It is used elsewhere in the New Testament of believers who are *not approved* by God in their present experience.

Paul used this same word in reference to himself, saying that he feared he might not persevere in the faith and as a result might be *disapproved* (1 Corinthians 9:27). While Paul knew he was eternally secure and accepted by God, he did not know if he would persevere in the faith and be approved by the Lord Jesus at His Judgment Seat (see 2 Corinthians 5:9-10). Similarly, in 2 Timothy 2:15 Paul used the opposite word, *dokimos*, meaning "approved," to urge Timothy, "Be diligent to present yourself *approved* to God, a worker who does not need to be ashamed, rightly dividing the word of truth."

Since in our text the word refers to the soil that produces thorns and briers, the leading dictionary of the New Testament and early Christian literature suggests that it should probably be translated here as "barren soil."[11] That yields the translation, "If [the earth] bears thorns and briers, it is *barren* and near to being cursed, whose end is to be burned." A barren believer faces temporal judgment, especially the believer whose barrenness results from falling away from the faith.

A Prescription to Avoid Apostasy

Here is my prescription for doctrinal wellness: read and study God's Word daily; be open before God, confessing those sins He reveals to you; have a regular prayer time; and do not forsake assembling with other believers in a sound Bible-teaching church. These things are vital to avoiding apostasy.

A steady diet of unorthodox teaching will cause your spiritual health to suffer. If you attend a church that does not clearly teach the fundamental doctrines of Scriptures, you can easily fall. Even prolonged casual contact with false teachings via radio, TV, books, and tapes can result in doctrinal apostasy.

Keep in mind that doctrinal defection is often preceded by moral decay. If a Christian falls into a lifestyle of willful sin, chances are he will stop reading his Bible, praying, and going to church. In such cases the person may eventually come to question doctrines he formerly held dear.

When someone falls away from the Christian faith, it is a lose-lose-lose situation. The person loses out on the joy of fellowship with God and with other believers. The church loses the participation of one of its members. And the Lord Himself loses the glory He should receive from His children.

Believers are like ground that yields either a good or bad harvest. With that in mind, how does your garden grow? Is it flourishing or is it full of weeds? You may recall the story of the farmer and the preacher. The preacher commented on what fine land that God had given the farmer. The farmer smiled and said, "Amen, preacher. But you should have seen the place when the Lord had it to Himself."

God could, of course, maintain a farm, or our faith, without any involvement on our part. However, He has chosen to give us a vital role to play. To keep our faith growing requires that we water and care for it. We need a daily intake of God's Word. Fellowship with other believers is vital to our spiritual health. And prayer and ongoing obedience are essential as well.[12]

It's a terrible mistake to assume that because we are clear on the gospel today we always will be. Any of us can fall. We must take care to stand firm in the faith and produce works that are pleasing to the Lord. That is the way to bring His blessing upon our lives.

CHAPTER 19

DANGEROUS ROAD AHEAD
2 Peter 2:18-22

HAVE YOU EVER noticed how often we compare people with animals? "He has the heart of a lion." "She is as sly as a fox." "He's a bear of a man." "She's as busy as a bee." Of course, not all comparisons are favorable. It certainly isn't flattering, for example, to call someone a pig.

The Bible also likens people to animals and some of the comparisons are not flattering. That is certainly the case in 2 Peter 2:18-22, where Peter compares people who have been duped by false teachers to dogs returning to their vomit and to pigs wallowing in the mire:

> For if, after they have escaped the pollutions of
> the world through the knowledge of the Lord and
> Savior Jesus Christ, they are again entangled in
> them and overcome, the latter end is worse for them
> than the beginning. For it would have been better
> for them not to have known the way of righteous-
> ness, than having known it, to turn from the holy
> commandment delivered to them. But it has hap-
> pened to them according to the true proverb: "A
> dog returns to his own vomit," and, "A sow,
> having washed, to her wallowing in the mire."
> —2 Peter 2:20-22

These verses are troubling to many believers because they appear to be talking about born again Christians ("they have escaped the pollutions of the world through the knowledge of the Lord and Savior Jesus Christ") who lose their salvation due to lack of perseverance ("they are again entangled in [the pollutions of the world] and overcome,[1] the latter end is worse for them than the beginning...").

Those who believe that Christians can lose their salvation

159

see no problem in these verses. However, that view has to be ruled out, since Peter clearly believed in and taught eternal security (Luke 10:20; John 13:10; Acts 10:43-48; 11:16-18; 15:7-11; 1 Peter 1:23-25; 2 Peter 1:9; 3:8-13).[2]

One way to harmonize this passage with the many that teach eternal security is by suggesting that the people in view weren't genuine believers.[3] This seems to eliminate the conflict with eternal security, but it doesn't adequately explain the fact that these supposed unbelievers had escaped the pollutions of the world and had come to know the Lord Jesus Christ and the way of righteousness.

This passage is not an easy one. However, with careful observation we will find its meaning becomes clear.

The False Teachers and Their Dupes

In order to understand this passage, it is vital to notice that there are two groups of people in verses 18 to 22. False teachers are discussed in verses 18 to 19 (and in verses 1 to 17) and those who would be duped by them are discussed in verses 18 to 22 (and in verses 2 and 3).

The false teachers are referred to four times in verses 18 and 19:

> they speak great swelling words of emptiness;
> they allure through the lusts of the flesh, through
> licentiousness;
> they promise [the dupes] liberty;
> they themselves are slaves of corruption.

Those who would be duped by the false teachers are referred to twice in verses 18 and 19 and five times in verses 20 to 22:

> the ones who have actually escaped;
> [the false teachers] promise them liberty;
> they have escaped the pollutions of the world
> through the knowledge of the Lord and
> Savior Jesus Christ;
> they are again entangled in [the pollutions of the
> world] and [are] overcome;

the latter end is worse for them than the
beginning;
it would have been better for them not to have
known the way of righteousness;
it has happened to them according to the true
proverb: "a dog returns to his own vomit," and,
"a sow, having washed, to her own wallowing in the mire."

We are now ready to sketch a picture of both groups of people.

• *Unbelieving false teachers.* Peter was talking about
unbelieving[4] false teachers "for whom is reserved the blackness of
darkness forever" (verse 17). There can be little question but that
"blackness of darkness forever" refers to hell (compare Jude 13).

It is wrong to conclude that Peter is saying that *all* false
teachers are unbelievers. Peter is not speaking *generally* about false
teachers but *specifically* about false teachers the Lord has revealed
to him who will soon deceive his readers. It is those false teachers
who will be unsaved.

In Second Peter 2, we see that these false teachers would
promote immorality, have "eyes full of adultery," and "promise
liberty." They would be real antinomians—people who say that there
is nothing wrong with violating God's revealed will—promoting
sexual immorality under the guise of freedom.

Sexual immorality has continued to be a teaching—and
lifestyle—of many false teachers throughout church history. Jim Jones
of the People's Temple took advantage of his followers by
promoting the notion that having sexual relations with him was holy
and right. Moses David taught the young women in the Children of
God that God wanted them to flirt with men, even have sex with
them, to lure them into the cult, thus coining the phrase *flirty fishing*.
David Koresh, head of the Branch Davidians, had fathered children
by many of the young women in his group and taught that this was
pleasing to God.

False teachers who deceitfully promise people liberty are themselves "slaves of corruption" (verse 19). The only true liberty is found in pleasing God. As even many non-Christians acknowledge, licentiousness and sexual immorality can be addictive. And just as alcohol and other drugs lead to ever-deepening despair, depression, and degradation, so does sexual addiction. The wages of sin is death.

• *Believing dupes.* What do we know of those who would soon be duped by these false teachers? First, we know they are believers since only believers "have actually escaped from those who live in error" (verse 18) and have "escaped the pollutions of the world through the knowledge of the Lord and Savior Jesus Christ" (verse 20).[5] Only believers know the Lord Jesus.[6] The word *knowledge* is used exclusively of believers in Second Peter (compare 1:2, 3, 5, 6).

Second, it is evident in all three chapters of Second Peter that the apostle was concerned that believers might fall into a sinful lifestyle through the wiles of false teachers. He urged his believing readers to be diligent to keep from stumbling and falling (1:5, 10; 2:18-22; 3:14, 17).

We must not read into Second Peter the idea that anyone who fell away would prove to be an unbeliever. Peter never questioned the faith of his readers. Rather, he acknowledged it. He began his second epistle with this strong statement: "To those who have obtained like precious faith with us by the righteousness of our God and Savior Jesus Christ"(1:1). Only believers have the same precious faith in Christ that the apostles had. What Peter questioned was *the progress of their sanctification.*

Third, Peter said nothing of restoration to fellowship for these believers who would fall. While we know from other passages that believers who fall into sin may turn back to the Lord (Galatians 6:1; James 5:19-20), there is no mention of that here. This may be because the Lord had revealed to Peter that those who would be duped by these false teachers would not repent. Or, perhaps Peter viewed their fall as so devastating that restoration to fellowship with God was unlikely.

It is important not to overgeneralize here. Peter was not saying that all who are duped by false teachers are believers—false teachers deceive many unbelievers too. However, the specific dupes to whom he was referring were believers in Jesus Christ.

We now turn to the heart of the apparent problem. If verses 20 to 22 are talking about genuine believers, why doesn't this lead to the conclusion that Peter is denying eternal security?

Peter Warns Christians of Judgment Here and Now

Many who read these verses think that Peter is warning that those who are misled by the false teachers will experience eternal judgment in hell. They point to verses 21 and 22 as proof texts. However, a careful reading suggests that temporal judgment is in view.

• *Eternal judgment is not mentioned.* Notice what *isn't* said. The apostle makes no reference to hell, the lake of fire, unending suffering, or any similar term or phrase. Look carefully at the passage:

> For if, after they have escaped the pollutions of the world through the knowledge of the Lord and Savior Jesus Christ, they are again entangled in them and overcome, the latter end is worse for them than the beginning. For it would have been better for them not to have known the way of righteousness, than having known it, to turn from the holy commandment delivered to them. But it has happened to them according to the true proverb: "A dog returns to his own vomit," and, "a sow, having washed, to her wallowing in the mire."

Nothing in these verses unequivocally refers to *eternal* judgment. In fact, as we look carefully at what is said, we will see that it is speaking of judgment here and now.

• *The latter end is worse than the beginning.* Peter had heard the Lord Jesus use this expression in the Parable of the Unclean Spirit

(Matthew 12:43-45; Luke 11:24-26). The parable clearly refers to a person's experience *in this life* becoming worse than it was before. It is worse to have seven demons than to have one.[7]

Compare also Matthew 27:64 for a similar thought, "The last deception will be worse than the first." Evidently this was a proverbial expression much like our modern expression, "Things went from bad to worse."

If a Christian falls into licentious living, his experience of life here and now will be worse than before he came to know "the way of righteousness."

• *Better not to have known the way of righteousness.* The word "for" at the start of the verse shows that verse 21 explains verse 20. At first, however, this seems to create more confusion, not less.

It is hard for many Christians to conceive of any way that it would be better for a Christian never to have known the way of righteousness. However, as I have taught this passage, I have found that people are quickly able to see Peter's point once they change their perspective.

Let me give you a simple example. My dad had a business card with some familiar words on it. The card urged the reader to read the words aloud. I urge you to do the same:

Paris	once	a bird
in the	in a	in the
the spring	a lifetime	the hand

How did you do? Did you see the repeated word in each expression? Most people don't—even after they read it out loud. People often only see what they expect to see. The same is true in this passage. To understand Peter's point, we must break out of our preconceived ideas and look carefully at what the text actually says.

Now think about the word "better" and the expression "the way of righteousness" in verse 21. Better *than what*? What is being compared? And what is "the way of righteousness"? Is it eternal life, being born again? Or is it the Christian life and progressive sanctification?

In light of the proverbial expression in verse 20 concerning the latter end being worse than the beginning, "better" here refers to better well-being *here and now* than in one's previous state. Therefore, even if the phrase "the way of righteousness" referred to regeneration—which it does not, Peter's point would be that if a person becomes a Christian and then lapses into licentiousness, his life will be worse than if he had never become a Christian. His life after death is not in view.

Maybe you've never been at a lower point as a Christian than before you were saved. However, I have met Christians who fell far lower, both morally and emotionally, than they had ever been as non-Christians.

The expression "the way of righteousness" is not a synonym for conversion or regeneration. Think about it. Why would Peter refer to salvation by grace through faith as "the way of righteousness"? That expression is talking about a road or path which one must remain on to be righteous in his experience. The justified person is completely righteous in his position. However, he is righteous in his experience only as he travels the righteous path.

Note the context. Peter is talking about having escaped from the pollutions of the world and then becoming entangled in them again. That is a clear reference to moral change in the life of a believer. If a person knows the way of righteousness in his daily experience, he knows Christ intimately (1 John 2:3-11). The way or path of righteousness refers to holy living. Climbing up the mountain of holiness on the path of righteousness is, for the Christian, a lifetime pilgrimage. It is possible to slip, even to fall off the path and down the mountain:

> You therefore, beloved, since you know this beforehand, beware lest you also fall from your own steadfastness, being led away with the error

165

of the wicked; but grow in the grace and knowledge of our Lord and Savior Jesus Christ.
—2 Peter 3:17-18a

Most likely Peter had both behavior and well being in mind.
Once a Christian suffers a major fall like this, his sense of well being
and his behavior are worse than if he had never begun a journey on
the path of righteousness.

People who work among the homeless find that a surprising
number at one time were successful salespeople, managers, doctors,
lawyers, and other professionals who fell into loose living and
became addicted to alcohol and other drugs. Some of these people
are believers who began to follow Christ in discipleship, and now
their latter behavior is worse than before they began on the path of
righteousness.

Few people are more miserable than believers who have
formerly known the joy of walking with Christ and now are not walking with Him. Regardless of any material prosperity they may have,
discontentment, frustration, and unhappiness characterize their lives.

This teaching grows out of the teachings Peter received directly from the Lord. The Savior instructed all who wish to follow
Him to count the cost, lest they find out after starting on the path of
discipleship that they aren't willing to pay the price (Luke 14:26-33). He
taught that it was better never to start on the path of discipleship than
to start on it and turn back. To do that is to be like a man who mind-
lessly starts to build a tower only to discover that he doesn't have the
money to complete the job. Or, like a commander of an army who
foolishly rushes into a military engagement he can't win.

We need to warn new believers that committing themselves
to discipleship is dangerous! While the rewards of following Christ
are great, the risk for those who fall is great as well. People should
not enter into discipleship flippantly. It should be a deliberate
commitment of a lifetime.

I guess it should come as no surprise that many today enter

discipleship with a let's-see-if-I-like-it attitude. That is often how they approach college, job, purchases, and even marriage. Many people enter commitments with the thought that they can always bail out if the going gets tough.

• *Filthy dogs and pigs.* Some people find it hard to believe that Peter would compare believers to dogs or pigs! But I believe that was his intent. Notice that the dog and the pig are said to have once been free from their filth. This surely illustrates Peter's point in verses 20 and 21 that these people had escaped from the pollutions of the world only to later become entangled again. Surely these proverbial expressions also look back to 2 Peter 1:9 where the apostle said his readers had been "cleansed from [their] old sins." Only believers who are in fellowship with God know the path of righteousness and only such believers live free from the sins that used to enslave them.

Whenever a believer ceases to walk with Christ and begins to walk in darkness, he has forgotten who he is (2 Peter 1:9) and has allowed his old habits to take center stage. Such a person is rightly compared to a dog that returns to his vomit or to a pig that has been cleaned up only to return to the mud. For a Christian to begin on the path of righteousness and then return to the pigsty of sin is a terrible affront to the name of Christ.

The Coffin Zone

Free soloing is a term rock climbers use for climbing without safety ropes. If they fall, they are either badly hurt or killed. The higher a climber goes, the more severely he will be hurt if he falls. At twenty-five feet a climber who falls will be injured, but will usually survive, as he bounces down the steep face of the rock. However, a fall from fifty feet or above is almost always fatal. For this reason, climber John Long calls free soloing at fifty feet or above "the coffin zone."[8]

Likewise, the higher a believer climbs on the path of

righteousness, the worse it will be if he or she falls. The old saying is true, "The bigger [or higher] they are, the harder they fall."

Striving to climb higher is the wisest thing a believer can do, but it's not free of danger. Peter is warning us to take care lest we fall. He wants us to be aware that there are charlatans, like the false teachers of whom he wrote who will seek to deceive us, promising liberty and joy yet delivering slavery and grief.

Though all believers are eternally secure, climbing the mountain of holiness on the path of righteousness will have serious consequences in our spiritual lives if we fall. Instead, we must cling to the Rock and keep on keeping on. Then we will climb ever higher on the dangerous but highly rewarding path of righteousness.

CHAPTER 20

OBEDIENCE AND DISOBEDIENCE
John 3:36

THROUGHOUT CHURCH HISTORY most professing Christians have thought that obedience is essential not only to living the Christian life but also to becoming a Christian in the first place.

The apostles dealt with the Judaizers (from the word *Judaism*) who said that in order to be saved a person had to believe in Jesus Christ *and* persevere in obedience to the Law of Moses (see, for example, Acts 15:1; Galatians 1:6-9; 3:1-5; 4:8-11; 5:1-12).

Over the centuries people have been told that they need to do more than believe in Christ to make it to heaven. Additional requirements mentioned include giving money to the Lord's work, attending church, confessing one's sins, obeying the golden rule, reading the Bible, praying, confessing one's faith in Christ, being baptized, and turning from one's sins. All of these things *are* commanded in Scripture. The question is, what must be done to gain eternal life? If obedience to God's commands is required, then we must discover *which commands* we need to obey to gain eternal life. There are hundreds of commands in Scripture. Finding exactly what we have to do to be saved is certainly the most important discovery we can make. John 3:36 sheds light on our search:

> "He who believes in the Son has eternal life;
> but he who does not obey the Son shall not see life,
> but the wrath of God abides on him."
> —New American Standard Bible

A few verses in the New Testament indicate that those who disobey the gospel are eternally condemned. "But *they have not all obeyed the gospel*. For Isaiah says, 'Lord, who has believed our report?'" (Romans 10:16); "It is a righteous thing with God...[to] tak[e] vengeance on those who do not know God, and on those *who do not obey the gospel* of our Lord Jesus Christ" (2 Thessalonians 1:6, 8); "Therefore, to you who believe, He is precious; but *to those who are disobedient*, [He is]...a stone of stumbling and a rock of offense" (1 Peter 2:7-8).[1]

John 3:36 is one of the most famous passages linking obedience to eternal salvation. Many pastors and theologians understand this passage as teaching that perseverance in obedience is required for a person to go to heaven.[2] Some say that if you don't persevere, you *lose your salvation*. Others claim that if you fail to endure in obedience, you *prove you never were saved* in the first place. The result, obviously, is the same. Failure to obey God to the end of your life will result in eternal damnation.

A good example of the importance some place on John 3:36 is found in John MacArthur's *The Gospel According to Jesus*. In this book he cites eleven verses five or more times; John 3:36 is one of those.[3] MacArthur understands John 3:36 as teaching that anyone who fails to persevere in obedience proves he never really was saved in the first place. He writes, "Thus the test of true faith is this: Does it produce obedience? If not, it is not saving faith. Disobedience is unbelief. Real faith obeys."[4] In another reference to John 3:36 he says, "Clearly the biblical concept of faith must lead to obedience."[5]

To say that saving faith necessarily results in ongoing obedience is the same as stating that obedience is a condition of eternal salvation. This was clearly asserted by the late Dr. John Gerstner, who held the view that ongoing obedience is an accompanying, though not meritorious, condition of salvation:

> Thus, good works may be said to be a condition for obtaining salvation in that they inevitably accompany genuine faith. Good works, while a necessary complement of true faith, are never the meritorious grounds of justification, of acceptance before God. *From the essential truth that no sinner in himself can merit salvation, the*

antinomian draws the erroneous conclusion that good works need not even accompany faith in the saint. The question is not whether good works are necessary to salvation, but in what way are they necessary. As the inevitable outworking of saving faith, they are necessary for salvation...[6]

Dr. Gerstner later chastised Dr. Charles Ryrie (a respected, moderate Calvinist, known for his many excellent books and *The Ryrie Study Bible*) for being unable to grasp the necessity of good works for salvation:

> That Ryrie cannot grasp the distinction between a necessary condition and a meritorious condition is apparent...Ryrie simply will not give up his Antinomianism or understand the biblical doctrine of sanctification...Instead of the perseverance of the saint, [Ryrie believes in] the preservation of the sinner.[7]

MacArthur makes a similar statement, "Salvation by faith does not eliminate works per se. It does away with works that are the result of human merit alone (Eph. 2:8)."[8]

The argument implied in these comments is logical. It goes something like this:

Major premise:	All true believers persevere in obedience.
Minor premise:	John Doe isn't persevering in obedience.
Conclusion:	John Doe isn't a true believer.

What do you think of that argument? It seems logical. But it is incorrect since the major premise is not biblical.

One of the tragic twists of the Reformation is that many today that call themselves *Protestant* and *Reformed* believe that perseverance in obedience is a condition of eternal salvation. They have effectively reversed the Reformation.

Obedience in John's Gospel

John's Gospel is the only book in the Bible whose stated purpose is evangelistic (see John 20:31). This makes it an ideal book in which to discern the role of obedience in salvation.

If the arguments advanced above were true, we would expect to find repeated references in John's Gospel to the fact that all truly saved people persevere in obedience. However, we find just the opposite—that the words *obey* and *obedience* do not occur even once in John's Gospel![9] Surely if obedience were a condition of salvation, it would be mentioned as such somewhere in the only evangelistic book in Scripture![10]

The only place in the Gospel of John where the word *disobey* occurs is in John 3:36. The second line of this verse is translated in a number of different ways.

> "*He who does not obey* the Son shall not see life" (NASB).
>
> "But *he who disobeys* the Son shall not see that life" (NEB).
>
> "*Whoever rejects* the Son will not see life" (NIV).
>
> "*He that believeth not* the Son shall not see life" (KJV).
>
> "*He who does not believe* the Son shall not see life" (NKJV).
>
> "*Those who don't believe and obey* him shall never see heaven" (TLB).

I personally feel that the NASB has the best rendering of the Greek verb *apeitheō*. This leaves the interpretive decision up to the reader. However, the real issue here is not translation but meaning. What does it mean in this context to disobey the Son?

He Who Disobeys the Son

The fact that the two halves of verse 36 are antithetical (opposites) makes it easier to understand what John the Baptist was saying. The first half deals with eternal salvation, the second with eternal condemnation. The condition of eternal salvation is believing in Christ. The condition for eternal condemnation, we would expect, is failing to believe in Him. Instead, however, John the Baptist declared that the condition of eternal condemnation is *disobeying* the Son of God.

It is reasonable to ask why John the Baptist didn't use the same verb in both halves of verse 36. Why did he switch from believe (*pisteuō*) to disobey (*apeitheō*)?

In this and other contexts (see below), the Greek verb *apeitheō* is an antonym of *pisteuō*, referring to *dis*belief. However, it is an antonym that conveys a powerful message. Disbelief is disobedience—indeed, the only disobedience for which people will be condemned.

The leading Greek lexicon of the New Testament makes this insightful comment about the verb translated "he who does not obey" (*apeitheō*):

> Since in the view of the early Christians, the supreme disobedience was a refusal to believe their gospel, *apeitheō* may be restricted in some passages to the meaning *disbelieve, be an unbeliever.* This sense, though greatly disputed (it is not found outside our literature [i.e., outside the New Testament, the Apostolic Fathers, and other early Christian literature]), seems most probable in John 3:36; Acts 14:2; 19:9; Rom 15:31.[11]

This word *apeitheō* is consistently used in the New Testament to refer to the disobedience of unbelief.[12] For example, commenting on the use of *apeitheō* in 1 Peter 2:7-8 and 4:17, Roger Raymer correctly points out that "to *disobey* the message (4:17) is to reject it; and to obey it is to believe ('obedience' in 1:14, 22 and 'obedient to the faith' in Acts 6:7). All who do not receive Christ as their Savior will one day face Him as their Judge."[13]

Failure to believe in Christ is not a morally neutral act. It is disobedience and sin. If a person never comes to faith in Christ, then he or she will never see life. That is why disobeying the Son is the gravest danger in the world.

Today we are bombarded with warnings about health hazards, risks to personal safety, dangerous weather conditions, etc. When it comes to our eternal destiny, the warning signs should be just as prevalent. Warning: those who do not obey the Son shall not see life, but the wrath of God abides on them.

Saving faith is an act of obedience to the command to believe in Christ for eternal life. John the Baptist, Jesus, and the apostles all called people to believe in Christ for eternal life. Probably the most famous question in the Bible, "Sirs, what must I do to be saved?" (Acts 16:30) was answered by Paul and Silas in this way, "Believe on the Lord Jesus Christ, and you will be saved" (Acts 16:31). The word *believe* is in the imperative mood. That is, it is a *command*. Anyone who believes in Christ obeys the command to believe in Him. It is that simple.

John 3:36 has nothing to do with ongoing acts of obedience being requirements of eternal salvation. Neither does any other verse. Salvation is "not of works, lest anyone should boast" (Ephesians 2:9).

Whoever believes in Christ has eternal life. Whoever disobeys the command to believe in Him is condemned now (John 3:18 says "already") and he will be eternally condemned unless he obeys that command before his earthly life is finished.

Obedience and Assurance of Salvation

Assurance of salvation is found in believing God's promise to those who believe in Christ, not in ongoing obedience. If a person thinks he has to persevere in obeying God's commands to go to heaven, then he doesn't believe Jesus' promise in John 6:47, "He who believes in Me has everlasting life." And he doesn't know for sure that he is going to heaven when he dies since he can't be certain he will persevere in obedience.

All people are sinners falling short of the glory of God

(Romans 3:23). Only by receiving God's grace, manifested in the death and resurrection of Christ, can anyone be justified before God (Romans 4:1-8).

There is no promise in Scripture that all true believers will persevere in obedience. In fact, there are examples throughout Scripture of believers who didn't persevere (for example, Solomon, Demas, and the believers of Luke 8:13, 1 Corinthians 11:30, and James 5:19-20). In addition, all of the commands in Scripture to persevere would be pointless if all believers persevere.

The obedience alluded to in John 3:36 refers to obeying the command to believe the gospel. If you know you've done that, you are sure that you have eternal life and that you will never come into eternal condemnation. John the Baptist said it so plainly, "He who believes in the Son has everlasting life." That promise is the basis of assurance.

Appendices

LORDSHIP SALVATION

JOHN MacARTHUR, a leading spokesman for the Lordship Salvation position, defines it this way: "The gospel call to faith presupposes that sinners must repent of their sin and yield to Christ's authority. That, in a sentence, is what 'lordship salvation' teaches."[1]

The Central Tenets of Lordship Salvation

There are four key aspects to Lordship Salvation: the inseparable relationship between justification and sanctification, the unique nature of saving faith, the high cost of salvation, and the subjective nature of assurance of salvation. Let's now consider each in turn.

• *Justification and sanctification are inseparably linked.* Progressive sanctification is the process whereby a believer grows more and more like Christ in his or her experience. According to Lordship Salvation, all truly saved people will progressively become more and more sanctified. While they never reach perfection this side of glory, people who are truly saved will persevere in the faith and will gradually become more and more like Christ.

This has direct bearing on evangelism. In this view, the call to follow Christ in discipleship *is* the gospel. To gain eternal life, one must count the cost of discipleship and commit himself to follow Christ. As MacArthur says:

> The gospel Jesus proclaimed was a call to discipleship, a call to follow him in submissive obedience...It put sinners on notice that they must turn from sin and embrace God's righteousness. It was in every sense good news, yet it was anything but easy-believism.[2]

Kenneth Gentry adds:

> What kind of trust or reliance is it that does not
> obey? To trust Jesus Christ, the Lord of the
> universe, must involve submission to Him as Lord
> and Master of one's life. *A person cannot be
> relying on Christ if he chooses to chart his own
> life course in opposition to Christ from the very
> outset of his faith relationship.*[3]

Similarly, James Boice, speaking of what a person must do to be
born again, writes:

> The minimum amount a person must give is *all*. I
> say, "You must give it all. You cannot hold back
> even a fraction of a percentage of yourself. Every
> sin must be abandoned. Every false thought must
> be repudiated. You must be the Lord's entirely."[4]

A while back I saw a church marquee that cleverly and
concisely conveyed this in one short statement, "The way to heaven
is to turn right and keep straight."

According to Lordship Salvation, justification and
progressive sanctification are so intertwined that in order to be
justified one must make a commitment to progressive sanctification.
And, if that commitment is not realized in one's experience, then the
individual will not make it to heaven; for only those who persevere
actually make it.

• *Saving faith is intricately tied to good works.* As can be
inferred from the preceding comments, Lordship Salvation teaches
that saving faith necessarily includes or results in good works. In
other words, if a person has faith in Christ, yet does not produce
enough good works, he will not be saved. True saving faith
necessarily results in perseverance in good works.

This means, then, that there are two types of faith in Christ:
saving faith and non-saving faith. Both believe the same facts. The
difference is that the saving variety produces a sufficient amount of
good works.

The non-saving variety may produce good works for years. However, eventually the person with non-saving faith will fall away and hence will show that he is not truly saved. Thus, according to Lordship Salvation good works are the acid test of the nature of one's faith. And, since one cannot be sure that his good works will last, or even that they are good enough now to infallibly prove one has the saving variety of faith, no one can be sure prior to death that he has saving faith.

• *Salvation is both free and costly.* According to Lordship Salvation eternal salvation is, in one sense, free, and in another sense, costly. Here's how one Lordship Salvation writer explains how salvation can be both free and costly:

> Eternal life is indeed a free gift (Rom. 6:23). Salvation cannot be earned with good deeds or secured with money. It has already been purchased by Christ, who paid the ransom with His blood. He has secured full atonement for all who believe. There is nothing left to pay, no possibility that our own works can be meritorious. But that does not mean there is no cost in terms of salvation's impact on the sinner's life. Do not throw away this paradox just because it is difficult. *Salvation is both free and costly...*
>
> That is what Jesus meant when He spoke of taking up one's own cross to follow Him. And that is why *He demanded that we count the cost carefully.* He was calling for an exchange of all that we are for all that He is. He was demanding implicit obedience—*unconditional surrender to His Lordship* (italics added).[5]

Under the heading "Paying the Cost," another writer says,

> The point of this examination of the cost of following Christ is not to discourage anyone from following Him, however. It is rather to encourage you to follow Jesus to the end. To do that we must count the cost, by all means, but then we must pay

it joyfully and willingly, knowing that this must be done if a person is to be saved."[6]

According to Lordship Salvation there is a price to be paid in order to gain eternal life. While this may be hard to reconcile with the biblical teaching that Jesus paid it all and that He gives eternal life as a free gift, this paradox is central to Lordship Salvation.

• *Believers can be confident, not certain.* As mentioned above, Lordship Salvation teaches that you cannot be sure that you are going to heaven.[7] Certainty is considered presumption.

This obviously follows from the connection between justification and sanctification and between saving faith and good works. If perseverance in good works is required to obtain final salvation, then in order to be sure of final salvation one would have to be sure he would persevere. Since this is impossible, so also is certainty of one's eternal destiny.

According to Lordship Salvation, fear of falling away and going to hell is vital in helping you to persevere. God uses this uncertainty to motivate the professing believer to keep trying his best to continue to produce good works.

What the Bible Says about Lordship Salvation

The only effective way to evaluate any theological view is to compare it to the teachings of Scripture. Let's consider the four pillars of Lordship Salvation now in light of the Bible.

• *Justification and sanctification are distinct.* Justification is a legal declaration by God that a sinner has right standing with Him. In essence it is a "not guilty" verdict. This forensic statement is made the moment anyone believes in Christ for eternal life. The apostle Paul said, "A man is not justified by the works of the law but by faith in Jesus Christ" (Galatians 2:16). And again, "Where is boasting then? It is excluded. By what law? Of works? No, but by the law of faith. Therefore we conclude that a man is justified by faith apart from the deeds of the law" (Romans 3:27-28). There is but one condition of justification before God: believing in Christ. All works, before and after justification, are excluded.

Progressive sanctification is the growth of a believer in Christlikeness and is clearly not the same as the legal declaration which occurs the moment one believes in Christ. To suggest that justification is dependent on subsequent sanctification is a radical redefinition of the gospel; justification by faith alone is converted to justification by faith plus works (or by faith that works, which is essentially the same thing).

The New Testament is filled with calls for justified people to obey God. Such challenges would be unnecessary if obedience was guaranteed. The justified person would be unable to disobey God.[8]

• *Saving faith is not tied to good works.* While believers should persevere in good works, they may not. Failure is possible at any point in the Christian life. When Paul wrote his first canonical letter to the believers in Corinth, most were still "babes in Christ" five years after their conversion (1 Corinthians 3:1-3). They didn't produce the types of works they should have. Indeed, their works were carnal, not spiritual. And some of the believers in that church had already died without ever having advanced to spiritual maturity (1 Corinthians 11:30).

It is also possible to start well and then later experience failure. A man named Demas was listed among Paul's trusted and faithful fellow workers on several occasions (Colossians 4:14; Philemon 24). Clearly he was a man of good works for a time. Yet at the end of Paul's life and ministry he lamented, "Demas has forsaken me, having loved the present world, and has departed for Thessalonica" (2 Timothy 4:10).

Saving faith is the conviction that Jesus is telling the truth when He guarantees, "He who hears My word and believes in Him who sent Me has everlasting life, and shall not come into judgment, but has passed from death into life" (John 5:24). Jesus promises eternal life now, no judgment in the future, and a past which includes having passed from the realm of the spiritually dead to the spiritually living. As we saw in the section on saving faith, there is no such thing as a type of faith in Christ that will not save. All who believe in Christ have eternal life, have passed from death into life, and will not come into judgment.

Clearly, believing is not the same as doing good works. While believers should persevere in good works, their faith is in no way dependent on doing works. Believers can be sure they have eternal life if they but believe Jesus' promise.

• *Salvation is free, not costly.* Paul said that salvation is "the gift of God, not of works, lest anyone should boast" (Ephesians 2:8-9). Jesus too spoke of salvation as "the gift of God" (John 4:10) and of the water of life which is absolutely free for the taking (Revelation 22:17).

Jesus paid the full and complete price for everyone's sins on the cross. There is no price whatsoever left to be paid. There is just a promise to be believed. Once the promise is believed, the free gift is received.

It is a contradiction to speak of salvation, which is both free and costly. It is like speaking of a square circle or a five-sided triangle. If something is free, there is no cost to the recipient. If something is costly, then it is not free. Costliness and freeness are mutually exclusive categories.

• *Believers can be certain, not merely confident.* When Jesus asked Martha, "Do you believe this?" (John 11:26) she didn't hesitate to say, "Yes" (John 11:27). She knew. There was no doubt. She was not fearful that she might not make it. She was certain she was eternally secure.

Assurance is nothing less than the certain knowledge that you personally have eternal life and are secure forever. All who believe Jesus' guarantee have that certainty. It is wrong to say that you can't be sure until you die. Lack of certainty is actually unbelief.

Most Evangelicals Need Evangelizing

What about all of the godly, moral, nice evangelical people who believe in Lordship Salvation?

Claiming to be a Christian does not make one a Christian. Nor does being a nice person and living a moral life. The proof of salvation is believing the gospel: that is, knowing that one has eternal life because Jesus guarantees it to all who believe in Him.

If a person holds to Lordship Salvation, then he doesn't believe that Jesus is the Guarantor of eternal life to everyone who simply believes in Him for it. He believes that other things, such as commitment, obedience, and perseverance, must also occur. Hence a person who believes in Lordship Salvation, no matter how moral, does not believe the gospel.

I am not saying, however, that all who believe in Lordship Salvation are unsaved. Actually, I am convinced that some of them are saved. The reason is simple. Jesus guarantees eternal life to all who come to faith in Him, even if they later stop believing in Him for eternal life. Thus, if a person believes the gospel and is then led astray by Lordship Salvation, he or she is still a Christian, albeit one who no longer believes the gospel.

Unless he indicates that he once believed in the Free Grace gospel, there is no way to tell if one who believes in Lordship Salvation is an unbeliever or a confused believer. However, we shouldn't let that deter us from witnessing. If someone is willing to listen, we should share the good news. Besides, it is not just the unbeliever who needs to hear and believe the gospel. Confused believers, while eternally secure, need to be won back to the gospel so that they can once again be sure they are saved, so that they are able to share the gospel clearly, and so that they have the proper foundation upon which to build the rest of their service for Christ.

A word of caution is in order. If you are a new believer, or if you are a believer unfamiliar with Lordship Salvation, you should first learn enough about Lordship Salvation that you don't end up being pulled into it by the person you were hoping to win. Keep in mind that in such situations the evangelism is two-way. They are trying to win you to their well-intentioned but false gospel, while you are trying to win them to the true gospel.

By the way, don't overlook those in full-time ministry. Many pastors, Bible College professors, seminary professors, and missionaries believe in Lordship Salvation and hence need to hear the gospel of grace. Don't assume that they are saved just because they are pastors of churches that have words like Grace, Faith, Believer, or Bible in the name. The key is what they believe.

In this age of toleration, with the chorus of calls to establish and maintain unity at just about any price, there is much pressure to accept all Evangelicals as brothers and sisters, regardless of what they believe about the gospel. We are told that we need to learn to brush aside doctrinal differences. Well, one doctrinal difference that we can't afford to brush aside is the gospel. It is nonnegotiable. We must be willing to make waves over the gospel if we are going to reach our friends, neighbors, and family members who are gripped by doubt, confusion, and fear. Take every opportunity to share the good news with all who aren't certain that they are going to heaven when they die. For the wonderful guarantee of the gospel is that anyone who believes it will never perish. At the moment of faith, the believer has everlasting life, which can never be lost.

BAPTISM AND SALVATION

T HE ROLE OF baptism in relation to salvation has long been a matter of intense interest. Both Eastern Orthodoxy and Roman Catholicism have traditionally taught that baptism is the means by which one enters the Church, the Body of Christ. In this way of thinking, there is no salvation apart from baptism because there is no salvation apart from the Church. Quite a few Protestant denominations teach variations of this as well, while others offer a mix of traditions, and a few do not practice water baptism at all. Thus, baptism is not an issue that affects only one or two branches of Christendom. The whole tree must deal with this question.

Even if you are not in a church that teaches *baptismal regeneration* (the necessity of baptism for salvation), you have probably been exposed to this teaching. During my four years in college ministry on staff with Campus Crusade for Christ, I was often confronted by students trying to convince me that baptism is required to be born again.

A few years ago I had a formal debate with a Protestant pastor in Baytown, Texas, a suburb of Houston, before 400 people from his church and denomination. He argued vociferously that no one could go to heaven apart from baptism by immersion for the remission of sins. That debate was a vivid reminder to me that many people believe submission to Christian water baptism is a condition of eternal salvation.

I have been baptized not once, but twice. A Serbian Orthodox priest christened me as a baby. Then, when I became a believer at age twenty, I was baptized again, this time by immersion, by a Baptist pastor.

The Case *for* Baptismal Regeneration

A handful of verses do seem to teach that one must submit to Christian water baptism in order to gain eternal salvation. I will cite the four passages mentioned most often,[1] explaining how proponents of baptismal regeneration use the verses.

Acts 2:38. "Then Peter said to them, 'Repent, and let every one of you be baptized in the name of Jesus Christ for the remission of sins; and you shall receive the gift of the Holy Spirit.'" Peter says that you must be baptized in order to receive the remission of sins and the gift of the Spirit, both of which occur at the point of regeneration. Hence, baptism is a condition of the new birth.

Acts 22:16. "And now why are you waiting? Arise and be baptized, and wash away your sins, calling on the name of the Lord." Ananias had told Saul of Tarsus, later the apostle Paul, that he had to be baptized to wash away his sins. Since the washing away of sins occurs at the new birth, baptism must be a condition of regeneration.

Mark 16:16. "He who believes and is baptized will be saved; but he who does not believe will be condemned." The Lord Jesus says here that salvation is for the one who believes *and is baptized.* Baptism is directly stated as a requirement for salvation.

1 Peter 3:21. "There is also an antitype which now saves us—baptism (not the removal of the filth of the flesh, but the answer of a good conscience toward God), through the resurrection of Jesus Christ." The apostle Peter says here than baptism saves us.

The Case *Against* Baptismal Regeneration

• *Many passages say that believing in Christ is the only condition.* A major problem with the argument for the necessity of baptism as part of salvation is that it contradicts many Scriptures that say that faith in Christ is the only condition for salvation. Because the Bible doesn't contradict itself, the verses cited above can't mean that baptism is a requirement of regeneration.

The Gospel of John, written after the birth of the church to tell church-age people how they might be born again (John 20:30-31), does not even contain the word *baptism*. And, while the verb form *to baptize* does appear, none of its occurrences remotely suggests baptismal regeneration. However, in overwhelming contrast, the word *believe* occurs ninety-nine times. Over and over again we learn that the one who believes in Jesus has everlasting life and will never perish (John 1:12-13; 3:14-16, 18, 36; 4:10ff.; 5:24; 6:47; 11:25-27; 20:31). Either these passages are wrong—more than believing in Christ is required—or else baptism is not a condition of eternal life.

• *Regeneration occurs at the point of faith, before water baptism.* The gospel does not change from person to person. If baptism is a condition of salvation for some, then it is a condition of salvation for all. If there is even one example in Scripture where a person was born again before undergoing Christian baptism, then baptism is not a condition of eternal life.

Consider, for example, the salvation of Cornelius and his household. Peter, considered by many an advocate of baptismal regeneration, was sent by God to Cornelius, a Gentile, to tell him how he might obtain eternal salvation ("Simon...will tell you words by which you and all your household will be saved," Acts 11:13-14). After preaching the death and resurrection of Christ, Peter said, "To Him all the prophets witness that, through His name, whoever believes in Him will receive remission of sins" (Acts 10:43). The very next verses say:

> While Peter was still speaking these words, the Holy Spirit fell upon all those who heard the word. And those of the circumcision who believed [Jewish believers] were astonished, as many as came with Peter, because the gift of the Holy Spirit had been poured out on the Gentiles also. For they heard them speak with tongues and magnify God.

> Then Peter answered, "Can anyone forbid water,
> that these should not be baptized who have received
> the Holy Spirit just as we have?"
>
> —Acts 10:44-47

Cornelius and his family were born again and received the Holy Spirit *before* they were baptized. At the very moment they believed in Christ they were born again.

• *Baptism is not a part of the gospel message.* The gospel message, not water baptism, is "the power of God to salvation for everyone who believes" (Romans 1:16). In First Corinthians, in a digression about water baptism, Paul said, "For Christ did not send me to baptize, but to preach the gospel, not with wisdom of words, lest the cross of Christ should be made of no effect" (1 Corinthians 1:17). If people are saved by hearing the gospel preached, and they are (Romans 1:16; 10:14), then Paul's statement here shows that eternal salvation is independent of Christian baptism.

• *Baptism does not mean immersion in water.* Most people do not know what the word *baptism* means. If they grow up in one type of church, they think it means sprinkling with water. If in another type, they think it means immersion in water. Actually, the term itself doesn't refer either to sprinkling or immersion in water.

The noun *baptisma*, translated—or actually transliterated— "baptism," most often refers not to Christian baptism, but to the baptism of John. And, even when *baptisma* does refer to Christian water baptism, it is not the designation *baptisma* all by itself which tells us this. It is only when immersion in water is indicated in the context that we conclude that water baptism is in view.

The truth of this is indisputable when we consider that *baptisma* is often used figuratively in the New Testament. For example, authors of Scripture quote Jesus five times referring to His approaching death as a baptism which He dreaded, "I have a baptism to be baptized with, and how distressed I am till it is accomplished!" (Luke 12:50; see also Matthew 20:22, 23; Mark 10:38, 39).

Obviously, this doesn't refer to Christian baptism! Nor does it refer to Jesus' own water baptism at the hands of John the Baptist—which occurred three years earlier at the beginning of Jesus' ministry. Jesus dreaded His "identification with" sinful man by His death on the cross.

Another figurative use of the word *baptize* is when Paul spoke of the new nation of Israel being baptized into Moses: "All were baptized into Moses in the cloud and in the sea" (1 Corinthians 10:2). Clearly this doesn't refer to immersion in water. It was the Egyptians, not the Israelites, who got wet! And the Israelites were not immersed in water when following the cloud that led them by day. The nation of Israel was "identified with" Moses and his faith in the cloud and in the sea.[2]

The basic sense of the term, a sense which includes both figurative and literal uses, is "to identify with," "to be placed into," or "to be immersed in." The context must reveal whether the usage is figurative or literal and what it is that one is being identified with, placed into, or immersed in.

The baptism of the Holy Spirit is another waterless baptism: "For by one Spirit we were all baptized into one body—whether Jews or Greeks, whether slaves or free—and have all been made to drink into one Spirit" (1 Corinthians 12:13; see also Romans 6:4; Colossians 2:12). Whenever a person is born again, the Holy Spirit baptizes him, or places him, into the Body of Christ, the Church. This is the baptism of the Holy Spirit.

The following chart describes the types of baptisms presented in the New Testament. Notice that only one of them refers to Christian baptism, and that none of them is a condition of eternal salvation. The baptism of the Holy Spirit occurs at the point of regeneration, except in the very early church when it sometimes occurred subsequent to regeneration through the laying on of hands by an apostle.

Type of Baptism	Purpose	Other
The Baptism of John (Matthew 3:6ff., etc.)	To prepare Israel for national repentance.	*Not for eternal salvation.*
The Baptism of Jesus (John 4:1-2)	To prepare Israel for national repentance.	John 4:1-2 is the lone reference—and Jesus didn't do the baptizing, His disciples did. *Not for eternal salvation.*
The Baptism Jesus Dreaded (Luke 12:50 and parallels)	To pay the price for our sins on the cross.	This "baptism" was Jesus' identification with us and our sinfulness. This had nothing to do with water. It refers to death on the cross *for our eternal salvation.*
Jesus' Baptism by John (Matthew 3:13-17 and parallels)	To fulfill all righteousness (Matthew 3:15).	Jesus submitted to John's baptism to endorse John's ministry and to motivate Israel to believe John and to turn to the Lord. *Not for eternal salvation.*
Being Baptized into Moses (1 Corinthians 10:2)	To identify with Moses.	Israel showed that it believed in Moses when it followed him through the Red Sea and under the leading cloud. *Not for eternal salvation.*
The Baptism of the Holy Spirit (1 Corinthians 12:13)	To place people into the Body of Christ.	This first occurred at Pentecost (Acts 2). In the initial stages of the church, it sometimes occurred after regeneration (e.g., Acts 2; Acts 8). Since then, at the moment of regeneration all are placed into the church (1 Corinthians 12:13). *Not for eternal salvation.*
Baptism for the Dead (1 Corinthians 15:29)	The purpose of this is unknown.	Possibly the Corinthians feared that unbaptized believers would miss the Millennium or certain rewards. *Not for eternal salvation.*

192

• *Christian baptism is the first step of discipleship, not a condition of salvation.* The purpose of Christian baptism was stated by the Lord Jesus in the Great Commission: "Go therefore and make disciples of all the nations, baptizing them in the name of the Father and of the Son and of the Holy Spirit, teaching them to observe all things that I have commanded you" (Matthew 28:19-20). In the Greek there is only one command: make disciples. It is surrounded by three attendant participles: going, baptizing, and teaching. As the disciples went out, they were to baptize and teach those who believed their gospel message.

Baptism is thus the first step in discipleship. It is an act of obedience to Christ's command. When we are baptized, we publicly identify ourselves as believers. This is why the candidate for baptism is commonly asked, "Do you believe in Jesus Christ?" or "Do you believe Jesus' promise that whoever believes in Him has everlasting life?"

Notice that Jesus didn't say, "Go therefore and save people by baptizing them and by teaching them." The means of gaining eternal salvation is by believing the gospel. The way one becomes a disciple of Jesus, something altogether different, is by being baptized and by learning Jesus' instructions.

Therefore, the purpose of Christian baptism is to identify oneself as a believer in Jesus Christ, as one who wishes to follow Him. Ideally, baptism is the first act in following Him. Unfortunately, today many new believers are not told of Christ's command to be baptized and so they put off baptism, sometimes for years or even decades. When I was a pastor I baptized one of the church leaders who had submitted to baptism as a teenager, but didn't believe the gospel until he was in his twenties. He had never considered the need to be baptized again until he realized that baptism was for believers.

Some born again believers put off Christian baptism because they just don't feel like doing it. The underlying problem, I believe, is that they don't understand its importance. It is a public testimony of one's faith in Christ and desire to follow Him in discipleship. If it was important enough that the Lord gave it to the Church as one of only two ordinances, baptism and the Lord's Supper, we should certainly obey Him in this. Though it is not necessary for eternal salvation, it is necessary to obey and please God.

• *Those tough texts don't teach baptismal regeneration.* Finally, what about those tough texts on baptism cited at the start of this appendix? Let's consider each of them.

Acts 2:38. "Then Peter said to them, 'Repent, and let every one of you be baptized in the name of Jesus Christ for the remission of sins; and you shall receive the gift of the Holy Spirit.'" There are various ways to explain this verse. Keep in mind that it can't be teaching baptismal regeneration, since Peter later told Cornelius and his household that all who simply believe in Jesus receive the remission of sins (Acts 10:43). They believed and received the remission of sins and "the gift of the Holy Spirit" before submitting to Christian baptism (Acts 10:44-48).

The key to understanding this passage and the next one is to recognize that regeneration is not mentioned here. Before Gentiles and Samaritans were incorporated into the early church, people were born again before they received the gift of the Holy Spirit.[3] Compare Acts 8:12-17 and Acts 19:2, 6.

Peter was speaking to Jews who had been in Palestine during the Passover. They were thus responsible for participating in crucifying the Messiah whom they thought of as an impostor. However, when Peter preached at Pentecost, they "were cut to the heart" (Acts 2:37)—that is, *they believed Peter's message* that Jesus was indeed the Messiah and the Savior—and they cried out, "What shall we do?" They already believed the saving message, that Jesus is the Christ, the Giver of eternal life (John 20:31). They were looking for a way to escape the terrible guilt of having crucified the Messiah.

Peter told them they must be baptized in order to receive the remission of all of the sins they committed against the Messiah, arresting Him, trying Him, scourging Him, beating and spitting upon Him, cursing Him, mocking Him, and crucifying Him. While it is true that the normative experience is for people to enter the Body of Christ with a clean slate in terms of fellowship forgiveness (1 John 1:9), these were exceptional people and exceptional times. They hadn't entered the Body of Christ yet, though they already believed and had eternal life. They also hadn't received fellowship forgiveness yet. For Jews guilty of crucifying the Messiah, they had to repent of those sins and submit to Christian baptism to receive fellowship forgiveness and to receive the Holy Spirit and be placed into the Body of Christ. In Acts 10:43-48, however, Peter presents the normative experience, one which soon became the experience of all, which is the reception of the Spirit and fellowship forgiveness at the moment of faith and regeneration.

Admittedly, this is not a widely held explanation of Acts 2:38. However, it is, I believe, what Peter meant. We know that Acts 2:38 is not an absolute statement of the condition for all people to receive the forgiveness of sins and the gift of the Spirit, since Peter told Cornelius and his household that all they had to do was believe in Christ for these things (Acts 10:43).

Acts 22:16. "And now why are you waiting? Arise and be baptized, and wash away your sins, calling on the name of the Lord." Ananias told Saul of Tarsus, the apostle Paul, that he had to be baptized to wash away his sins. Saul was also a Palestinian Jew guilty of crucifying the Messiah. He too needed fellowship forgiveness, what Ananias calls the washing away of sins. We know from Galatians 1:11-17 that Paul, by his own testimony, did not receive the gospel from men, but directly from Jesus Himself. He believed the gospel and received eternal life on the road to Damascus when Jesus appeared to him and led him to faith.

Mark 16:16. "He who believes and is baptized will be saved; but he who does not believe will be condemned." Many commentators have noticed that the Lord specifically says that condemnation

195

is for disbelief (Jesus made the same point in John 3:18), not for disbelief plus failure to be baptized. Thus whatever the first half of this verse means, the second half clearly indicates that the basis of escaping eternal condemnation is merely believing in Christ.

There are several ways the first half of the verse can be understood. Some suggest that the baptism here is Holy Spirit baptism.[4] Thus the point would be that those who believe in Christ and are placed into the Body of Christ by the Holy Spirit will be saved.

Zane Hodges suggests that the salvation spoken of here refers to more than the reception of eternal life.[5] Whenever Luke and Paul use the word *save*, they always use it to refer to the full package, eternal life, forgiveness of sins, and reception of the Holy Spirit. Since Jews who were in Palestine during Jesus' crucifixion needed to believe and be baptized to receive the full package, the Lord in this summary statement includes faith and baptism for reception of the "salvation."

While both of these views are possible, I am inclined to a third view. The expressions *salvation* and *save* refer to deliverance of some kind. This most likely refers to salvation from the wrath of God eternally *and here and now*, a point Paul made in Romans 10:9-10. To escape the wrath of God eternally requires only belief in Christ (Mark 16:16b; Romans 10:10a). To escape it here and now requires belief and obedience (Mark 16:16a; Romans 10:10b), which includes, and is symbolized by, baptism or by confessing Christ.[6] Therefore, Jesus is speaking in a summary statement of the conditions of escaping the wrath of God eternally, by believing, and temporally, by believing and obeying.

1 Peter 3:21. "There is also an antitype which now saves us—baptism (not the removal of the filth of the flesh, but the answer of a good conscience toward God), through the resurrection of Jesus Christ." Two questions must be answered. What type of salvation and what type of baptism are in view here?

First, what kind of salvation and deliverance does Peter have

196

in mind? The type behind the antitype is the salvation of Noah and his family *from physical death* through the ark. This had nothing to do with spiritual salvation from hell. Likewise, Peter was almost surely speaking of believers being saved here and now from the judgment of God. The apostle Peter said here than baptism saves the believer from God's judgment here and now. As Noah was already a believer, so too were the people mentioned in 1 Peter 3:21 who needed salvation or deliverance.

Second, is this referring to Holy Spirit baptism or Christian water baptism? Most likely Christian water baptism is in view, since it is "the answer of a good conscience toward God." When a believer is baptized he is taking the first step of discipleship. That step is "the answer of a good conscience toward God." If a believer keeps taking steps of obedient discipleship, following through with the implicit commitment made at baptism, then he will be saved from God's judgment here and now.

The four texts we have considered must harmonize with other Scriptures which say that eternal life is conditioned solely on believing in Christ.[7] It is unwise to develop a doctrine using difficult texts and then twist the meaning of simple texts to fit that understanding. Instead, we must develop our doctrine based on the simple texts and let that understanding guide us in interpreting the tough texts.

Be Baptized, But Not to Gain Eternal Life

The bottom line is this: if you are a believer in Jesus Christ, you should be baptized as soon after you come to faith as is feasible. Since only those who believe in Christ are to be baptized, and since all believers already have eternal life (John 3:16), only people who are already born again are to be baptized.

As I mentioned, I was baptized at age twenty, shortly after I came to faith in Christ. The reason I chose to be baptized was not to be born again. It was because I was so grateful for the eternal life that Jesus had given me that I chose to obey Him and be baptized.

Don't be confused. If you think you must be baptized to go to heaven, you don't believe Jesus' promise, "He who believes in Me has everlasting life" (John 6:47). He didn't say, "He who submits to Christian baptism has everlasting life." The sole condition is to believe in Him for eternal life. Believe His promise and you will know you have eternal life. Then, by all means, be baptized in order to please the One who has given you such a marvelous gift.

REPENTANCE AND SALVATION

I N THE GOSPEL debate repentance is a hot topic. One of the most famous questions in the Bible is "What must I do to be saved?" (Acts 16:30). The correct answer to that question is a matter of life and death, eternal life and eternal death.

Must a person repent in order to be saved? If the answer is yes, then what specifically is repentance? If the answer is no, then what *is* the purpose of repentance? Why does God call all men everywhere to repent? (Acts 17:30).

I wrote my doctoral dissertation on this very issue, because it is arguably the single most confusing area regarding the gospel. In this appendix we will consider the meaning and benefits of repentance.

What Must I Do to Be Saved?
The Place of Repentance in Eternal Salvation

Paul's answer to the question, "What must I do to be saved?" was simple, straightforward, and clear, "Believe on the Lord Jesus Christ, and you will be saved" (Acts 16:30-31). The Lord Jesus and His apostles were united on this point. There is but one condition of eternal salvation, faith in Christ (see, for example, John 3:16-18; 5:24; 6:47; 11:25-27; 20:31; Acts 10:43; Ephesians 2:8-9). Another way of saying this is that there is but one condition of justification before God, faith in Christ (see, for example, Romans 3:28; 4:1-8; Galatians 2:16; 3:6-16). Justification is by faith alone, *sola fide* as the Reformers put it so succinctly in Latin.

Since eternal salvation is by faith alone, what is the role of repentance in eternal salvation? There are three options:

> 1. Repentance is a condition of eternal salvation since it is a synonym for faith in Christ. Thus, "He

who believes in Me has everlasting life" is
identical to "He who repents has everlasting life."

2. Repentance is a condition of eternal salvation
since it is a necessary precursor to faith in Christ.
Thus one cannot believe in Christ until he first
repents; that is, until he first recognizes his
sinfulness and need of a Savior.

3. Repentance is not a condition of eternal
salvation and is neither a synonym for faith in
Christ nor a necessary precursor to faith in Christ.

If we can determine what repentance is, then it will be clear
which of these three possibilities is indeed correct. Let's turn now to
the meaning of repentance.

What Is Repentance?

The meaning of words is determined by examining their
usage. Thus to determine the meaning of repentance, we need to look
at some of the fifty-eight New Testament uses of *repent* and
repentance.

Jesus said to a Jewish audience, "The men of Nineveh will
rise up in the judgment with this generation and condemn it, because
they repented at the preaching of Jonah; and indeed a greater than
Jonah is here" (Matthew 12:41).

Jesus was here rebuking the people of Israel, most of whom
failed to repent even at the preaching of the Son of God! The men of
Nineveh repented centuries earlier under the preaching of a much
lesser prophet than Jesus. Jonah was a reluctant prophet who didn't
want the Ninevites to repent.

What the Lord Jesus means by repentance here is evident
when we look at the repentance of the Ninevites. In response to Jonah's
proclamation of coming judgment, all of the people of Nineveh fasted
and put on sackcloth (Jonah 3:5) and "turned from their evil way"
(Jonah 3:10). The repentance of the Ninevites was not faith in Christ,

nor was it a necessary precursor to faith in Christ. They decided to turn from their sins because they hoped to escape the destruction of their city and the widespread loss of lives which Jonah had proclaimed: "Who can tell if God will turn and relent, and turn away His fierce anger, so that we may not perish?" (Jonah 3:9).

The apostle John wrote prophetically about what will happen in the coming Tribulation, "And they did not repent of their murders or their sorceries or their sexual immorality or their thefts" (Revelation 9:21). Once again, repentance is not faith in Christ or a necessary precursor to that, but it is a decision to turn from one's sinful ways, which the people in question did not do, in spite of the terrible Tribulation judgments they were experiencing.

Jesus taught the apostles about repentance when He said, "If your brother sins against you, rebuke him; and if he repents, forgive him. And if he sins against you seven times in a day, and seven times in a day returns to you, saying, 'I repent,' you shall forgive him" (Luke 17:3-4). Again, repentance here is neither faith in Christ, nor a necessary precursor to faith in Christ, it is a decision to turn from one's sins.

All fifty-eight New Testament references to repentance bear this out. In each case repentance is a decision to turn from one's sins. It is never a synonym for faith in Christ or a necessary precursor to faith.

Further Evidence That Repentance Isn't Faith
Or a Necessary Precursor to Faith

• *Since repentance isn't in John's Gospel, it isn't a condition.* The word *repentance* isn't found in John's Gospel. Yet the Fourth Gospel is the only book in all of Scripture whose stated purpose is evangelistic, that is, to tell unbelievers what they must do to have eternal life (John 20:31). Therefore, it is extremely telling that the words *repent* (*metanoeō*) and *repentance* (*metanoia*) do not occur there. This shows that repentance is *not* a synonym for faith in Christ and that it is *not* a necessary precursor to faith in Christ. If either were the case, *the* book on evangelism would have said so.

The apostle John had to exert considerable effort to avoid any reference to repentance, since he heard both John the Baptist and the Lord Jesus preach repentance. John was careful to include various synonyms for faith, yet he never mentioned repentance. If repentance were a condition of eternal life, John would have said so. That he doesn't proves that it isn't.

Some object that this is an argument from silence. However, it is really an argument *about* silence. Let's say that a retired colonel who served under General Patton in World War 2 wrote a book about the greatest generals of the twentieth century and yet he never mentioned General Patton in his book. Wouldn't an obvious conclusion be that this writer did not consider General Patton to be one of the greatest generals of the twentieth century? In fact, wouldn't it be a certain conclusion?

So, too, when John is writing to tell people what they must do to have eternal life, and he doesn't even mention repentance, a subject he was very familiar with, and one he was even commanded by our Lord to proclaim (Luke 24:47), it is certain that repentance isn't a condition of eternal life.

• *Since repentance isn't in the Book of Galatians, it isn't a condition.* The Book of Galatians is Paul's defense of his gospel. He repeatedly mentions that faith in Christ is the only condition of justification. He never once mentions repentance. Surely if repentance was a necessary precursor to faith in Christ, or a synonym for faith in Christ, Paul would have indicated this in his defense of his gospel.

• *The belated repentance of believers in Ephesus shows it isn't a condition.* Ephesus was a city known for its occult practices. When the seven sons of Sceva, the Jewish chief priest, tried to exorcise a demon using those practices by substituting the name of Jesus for the normal secret appellations they would have used, the evil spirit attacked them (Acts 19:14-16). When the report of the incident got out, fear fell upon all the inhabitants of Ephesus, including the believers there. Note how *the believers* responded, "And many *who had believed* came confessing and telling their deeds. Also, many of those who had practiced magic brought their books together and burned them in the sight of all. And they counted up the value of them, and it totaled fifty thousand pieces of silver" (Acts 19:18-19, emphasis added).

The ones confessing their deeds and burning their magic books were those "who had believed." Past tense. Paul ministered and led people to faith in Christ in Ephesus for two years (Acts 19:10). Thus, those who repented had been Christians for up to two years before they gave up their magic books! Few sins are more grievous than occultism. Yet these people came to faith in Christ without giving up their occult practices and books first! Clearly their repentance followed their faith and regeneration.[1]

Commonly Asked Questions about Repentance

• *Didn't Jesus say that those who don't repent will perish?* Yes, He did. In Luke 13:3, 5, He said, "Unless you repent you will all likewise perish." However, the word *perish* does not always refer to eternal condemnation (as it does, for example, in John 3:16). In many contexts it refers to temporal judgment and death.[2] That is surely the case here, as the context makes crystal clear.

Notice the word *likewise* in the statement by the Lord. The occasion for Jesus' remark was that some "told Him about the Galileans whose blood Pilate had mingled with their sacrifices" (Luke 13:1). In other words, Pilate killed some worshippers. In Luke 13:3, 5, "perishing" refers to physical destruction and death. And, in fact, Israel did not repent and during the Jewish Wars (66-70 A.D.) the nation was destroyed and many in the nation died.

• *Doesn't the Parable of the Prodigal Son teach that repentance is necessary for eternal salvation?* Well, many understand it in precisely that way. Yet the context suggests a

203

completely different understanding. A fact most fail to take into account is that the prodigal was a son of his father before he went to the far country, when he was in the far country, and when he returned from the far country. He didn't become a son of his father when he repented.

Since the father in the parable surely represents God, the son illustrates a child of God who has strayed and who needs to repent to get back in fellowship with God. Whenever a believer is out of fellowship, God waits with open arms to take him back, if he but comes to his senses.

• *Doesn't the Great Commission in Luke include the preaching of repentance?* Yes. Jesus told His followers "that repentance and remission of sins should be preached in His name to all nations, beginning at Jerusalem" (Luke 24:47). However, we must remember the Great Commission was not merely a commission to evangelize. It was also a commission to disciple those who believe. In fact, in some expressions of the Great Commission the Lord only spoke of discipleship.

In Matthew 28:18-20 the Lord told the disciples to make disciples by baptizing them and teaching them to observe all that He had taught them. We don't conclude from that, do we, that baptism and instruction in discipleship are conditions of eternal life? In the same way, the Great Commission in Luke concerns discipleship. Repentance is indeed a condition of fellowship with God and of the forgiveness associated with that fellowship (see Luke 5:32; 15:4-32). We know from 1 John 1:9 as well that believers need ongoing fellowship forgiveness from God.

• *Didn't Paul say that repentance leads to salvation?* Yes, he did. In 2 Corinthians 7:10 Paul wrote, "Godly sorrow produces repentance leading to salvation." However, we must observe the context to see what type of "salvation" or deliverance is in view. Paul was speaking of the deliverance *of believers* from temporal judgment, not of the deliverance of unbelievers from eternal judgment. Those whom Paul was addressing were "beloved" (verse 1). He wrote them a previous letter rebuking them for tolerating blatant sin in their midst. Paul said, "Even if I made you sorry with my letter, I do not regret it." Why? Because "your sorrow led to repentance...that you might suffer loss from us in nothing. For godly sorrow produces repentance leading to salvation, not to be regretted; but the sorrow of the world produces death" (2 Corinthians 7:8-10).

Paul's point is that if a person is sorry for his sins, but doesn't repent, he is on the path of death. God judges unrepentant sin. Sorrow for sin won't win any release from the punishment. However, the person who is both sorry for his sin and repents is on the path of life. God delivers him from ongoing temporal judgment, just as He delivered the Ninevites from judgment when they repented.

• *Didn't both John the Baptist and Jesus say, "Repent, for the kingdom of heaven is at hand"?* Yes, they did. Compare Matthew 3:2 and 4:17. However, it is wrong to conclude that what they meant was that in order for an individual to enter God's kingdom, he or she must repent.

John the Baptist and Jesus were preaching to national Israel. They were calling the entire nation to repent in light of the nearness of the kingdom.

God has given only one condition for individuals to enter God's kingdom, faith in Christ. However, He has given *two conditions* for the kingdom to come to the nation of Israel: faith in Christ and repentance. Jesus stated both of these conditions in Mark 1:15, "Repent, and believe in the gospel."

At the end of the Tribulation the only Jews who will be alive will be repentant believers. If Israel had responded to the preaching of Jesus and John the Baptist, then the kingdom could have come to national Israel then, rather than later.

• *Isn't the change-of-mind view clear on the gospel?* This view defines repentance as a change of mind, not as a decision to turn from one's sins. It suggests that repentance is sometimes given in

205

Scripture as a condition of eternal salvation and that there the change of mind in view is a change of mind about Christ. In other words, in this understanding repentance is sometimes a synonym for faith in Christ.

As one who held the change-of-mind view for a long time, I certainly agree that it is a view that maintains the clarity of the gospel. Many Free Grace people hold that view and find great comfort in it.

However, as I reflect on the way I presented the gospel when I held that view, I realize that I didn't bring up repentance. I told people that in order to have eternal life they simply had to believe in Christ. The only time I would discuss repentance with someone when witnessing would be when he or she brought it up.

I suspect this is the case for most Free Grace people who hold the change-of-mind view. If believing in Christ is the sole condition, it makes sense to tell people to believe.

I realized even when I held the change-of-mind view that there was a risk in even admitting to someone that they had to repent to have eternal life. Most people think of repentance as a decision to turn from one's sins. Thus when I would say that repentance is indeed a condition, they could reject my definition of repentance (as being clearly contradicted by the context), and yet accept my statement that repentance is required.

While the change-of-mind view is not contrary to the gospel, it is contrary to Scripture in the sense that it is not taught in the Bible. The Lord used His Word to cause me to abandon that view. And, for that reason I now encourage others to change their minds about repentance as well.

Why, Then, the Calls to Repentance?

If the calls to repentance were not calls to eternal salvation, what were they calls to? There are, as we have seen above, four reasons why people, individually and nationally, should repent.

• *For believers and unbelievers to escape temporal judgment.* As we have already seen, the Ninevites escaped temporal judgment because they repented at the preaching of Jonah. Both believers and unbelievers are wise to repent so that they escape judgment in this life. This is true not only individually, but nationally as well.

• *For Israel to receive the kingdom.* When John the Baptist and Jesus said, "Repent, for the kingdom of heaven is at hand" (Matthew 3:2; 4:17), they weren't telling the individuals present that they had to repent to have eternal salvation. Individuals are guaranteed eternal life simply on the basis of faith in Christ. Actually, Jesus and His forerunner were calling *the nation* to turn back to the Lord so that the kingdom might come to Israel at that time.

Both the Old and New Testaments say that the Messiah will not set up His kingdom until the nation has come to faith in the Messiah *and* has turned from its wicked ways. While individuals are guaranteed participation in the coming kingdom just by believing in Christ, the national participation of Israel in that kingdom requires both faith *and* repentance. Jesus told the nation, "Repent, and believe in the gospel" (Mark 1:15). Jesus called for more than believing the gospel. If believing the gospel is sufficient for justification, and it is, then the Lord was clearly calling for more than justification here. He was calling for justification *and* sanctification. Faith and repentance.

During the Tribulation, the nation of Israel will indeed do both of these things. It will come to faith in the Messiah and it will turn from its wicked ways. The coming of the millennial kingdom will follow Israel's repentance and faith.

• *For believers to return to fellowship with God.* If a believer turns his back on God and fails to confess his known sins (1 John 1:9), his fellowship with God is broken. In order to restore that fellowship a believer must repent (Luke 15:11-32). While there is but one condition of eternal salvation, there are two conditions of restoring fellowship with God, faith and repentance.[3] The calls to repentance are invitations to renewed fellowship with God, not proclamations of the gospel.

• *For unbelievers to get right with God.* While repentance is not a condition of eternal salvation, God is indeed a rewarder of those who diligently seek Him (Hebrews 11:6). Let's say that an unbelieving couple has two small children who have never been to church. It's been years since the parents prayed, read the Bible, or went to church. Now they decide for the good of the family to get right with God. They start going to church, reading the Bible to their kids, and praying together as a family. Does this guarantee the family's eternal salvation? No. However, it makes them more likely to hear and believe the message that will save them.

Cornelius was a God-fearing Gentile who, before he came to faith in Christ, diligently sought God through prayer and the giving of alms. And, while those things are not conditions of eternal life, they did get God's attention. He sent an angel to tell him, "Your prayers and your alms have come up for a memorial before God. Now send men to Joppa, and send for Simon…He will tell you what you must do [to be saved]" (Acts 10:4-6; compare Acts 11:14, "[Simon] will tell you words by which you and all your household will be saved"). When Peter came, he led Cornelius to faith in Christ and eternal salvation (Acts 10:43-48). There is no doubt in the Acts 10 account that Cornelius' prayers and alms motivated God to bring him the message of how to be saved.

Make no mistake about what I'm saying here. The only condition of eternal life is faith in Christ. However, repentance may make a person more receptive to the gospel and may incline God to bring the gospel to that person.

Sadly there are many who repent of their sins, yet who never come to faith in Christ. The reason for this, I believe, is that they are not actually seeking God. Though they may not realize it, they are seeking the praise and approval of man.

I was such a person for years. I tried so hard to be good enough to be saved. This was repentance, but it was self-righteous repentance. I was like Paul's fellow Jews who had a zeal for God, but not according to knowledge (Romans 10:1). I was seeking the praise and approval of the religious club to which I belonged. I thought their approval guaranteed entrance to heaven.

However, God in His grace sent someone to challenge me to reconsider my view of the gospel. Shortly after that I came to faith in Christ. Was there something in my heart that indicated to God that I was genuinely seeking Him? I don't know. However, I know that I have eternal life because I have believed in Jesus Christ for it, not because of any repenting I did before or after my spiritual birth.

If an unbeliever decides to turn from his sins in order to get right with God, then he will be more open to the gospel. If he is sincerely seeking to get right with God, his repentance will ultimately result in his coming to hear and believe the gospel of grace.

How Did We Ever Get in This Mess?

Why all this confusion over repentance? Ultimately, it goes back at least to the rabbis who taught that people had to turn from their sins to enter God's kingdom (Luke 18:9-14). Soon after the deaths of the apostles, the second-century church leaders picked up that idea, contrary to the gospel of the apostles, and made it a cardinal doctrine of the Church.

During the latter part of the second century, the Church taught that a person could go to a priest only once in his life, to confess his sins and be granted forgiveness by means of doing prescribed penance. However, this led people to put off repentance until their deathbeds. The church changed the doctrine to allow multiple confessions and penance. Eventually people could even buy advanced penances, receiving forgiveness for sins not yet committed. These were called indulgences.

The Reformers responded to such abuses and said that salvation is *sola fide*, by faith alone. However, their followers have taken this cry and managed to find a place for repentance as well. They say either that true faith *includes* repentance, or that it necessarily *results in* repentance. Either way, they say that no one can get into heaven without repenting.

The bottom-line reason for this mess is that the way is narrow that leads to life and the way is broad that leads to destruction (Matthew 7:13-14). The vast majority of people both within and outside of Christendom are seeking to gain entrance to God's kingdom by their works. No matter how well intentioned, no one can be born again by works. Only by believing in Christ for eternal life can anyone be regenerated.

What's the Solution?

The solution is simple: don't confuse justification and sanctification. Tell unbelievers that if they simply believe in Christ they will at that moment have eternal life. That is justification by faith alone. Tell believers to repent of their sins in order to escape temporal judgment and to be in fellowship with God. That is progressive sanctification.

If an unbeliever asks if he must give up his sinful ways to have eternal salvation, tell him no. The only condition is faith in Christ. Tell him, however, that sin never pays, for the believer or the unbeliever, and that he should turn from his sinful ways whether or not he is convinced that Jesus gives eternal life to all who merely believe in Him for it. The passing pleasure of sin is far outweighed by its long-term pain. Just ask any alcoholic or drug addict, or any member of their family.

Paul's answer to the question, "What must I do to be saved?" was, "Believe on the Lord Jesus Christ, and you will be saved" (Acts 16:30-31). If repentance is the condition, then Paul got it wrong! That is, of course, absurd. The only condition is to believe in Christ. Believe. Not repent. Not believe plus repent. Just believe. It's that simple.

APPENDIX 4

MY APPROACH TO UNDERSTANDING GOD'S WORD

W HILE I HOPE many pastors, missionaries, and theologians read this book, I am writing primarily for the layman who wants help in understanding the Scriptures—especially those passages which seem to cause confusion concerning the gospel. To help you get the most from this book, I want to explain my basic approach to understanding the Scriptures.

Use Scripture to Interpret Scripture

An important principle of biblical interpretation or hermeneutics is that we use Scripture to interpret Scripture. We understand difficult passages in light of simpler ones which are dealing with the same subject. This is called the analogy of faith.

For example, let's say we have a clear passage indicating that Jesus is God and a difficult one which might seem to deny Jesus' deity. By the analogy of faith we know that the second passage does not deny His deity. We must look for another interpretation consistent with the teaching of clear Scripture.

Remember That Most Words Have Multiple Meanings

It is a mistake to think that words are like fingerprints, each one having a distinct and unchanging identity. Actually, terms are like chameleons that change, depending on their environment. They have what linguists call *fields of meaning*. Thus, the meaning of a given word depends on the context in which it is found.

"Write a definition of the word *trunk*." This was the assignment one of my professors in seminary gave to a large class. When we compared answers, we discovered that there were many correct answers: a type of suitcase, a compartment in a car, the base of a tree, the torso of one's body, or the nose of an elephant. Depending on the context, *trunk* could mean all of those things, and more.

Now let's say that a person thought *trunk* always meant the nose of an elephant. Look at the confusion he would have over this sentence: "Dave put his golf clubs in the trunk."

The same is true with expressions that are used in the Bible, especially of words used in contexts dealing with eternal salvation. When those words occur in contexts not dealing with eternal salvation, as they *often* do, confusion abounds for those who think they always refer to eternal salvation. Let's consider four such words: *salvation, fire, burning,* and *soul.*

• *Salvation doesn't normally refer to deliverance from eternal condemnation.* It is unfortunate that in Christendom today the word *salvation* has come to be seen as synonymous with *deliverance from eternal condemnation.* While it is used in that way at times in Scripture, it is much more often used to refer to *deliverance from difficulties in this life.* Thus whenever we see the term *salvation* in the passages we consider, we will ask, "Salvation from what?"

The apostle Paul wasn't saying anything about heaven and hell when he told the captain of a ship that was about to crash, "Unless these men stay in the ship, you cannot be saved" (Acts 27:31). Neither was James when he said, "The prayer of faith will save the sick, and the Lord will raise him up [from his sickness]" (James 5:15), or Peter when he was afraid he was about to drown and cried out, "Lord, save me!" (Matthew 14:30). When unbelieving Jews mocked Jesus saying, "Save Yourself, and come down from the cross!" (Mark 15:30), they were challenging Him to deliver Himself from physical death.

The way to determine what type of deliverance is in view is to carefully consider the context. Consider this verse, for example: "Now when neither sun nor stars appeared for many days, and no small tempest beat on us, all hope *that we would be saved* was finally given up" (Acts 27:20, italics added). The person who thinks that salvation *always* refers to deliverance from eternal condemnation has tremendous problems with this verse. However, if we ask "Salvation from what?" we conclude that Luke was saying that all hope was lost of physically surviving that terrible storm.

• *Fire and burning don't normally refer to hell.* Fire and burning can refer to eternal condemnation, but that is not often the case. Fire and burning most frequently refer to judgment here and now, in this life. Believers can experience fiery judgments, even though they can't experience eternal condemnation.

Proverbs 25:21-22, cited by Paul in Romans 12:20, says, "If your enemy is hungry, feed him; if he is thirsty, give him a drink; for in so doing you will heap coals of fire on his head." This speaks figuratively of causing your enemy emotional pain now by returning his evil with good.

Paul uses fire and burning to refer to the judgment of believers' works at the Judgment Seat of Christ. "If anyone's work is burned, he will suffer loss; but he himself will be saved, yet so as through fire" (1 Corinthians 3:15).

Unless the context clearly indicates that eternal condemnation is in view, fire and burning in Scripture refer either to literal fire and burning or figuratively to some type of judgment. Recognizing this simple truth eliminates much confusion.

• *Soul most often refers to one's physical life here and now.* *Psychē* is the Greek word translated as *soul* in the New Testament. However, it is also translated as *life* (Matthew 2:20; 6:25; 20:28; etc.), *living creature* (Revelation 8:9; 16:3), *heart* (Ephesians 6:6; Colossians 3:23), *mind* (Acts 14:2; Philippians 1:27), and sometimes merely as a personal pronoun such as *I, us,* or *you* (Matthew 12:18; John 10:24; 2 Corinthians 12:15).[1] And while *soul* is its most frequent translation, *life* occurs nearly as often.[2] We derive many English words from *psychē* including psychology, psychotherapy, psychiatry, etc.

Unfortunately, many people mistakenly think that the word *soul* always refers to one's eternal being. Actually, it rarely has that meaning. When *psychē* is translated *soul*, it refers most often to *person, life,* or *inner self.*

Thus, many erroneously think that saving one's soul means going to heaven and losing one's soul means going to hell. This, however, is a major misunderstanding based on a failure to understand the field of meaning of the word *psychē*. Whenever the expression *saving the psychē* occurs in the New Testament, it refers to saving one's *life*, either from physical death or from loss of joy and significance.[3]

Note how confusing the following verses are if you think *soul* always means *the eternal self:* "Let every soul be subject to the governing authorities" (Romans 13:1); "in the days of Noah...eight souls were saved through water" (1 Peter 3:20); "Then fear came upon every soul" (Acts 2:43). Clearly in each of those cases the designation *psychē* means *person*, not *eternal self*. And, did you notice that the salvation spoken of in 1 Peter 3:20 is not deliverance from eternal condemnation? That speaks of the case of Noah and his wife and three sons and their wives who were all delivered from the flood and certain physical death.

Probably the most telling example is that the Lord Jesus Himself laid down His "soul," His *psychē for us*. Consider these texts:

> "The Son of Man did not come to be served, but to serve, and to give His life [*psychē*] a ransom for many" (Matthew 20:28).

> "The good shepherd gives His life [*psychē*] for the sheep" (John 10:11).

> "Therefore My Father loves Me, because I lay down My life [*psychē*] that I may take it again" (John 10:17).

Clearly Jesus didn't give up *His eternal self!* What He gave up was His physical life. He died for us. He laid down His *psychē,* His life, for us. Of course, He not only laid it down, He also took it up again when He raised Himself from the dead ("I take it up again"; compare John 10:18, "I have power to lay it down, and I have power to take it again").

Watch for Synonyms for Faith

While faith is the only condition of eternal salvation, the Bible sometimes employs synonyms or figures of speech to refer to faith.

• *Hearing Jesus' voice.* Sometimes *hearing* is used figuratively in the New Testament to refer to responding favorably to something. In one gospel context Jesus referred to believing in Him as hearing His voice: "He who hears My word and believes in Him who sent Me has everlasting life, and shall not come into judgment, but has passed from death into life," (John 5:24; see also verses 25-29).[4]

• *Drinking living water.* Jesus told the woman at the well that He had living water which would forever quench her thirst (John 4:10ff.). As she learned in the ensuing conversation, He was using drinking as an illustration of believing. The one who appropriates Christ by faith will never thirst again spiritually. That is, he or she is eternally secure.

• *Following the Good Shepherd.* Sheep following a shepherd is a figure of trust and Jesus once illustrated faith in Him in that way. He is the Good Shepherd, and those who follow that Shepherd, that is, those who trust in Him for eternal life, are eternally secure (John 10:27-30). This figure says nothing about following Jesus in discipleship. It is a specific reference to believing in Him for eternal life.

• *Obeying God's command to believe the gospel.* God commands all persons to believe the gospel. Thus faith in Christ is an act of obedience. For example, Peter contrasts believing in Christ with disobeying the command to do so, "Therefore, to you who believe, He is precious; but to those who are disobedient, [He is] ...a stone of stumbling and a rock of offense" (1 Peter 2:7-8). Great confusion results if a person mistakenly understands these verses to be saying that those who obey God's commandments are saved. Only one command, the command to believe the gospel, is in view. The only act of obedience that is a condition of eternal life is to believe in Christ for it.

• *Doing the will of the Father.* This is merely a variation on obeying the gospel. Near the end of the Sermon on the Mount, Jesus said, "Not everyone who says to Me, 'Lord, Lord,' shall enter the kingdom of heaven, but he who does the will of My Father in heaven" (Matthew 7:21). While many have mistakenly understood doing the will of the Father here as referring to keeping the commandments of God, the context and other uses of this expression show that it refers to believing in Jesus for eternal salvation.

In the very next verse the people who hadn't done the will of the Father say, "Lord, Lord, have we not prophesied in Your name, cast out demons in Your name, and done many wonders in Your name?" They thought their *works* guaranteed them kingdom entrance. Our works can't do that. In fact, as this passage shows, anyone who thinks they can does not believe the gospel! Kingdom entrance is only guaranteed by believing in Jesus. According to Jesus' own words, this is what is meant by doing the will of the Father, "*This is the will of Him who sent Me*, that everyone who sees the Son and believes in Him may have everlasting life; and I will raise him up at the last day" (John 6:40, italics added).

• *Receiving Christ.* In the pinnacle of his prologue John said, "He came to His own, and His own did not receive Him. But as many as received Him, to them He gave the right to become children of God, even to those who believe in His name" (John 1:11-12). To receive Christ is to "believe in His name." Great confusion is caused when people mistakenly think that receiving Christ is something other than believing. Receiving Christ does not mean inviting Him into one's heart, praying a prayer, etc. The only way to receive Christ is to believe in Him.

Watch the Context Carefully

Many other expressions could be cited which are often confused and which lead to confusion on the gospel. *Perishing* sometimes refers to eternal condemnation and sometimes to physical destruction here and now. *Life* sometimes refers to life eternal and sometimes to life here and now. *Death* sometimes refers to eternal separation from God and sometimes to separation of the body from the spirit in physical death. We always need to watch the context. A text without a context is a pretext.

Beware of Dogmatic Interpretation

Dogmatic interpretation occurs when you determine the meaning of a verse or passage based on what your denomination, church, pastor, parents, or friends tell you it means. This makes understanding the Bible very simple—you just rely on someone else's study of the passage.

One danger of this is that difficult passages can have five or even ten or more different interpretations. If you accept someone else's view without studying for yourself, you very possibly will be adopting a wrong view.

God holds each of us personally accountable for our own understanding and application of Scripture. He expects each of us to seek Him diligently and prayerfully. Dogmatic interpretation eliminates the need to depend on God for understanding of His Word. All we need to do is take some group's interpretation.

I want no one to adopt my views of Scripture unless they can see *why* I take them and then become personally convinced that this is what God's Word teaches. Each person should study the Scriptures for himself. Each one should pray every time he studies God's Word, asking Him to open its meaning. The Bible is spiritually appraised, and everyone needs God's Spirit to unlock its meaning. Blithely accepting someone else's interpretation is a poor way to determine our understanding of Scripture.

Develop a Biblical Mind-Set

I must confess that I don't come to each new passage of Scripture I study with a completely open mind, for the Word of God has already influenced my mind. And this is how it should be. Once a person has studied the Bible for himself, then he has a frame of reference for understanding it. All knowledge proceeds from the known to the unknown. Our knowledge of Scripture grows as we apply what we know to what is still unknown to us.[5]

It is my prayer that this book will help you grow in your understanding of God's Word and in the development of a spiritual mind-set. I have emphasized foundational doctrines—eternal security, assurance, saving faith, and perseverance. While I have dealt with only a small number of tough texts, the principles I demonstrate in interpreting those will, if applied, allow you to understand other tough texts as well.

DEFINITIONS

S INCE CHRISTIAN WRITERS today use the same words with different meanings, it is important to know what any given author means by key theological words. The following definitions explain the way I use various terms in this book.

Antinomianism. Literally "against law." Technically, anyone who believes that justification is by faith, totally apart from works, is antinomian. However, it is most often used in a non-technical sense to refer to those who promote licentious behavior. Free Grace people are often charged with being antinomian. If by this it is meant that they deny the necessity of good works for eternal salvation, the charge is true. If by this it is meant that they promote licentiousness, the charge is false (except in a few extreme cases).

Arminianism. This is a system of modified Calvinism named after Jacob Arminius, a sixteenth and early seventeenth century Calvinist. While a professor at the University of Leyden in Holland (1603-1609), he had an ongoing debate over Calvinism with fellow professor Francis Gomar, a staunch Calvinist. When Arminius died forty-six ministers assented to a document called the Remonstrance. This document took different positions on the main points of Calvinism. The most prominent aspects of Arminianism are the beliefs that election to eternal life is conditioned upon good works in this life, that eternal life once gained can be lost, and that Christ died for all people. Whereas Calvinism stressed God's sovereignty, Arminianism stressed man's free will.

Assurance. The certain knowledge that one is eternally secure in Christ. There are no degrees of assurance, since assurance is certainty. Assurance is based solely on God's promise in the gospel. Good works are not indispensable to assurance, though they may have a secondary, confirmatory value to what the believer already knows to be true.

Baptism. To be placed into, immersed in, or identified with. Jesus spoke of His approaching death on the cross as a baptism or identification with sinful man, which He dreaded (Luke 12:50). Paul spoke of Israel being baptized into, or identified with, Moses in the cloud and in the sea (1 Corinthians 10:2). Christian baptism is immersion in water as a public identification of one's faith in Christ. Since faith in Christ is the sole condition of eternal life, Christian baptism is not a condition of eternal salvation. See appendix 2 for a discussion of baptism and salvation.

Believe. To be convinced that something is true. To believe in Christ in the biblical sense is to be convinced that He indeed guarantees eternal life, that is, an eternally secure life, to all who simply believe in Him for it. See John 11:25-27. Committing one's life and obeying God's commands are not saving faith. Those are discipleship issues. For further discussion of saving faith, see chapter 1.

Calvinism. Named after the theology of John Calvin (1509-64). However, there is much debate today about how much of modern Calvinism he would have embraced as true. It is far from clear, for example, that Calvin believed in limited atonement, and he, unlike most Calvinists, believed that assurance of salvation was of the essence of saving faith. See TULIP for an explanation of the five points of Calvinism.

Carnality. Living like the unsaved live (1 Corinthians 3:3). All believers begin the Christian life as carnal people, as babes in Christ. Our aim is to grow to maturity and then keep on growing more and more like Christ for the rest of our lives. It takes time to grow to spiritual maturity. The spiritual believer is one whose habits are now based on a spiritual mind-set (Romans 8:5-6).

Cheap Grace. A pejorative expression used by Lordship Salvation adherents to caricature Free Grace Salvation. It implies that the Free Grace view cheapens the grace of God by leaving out the stringent demands of justification, which supposedly include denying oneself, taking up one's cross, and following Christ. Of course, if those things are the demands of discipleship and not justification, then the argument is invalid. Indeed, if Jesus paid the entire price of our salvation, then the Free Grace view is not accurately described as *Cheap Grace*, but instead as *Free Grace*.

Confession. To declare or acknowledge something to be true. To confess our sins is to acknowledge to God that we have done wrong when we become aware of wrongdoing (1 John 1:9). To confess Christ is to publicly declare Him as the Guarantor of eternal life. Confessing our sins and confessing Christ are conditions of fellowship with God, but not of eternal salvation.

Easy Believism. Another pejorative expression used by Lordship Salvation advocates (see Cheap Grace) to describe the Free Grace view of salvation. It suggests that Free Grace Salvation is too easy, that more than just believing in Christ for eternal life is required. Lordship Salvation is seen as more difficult because it requires commitment of life and perseverance in good works for gaining entrance to God's kingdom. Of course, if believing in Christ is too easy, one wonders why the only evangelistic book in the Bible, the Gospel of John, repeatedly says that it is the one and only condition of eternal life (e.g., John 1:12; 3:14-18, 36; 6:47; 11:25-27; 20:30-31).

Eternal Life. This is God's kind of life. It is the life He gives to all who believe in Christ. As the name suggests, eternal life is eternal and cannot be lost. See eternal security.

Eternal Security. The doctrine that all who have been born again are forever secure in that new life. Eternal life is, as the name suggests, eternal. Eternal security is true because God guarantees it, not because all believers persevere in good works (which they don't). This is also called "Once saved, always saved."

Free Grace Salvation. The view that the sole condition of eternal salvation is believing in the Lord Jesus for it. See Believe.

Gift. Something received at no cost to the recipient. The giver pays the entire price of the gift, or else it is not a gift. Eternal salvation is a gift. The purchase price for eternal salvation was the shed blood of Jesus Christ on the cross of Calvary. He paid the entire price for our salvation. There is nothing for us to pay.

Grace. The bestowal of favor upon a person. In the case of eternal salvation God's grace is unmerited favor. We do nothing to merit eternal life. God justifies the ungodly, not the godly (Romans 5:8; see also Romans 4:4-5). The person who thinks or hopes that God owes him salvation for the work he has done is sadly misguided and does not believe the gospel of God's grace.

Great White Throne Judgment. The judgment of all of the unsaved of all time (Revelation 20:11-15). All unbelievers will be given their day in court. They will be shown that they fall short of God's glory and that their condemnation is just. Their names will not be found in the Book of Life, since only those who have come to faith in Christ have their names written there. They will be judged according to their deeds, and their degree of suffering in hell will be related to their deeds, and especially to the amount of light they rejected.

Hope. Biblical hope, unlike the common use of the word today, refers to something which one is sure will happen, but which is yet future. Thus believers hope in the return of Christ. We are sure He is coming back soon, but we don't know precisely when.

Inerrancy. Literally, "without error." The Bible is inerrant.

Inheriting the Kingdom. An expression which refers either to getting into the kingdom or to ruling in it. All believers will inherit the kingdom in the sense that they will enter it. This is sometimes called *passive inheritance* since nothing other than coming to faith in Christ is required. However, only those believers who persevere in faith and spiritual maturity will inherit the kingdom in the sense of ruling with Christ and being His co-heirs. This is sometimes called *active inheritance* since it requires perseverance on our part. Romans 8:17 lists both types of inheritance.

Intellectual Assent. An expression often used in a pejorative sense, referring to the view that saving faith is nothing more than being convinced that the gospel is true—that Jesus guarantees eternal life to all who merely believe in Him for it. Yet, that is indeed what saving faith is. Intellectual assent as commonly used falsely suggests emotional detachment, disinterest, and a stuffy academic air. While emotions vary, no one is totally emotionally detached or disinterested at the moment of gaining eternal salvation and knowing he is secure forever. See chapter 1 for more on intellectual assent.

Judgment Seat of Christ. Also called the Bema, after the Greek word which means *judgment seat*. While eternal life is absolutely free, believers are held accountable for their actions, not only now, but also after this life is over. Every believer will appear at the Judgment Seat of Christ to be judged for what he did in this life (2 Corinthians 5:10). Some will be praised by Christ with the words, "Well done, faithful servant." Others will be rebuked by Christ with the words, "You wicked servant." See Luke 19:11-26. Whether a believer rules with Christ, and how much treasure he has, is directly related to how he fares in this judgment.

Legalism. The view that one is justified or sanctified by keeping God's laws. Justification is by faith, not by obeying God. And, while progressive sanctification results in the keeping of God's commands, it is not accomplished by focusing on His commands. The focus of the believer is to be on Christ, not on His commands (Galatians 2:20; 3:26-29). Fixation on the commands results in defeat, not victory (Romans 7).

Lordship Salvation. The view that commitment and obedience to God's commands are required to make it to heaven. Anyone not committed to Christ's Lordship is probably unsaved, since regenerate people are committed to Christ most of the time. This view, though well intentioned, garbles the gospel, and shifts the focus off of Christ and His trustworthiness and moves it onto the sinner and his purported faithfulness.

Perseverance. To persevere is to endure, to hang in there. Biblical perseverance is continuing to abide in Christ to the end of life. It is to remain in fellowship with Him. While perseverance is the aim of the Christian life, it is not guaranteed. Those Christians who do persevere will rule with Christ forever (2 Timothy 2:12).

Repentance. A decision to turn from sins. This is a condition of deliverance from temporal judgment and of fellowship with God. It is not a condition of eternal salvation. (Note: many who are clear on the gospel understand repentance as a change of mind about self and Christ, recognizing self as a sinner and Christ as one's sure ground of eternal life. In that case, repentance would be a condition of eternal life. However, the biblical evidence does not, in my estimation, support that definition of repentance as "a change of mind about self and Christ." See, for example, Matthew 12:41.) See appendix 3 for more about repentance.

Rewards. While eternal life is a free gift received by faith in Christ, temporal and eternal rewards are earned for work done. While all believers will spend eternity in God's kingdom, only faithful believers will rule with Christ and have a special abundance of life. There are two types of rewards, which I call instant winners and perseverance prizes. The moment any believer does a good work with a good motive, he has laid up treasure in heaven. This is an instant winner. However, in order to get the perseverance prizes, which include ruling with Christ and being able to eat the fruit of the Tree of Life, believers must endure in their confession of faith to the end of their Christian lives. See Matthew 6:1-21; 2 Timothy 2:12; Revelation 2–3.

Salvation. Deliverance from something. In the Old Testament the word *salvation* refers to deliverance from temporal difficulties like enemies, physical death, and the like 95 percent of the time. In the New Testament it refers to temporal deliverance about 50 percent of the time. *Eternal salvation* refers to deliverance from eternal condemnation. Whenever one sees the word *salvation* in Scripture, he must be careful to ask, "Salvation from what?"

Spirit Baptism. The work of the Holy Spirit whereby He places believers in the Body of Christ. This occurs at the moment of spiritual birth and is true of every believer (1 Corinthians 12:13). From that moment onward, every believer is indwelt with the Holy Spirit who enables him to live for God.

TULIP. The five points of Calvinism. They include Total depravity, Unconditional election, Limited atonement, Irresistible grace, and Perseverance of the saints. While there is some truth in all but the third of these, the points are potentially misleading and lead to what we might call DAISY theology: "He loves me; He loves me not; He loves me…" Most who call themselves five-point Calvinists are not sure they themselves are eternally secure, even though they believe in eternal security, because they don't know if Christ died for them or if they will persevere in the faith (which, according to TULIP theology, all "true" believers will do).

Works. In the Pauline sense works are those things which we do in an effort to obey God and keep His commands. Eternal salvation is by grace through faith and is not the result of works, lest anyone should boast (Ephesians 2:8-9). Works and faith are antithetical methods of justification. While good works *should* spring from the life of the believer, they are not a condition of eternal life, and perseverance in good works is not guaranteed.

Study Guide

STUDY GUIDE

T HE FOLLOWING QUESTIONS are designed for group or individual study. While some of the answers are found in the chapters, many are not. Those questions will require you to think (ouch!) and to come to your own conclusions. See Acts 17:11 for a biblical example of the importance of searching the Scriptures to see if any given teaching is true.

Chapter 1
Saving Faith in Focus

1. What is faith? Give a definition and two or more illustrations.
2. What must a person believe in order to have eternal life?
3. Is it possible to believe that Jesus died on the cross for your sins and yet not believe that Jesus freely gives eternal life to all who simply believe in Him? Why or why not?
4. How were people saved in the Old Testament, before Jesus came? (See Romans 4:1-8; Galatians 3:6-14; and Hebrews 10:1-18.)
5. You can look at a chair and believe it will hold you up, but you don't *really believe* it will hold you up until you sit in it. Is that a good illustration of saving faith? Why or why not?
6. In what ways is saving faith like everyday faith and in what ways is it different?
7. In light of John 3:16, 6:47, 11:25-27, and other verses like these, is it possible that at the moment of saving faith a person might believe in Jesus for eternal life and yet not know if he really had eternal life? Why or why not?
8. If faith is the conviction that something is true, what is false faith?

Chapter 2
The Original Nic at Nite (John 3:16)

1. Why is John 3:16 a difficult verse for those who believe that good works are necessary to have eternal life?
2. Explain what Jesus meant by "born of water and the Spirit" (verse 5).
3. Was Nicodemus seeking God that night? If yes, how can this be harmonized with the teaching of Romans 3:11 that no one seeks God?
4. What do you think Nicodemus would have said if *at the start* of their conversation Jesus had asked him, "What would you say if God asked you, 'Why should I let you into My kingdom'"? Would his answer have been different *after* their conversation?
5. What is a *type* and how is the uplifted serpent a type of Christ and salvation by faith in Him?
6. What is eternal life and when does it begin?
7. If you had only John 3:14-18 to go on, how would you define saving faith?
8. In light of John 3:14-18, how can you be sure that you have eternal life and will never experience eternal condemnation?

Chapter 3
Faith on the Rocks (Luke 8:11-13)

1. Is the belief referred to in verse 12 ("lest they should believe and be saved") saving faith? Why or why not?
2. Many assume that the belief referred to in verse 13 is not saving faith. Yet Jesus clearly indicates that the people of verse 13 believed something for a time. What did they believe? Defend your answer.
3. How long does a person need to believe the gospel in order to be saved?

4. If a person dies in a car accident one minute after believing the gospel, will he go to heaven or hell? Why?

5. If the person mentioned in the previous question survived the accident and walked with Christ for fifty years, but in his fifty-first year became depressed or ill and stopped believing, and then died while still in unbelief, would he go to heaven or hell? Why?

6. Which of the following items best describes the relationship between saving faith and fruit-bearing as indicated by the parable of the four soils? Defend your answer.

    A. All who have saving faith bear fruit.

    B. While all believers do some good deeds, only some believers produce what Jesus here calls *fruit*.

7. Agree or disagree: In the parable of the four soils, the germination of the seeds illustrates regeneration. Why or why not?

8. Are you sure that you have exercised saving faith? Why or why not?

Chapter 4
Will the Real Believer Please Stand Up? (John 12:42-43)

1. Make your best case for the view that the people in John 12:42-43 didn't really "believe in Him."

2. Now make your best case for the view that the people listed in John 12:42-43 really did "believe in Him."

3. Which is it? Did they really believe in Christ? Why or why not?

4. What does John mean when he says that they were not confessing Christ? Is failure to come forward at an evangelistic meeting what John had in mind in 12:42-43? Failure to submit to public baptism? Why or why not?

5. Compare the three appearances of Nicodemus in John 3:1-21; 7:45-52; and 19:38-42. He is sometimes called John's example of a "secret believer." Do you think that is an accurate designation? Do you think Nicodemus might be one of the people referred to in 12:42-43. Why or why not?

6. When have you ever loved the praise of people more than God's praise?

7. Give a modern illustration of the struggle faced by these leaders who "believed in Him." What could this look like in *your* life?

8. What is the application for believers today if these verses concern genuine believers?

Chapter 5
Free at Last! (John 8:30-32)

1. Make the best case you can that those addressed in verses 30 to 32 were not true believers.

2. Make the best case you can that those addressed in verses 30 to 32 were true believers.

3. Which is it? Were they true believers? Why or why not?

4. Explain the apparent contradiction between verses 30 to 32 and verse 45. How would John speak of people who believed Jesus and then a few verses later quote Jesus rebuking people that didn't believe Him?

5. How does a person abide in Christ's word?

6. Are you abiding in Jesus' word? Why or why not?

7. What is a disciple? Are all believers disciples? Why or why not?

8. When you see the words *believe* or *faith* in Scripture, how do you decide whether saving faith is in view?

Chapter 6
Assurance in Focus

1. How are the Arminian and Calvinist views of assurance similar? Dissimilar?

2. Name three people in the Bible who knew for sure that they were eternally secure. Support your answer with Scripture.

3. If some people in Scripture were absolutely sure that they were eternally secure, wouldn't God want everyone to have that certainty? Why or why not?

4. Agree or disagree: A person who is out of fellowship with God can't be sure he is eternally secure. Why or why not?

5. How could a person who was sure he was eternally secure lose that certainty?

6. What possible benefits are there in knowing for sure that you are eternally secure?

7. Explain why you would be calling God a liar if you said you believed in Jesus, and yet you weren't sure that you had eternal life (1 John 5:10).

8. Are you sure that you have eternal life and that you can never lose it? Why or why not?

Chapter 7
Assurance and God's Approval (2 Corinthians 13:5)

1. Briefly explain the assurance-of-salvation view of 2 Corinthians 13:5.

2. Evaluate the evidence from First and Second Corinthians that Paul affirmed the salvation of his readers apart from their works. If you find that he did, how would this influence your understanding of 2 Corinthians 13:5?

3. Evaluate the two different ways of understanding "in the faith" and "Christ in you." Which view do you feel best fits the context and why?

4. Discuss the significance of the repetition of the related words "proof" (KJV, NKJV, NIV, NASB) in verse 3 and "prove" (KJV) or "test" (NKJV, NIV, NASB) in verse 5.

5. The word "disqualified" (Greek: *adokimos*) occurs only one other time in Paul's two epistles to the Corinthians outside of this passage where it occurs three times (once each in verses 5, 6, and 7).

How does the use of *adokimos* in 1 Corinthians 9:27 influence your understanding of its meaning here?

6. If, as some suggest, 2 Corinthians 13:5 is about assurance of salvation by self-examination, then when could you be *certain* that you were saved? Keep in mind that those who understand this verse in that way suggest that this self-examination must be repeated over and over again.

7. Can a new Christian be certain he or she is saved if the assurance-of-salvation view of 2 Corinthians 13:5 is correct? Keep in mind that new believers have not yet done any Spirit-produced good works.

8. In what way(s) would the assurance-of-fellowship view have a different impact on your life than the assurance-of-salvation view?

Chapter 8
The Place of Feelings in Assurance (Romans 8:15-16)

1. Explain and evaluate the fact, faith, and feeling illustration.

2. If the Westminster Confession of Faith is correct on the issue of assurance, is certainty that you will end up in heaven possible prior to death? Why or why not?

3. Does the Holy Spirit bear witness *with* our spirit or *to* our spirit? Explain the difference and defend your answer from the scriptural context.

4. What does *Abba* mean? What does this suggest about the type of relationship we have with God?

5. Is the birth certificate illustration a good example of the objective nature of assurance of salvation? Why or why not?

6. Have you ever had a special time of fellowship with God when you felt His presence in a particular way? If so, would you say that experience was sufficient to infallibly prove to you once and for all that you are a child of God? Why or why not?

7. Have you ever felt so depressed, so angry, so guilty, or so afraid that you doubted you were a child of God? If so, why did you doubt? What were you thinking that led you to the conclusion that you probably weren't a child of God?

8. Agree or disagree: Feelings can and sometimes do *confirm* what you already know to be true from the objective promises in God's Word. Why or why not?

Chapter 9
Confirming Your Call and Election (2 Peter 1:10-11)

1. Briefly explain the biblical doctrine of election in terms of God's sovereignty and human responsibility.

2. How can a person be sure he is one of God's elect?

3. Do you think that the election spoken of in this passage is election to eternal salvation or election (or being chosen) to rule with Christ? Defend your answer.

4. Is eternal salvation received by faith alone or by faith plus the addition of perseverance, love, and other character qualities? Defend your answer.

5. Explain the abundant or rich entrance to the kingdom spoken of in verse 11.

6. How does 2 Peter 1:19 help us understand 1:10?

7. How does 2 Peter 3:17-18 help us understand 1:10?

8. Is 2 Peter 1:10 a verse about personal assurance of salvation? Why or why not?

Chapter 10
Believer, Do You Know God? (1 John 2:3-6)

1. Defend the interpretation that 1 John 2:3-6 is telling believers how they might have assurance of *salvation.*

2. Defend the interpretation that 1 John 2:3-6 is about assurance of *fellowship*.
3. Which of these two views do you believe is correct and why?
4. Place the following references to "knowing God" into one of three categories: *positional* (therefore, "knowing God" equals "being regenerate"), *experiential* (therefore, "knowing God" equals being His friend, being in fellowship with Him), or *other* (for verses in this category, briefly explain what knowing God/Him/ Christ means there): Job 18:21; 24:1; 36:26; Luke 22:57; 24:16; John 15:21; Galatians 4:8, 9; 1 Thessalonians 4:5; 2 Thessalonians 1:8; Titus 1:16; 2 Peter 1:8; 2:20; 3:18; 1 John 2:13, 14; 3:6; 4:6, 8.
5. Agree or disagree: It is possible for believers to grow in their knowledge of God. Why or why not?
6. What is the biblical relationship between obeying God's commandments and knowing God?
7. Do carnal believers know God? Defend your answer.
8. Do you know God? Defend your answer.

Chapter 11
Eternal Security in Focus

1. Define eternal security.
2. What are the best logical arguments for and against eternal security? Why?
3. If a person can lose his salvation, what specifically would he have to do to lose it?
4. Have you listed *everything* that could cause a person to lose his salvation? If so, how are you sure? If not, how could you become sure? If you don't think you can be sure you've listed everything, what does this say about assurance of salvation?
5. Have you ever seen examples of people who didn't believe in eternal security who were gripped by fear? If yes, please explain.

6. Many ask, "If I believed that I was eternally secure no matter what, why wouldn't I go out and live like the devil?" How would you answer them?

7. Agree or disagree: Scripture can't contradict itself. If any passage unmistakably teaches eternal security, then no other passage actually teaches against it. Why or why not?

8. Have you ever known anyone who believed in eternal security and lived a godly life? If so, please elaborate.

Chapter 12
A Punishment Worse Than Death (Hebrews 10:26-31)

1. Agree or disagree: Born again people, believers in Jesus Christ, are in view in Hebrews 10:26-31. Defend your answer from the text.

2. Agree or disagree: A "worse punishment" than the death penalty must be eternal condemnation. Defend your answer from the text.

3. Does God "repay" (verse 30) Christians when they fall away from Him? Support your answer from Scripture.

4. Compare this passage with 1 Corinthians 11:30 and James 5:19-20.

5. Do you think that verse 26 applies only to the specific sin of doctrinal apostasy (verse 29), or does it refer to all willful sin? Defend your answer from the context and from other Scripture.

6. Why does the author say, "There no longer remains a sacrifice for sins"? Compare Hebrews 9:25-28 and 10:1-4, 11-14, 18.

7. Are you afraid of falling away from the gospel? Why or why not?

8. If you are afraid of falling away from the gospel, what can you do to avoid falling away?

Chapter 13
The Burned Branches (John 15:6)

1. In what sense are believers like branches and the Lord Jesus like a vine?
2. In viticulture why do they burn branches that are no longer connected to the vine?
3. When Jesus says, "You are already clean" (verse 3), what does He mean? Compare John 13:10.
4. How does the vine-branch illustration inform our understanding of abiding in Christ?
5. Do all believers "bear much fruit"? Why or why not?
6. To what does this burning refer? Defend your answer.
7. Do you fear that if you are unfruitful and not abiding in Christ He will cast you out and throw you into the fire, figuratively speaking? Why or why not?
8. How do other passages in John such as 4:10, 5:24, 6:39-40, 10:28-29, and 11:25-26 influence our understanding of this passage?

Chapter 14
Falling from Grace (Galatians 5:4)

1. Name some of the things a person might do to "attempt to be justified by law."
2. What is falling from grace?
3. Is Paul warning believers or unbelievers about falling from grace? Defend your answer.
4. Name three specific instances that have occurred in the past year in which you were tempted/encouraged to fall from grace.
5. Why would God allow His children to be tempted to fall from grace? Why doesn't He make us immune to such temptation?
6. How do you identify a person who has fallen from grace, by their actions, their beliefs, or both? Defend your answer.

7. Should you fear falling from grace? Why or why not?

8. Do you think it is possible for a committed Christian such as a missionary or a pastor to fall from grace? Why or why not?

Chapter 15
Erasers in Heaven? (Revelation 3:5)

1. What is the Book of Life?

2. Is your name in the Book of Life? How do you know?

3. Define "overcoming."

4. Does Revelation 3:5 imply that God will blot the names of believers who don't overcome out of the Book of Life? Why or why not?

5. If this isn't a warning about hell, then what would be the motivation to overcome in our Christian experience?

6. Defend the interpretation that Revelation 3:5 claims, by means of understatement, that the Lord Jesus will exalt the name of the overcomer.

7. Paraphrase Revelation 3:5.

8. Compare Revelation 3:5 with 1 Corinthians 9:27; 2 Timothy 2:12; Revelation 2:17, 26; and Revelation 3:12, 21.

Chapter 16
Perseverance in Focus

1. Please compare the Reformed doctrine of the perseverance of the saints with the Arminian doctrine of perseverance. Practically speaking, are they basically similar or dissimilar?

2. Why do you think that the New Testament fails to give a lot of examples of people who persevered? Of people who didn't persevere?

3. What is the proper biblical relationship between perseverance and assurance of salvation?

4. If the Reformed doctrine of the perseverance of the saints isn't true, then abuses of grace by genuine believers are possible. Why might God leave open the possibility that regenerate people would displease and dishonor Him?

5. If the Reformed doctrine of the perseverance of the saints is true, then God greatly limits the amount of sin any believer can commit. If God so restricts our sinning, why doesn't He *completely* stop it? After all, we will be sinless once this life is over.

6. Do you *want* to persevere? Why or why not?

7. Are you sure that you will persevere? Why or why not?

8. What would the Bible have us do in order to keep ourselves in a state of perseverance?

Chapter 17
Are Believers Free of All Bad Habits? (2 Corinthians 5:17)

1. The Greek leaves out some words in 2 Corinthians 5:17. What is a literal rendering of the first half of the verse, leaving out the unstated words?

2. What are the options for words which could be supplied, and which option do you prefer and why?

3. Agree or disagree: If you are born again, you no longer have any temptation to sin because old things have passed away. Defend your answer.

4. If 2 Corinthians 5:17 is talking about transformation of life, then how much transformation is indicated? How much sin would we see in a person whose old behavior had ceased?

5. How do the following passages impact your understanding of verse 17: 1 Corinthians 9:24-27, 2 Corinthians 5:9-10, 2 Timothy 2:15, 1 John 2:28, and 1 John 3:2?

6. Are holiness and transformation of life automatic and irresistible for the believer?

7. What practical value could there be in viewing unbelievers as lost and needing salvation and believers as brothers and sisters in Christ who are fellow members of God's family?

8. Does 2 Corinthians 5:17 guarantee that all born again people will persevere in the faith? Why or why not?

Chapter 18
The Danger of Falling Away (Hebrews 6:4-8)

1. Agree or disagree: Born again people, believers in Jesus Christ, are in view in Hebrews 6:4-8. Defend your answer from the text.

2. Define repentance.

3. Does the impossibility of renewing a person to repentance mean that it is impossible to bring him or her back to Christ and salvation? Defend your answer from the text.

4. Are verses 7 and 8 saying that true saving faith always results in fruitful lives characterized by good works? Defend your answer.

5. Does the burning of verses 7 and 8 refer to temporal or eternal judgment? Defend your answer from the text.

6. Name three passages of Scripture that clearly show that God sometimes takes believers home prematurely due to sin in their lives.

7. What bearing do the following texts from John's Gospel have on our understanding of this passage: John 4:14 ("will never thirst"); 5:24 ("shall not come into judgment"); 6:47 ("he who believes in Me has everlasting life"); and 10:28-29 ("they shall never perish; neither shall anyone snatch them out of My hand...[or] out of My Father's hand")?

8. Look up the word *curse* in a Bible concordance. (See especially Genesis 8:21; Deuteronomy 11:28; 28:16-19; Proverbs 30:10; Romans 12:14.) Does it always refer to eternal condemnation, always refer to some judgment in this life, or sometimes refer to eternal condemnation and sometimes to temporal judgment? Defend your answer by listing passages where the word occurs.

Chapter 19
Dangerous Road Ahead (2 Peter 2:18-22)

1. The words *they* or *them* occur ten times in this passage. Next to each of these, indicate if Peter is talking about the false teachers, or their dupes.

> For when *they* speak great swelling words of emptiness...
> ...*they* allure through the lusts of the flesh, through lewdness...
> While *they* promise them liberty...
> *They themselves* are slaves of corruption...
> After *they* have escaped...
> ...*they* are again entangled...
> ...the latter is worse for *them* than the beginning.
> It would have been better for *them*...
> ...the holy commandment delivered to *them*.
> It has happened to *them* according to the true proverb...

2. Do you think it is possible for a believer to have a worse experience in this life after a moral fall than when he was a new believer or even an unbeliever? Why or why not?

3. What can you do to keep from falling "from your own steadfastness, being led away with the error of the wicked" (2 Peter 3:17)?

4. Agree or disagree: All false teachers promote immorality. Defend your answer.

5. Have you ever counted the cost of following Christ on the path of righteousness? What does that mean?

6. What is true freedom (liberty)?

7. Does 2 Peter 2:18-22 teach that all born again people persevere on the path of righteousness? Why or why not?

8. Can believers in any sense ever be rightly called "dogs" and "pigs"? Defend your answer.

Chapter 20
Obedience and Disobedience (John 3:36)

1. Is persevering in a life of obedience identical to believing in Christ for eternal life? Why or why not?

2. Is ongoing obedience a condition of eternal life? Why or why not?

3. Compare how the current condition and ultimate fate of believers and unbelievers are stated in John 3:18 and 3:36.

4. In his first epistle Peter contrasted "you who believe" with "those who are disobedient" (1 Peter 2:7). In light of the context and the contrast, is the disobedience in question a general reference to an overall lifestyle of disobedience or a specific reference to failing to believe in Christ? Defend your answer.

5. Have you obeyed the Son in the sense spoken of in John 3:36? How do you know?

6. Agree or disagree: If eternal life can be lost, it has the wrong name. Why or why not?

7. Agree or disagree: In light of the fact that "he who believes in the Son has everlasting life" (John 3:16; 6:47), eternal life begins at the moment of faith, not when we die. Why or why not?

8. Agree or disagree: The vast majority of people in Christendom believe that obeying God's commands is necessary to get into heaven. Surely all of them can't be wrong. Why or why not?

Endnotes

ENDNOTES

Introduction

1. My dad went by Bob, as I do. I am not Robert Faris Wilkin, Jr. for I have a different middle name. My full given name is Robert Nicholas Wilkin.

Chapter 1: Saving Faith in Focus

1. An exception is universalism. Universalists say that God is so loving and gracious that the death of Christ saves everyone, regardless of what they believe.
2. One evangelist who has been in the ministry for 51 years recounted his testimony by quoting from a letter he wrote shortly after his conversion: "It has been over nine days since I smoked a cigarette...I am now taking part in all the church work I can...I have been born again. You may think I will get over this in a few days and be back to normal but I will never be the same again. I had not been born again before now. *I did believe but I did not have the love of God*" (*Challenge to Evangelism Today* [Fall 1997]: 1, emphasis added). Clearly for this evangelist believing, while necessary, is not enough. One must also love God by living an obedient life.
3. This is sometimes called Lordship Salvation. It is the view that to be saved you must not only believe in Christ for eternal life, but you must also yield to His Lordship over your life. While Lordship Salvation typically refers to Calvinists who believe in salvation by faith that works, it applies equally well to Arminians who believe in salvation by faith plus works. See the appendix on Lordship Salvation for more details.
4. The word translated *difficult* (*thlibō*) actually is better translated as *confined* or *narrow*. See *A Greek-English Lexicon of the New Testament and Other Early Christian Literature,* by William F. Arndt and F. Wilbur Gingrich, Second edition, revised and augmented by F. Wilbur Gingrich and Frederick W. Danker from Walter Bauer's Fifth Edition, 1958 (Chicago: The University of Chicago Press, 1979), 362. Both the gate and the road to which it leads are narrow. Since a different Greek word, *stenē* is used for the gate, a word which also means *narrow*, it is probably best to refer to the way as *confined*, a synonym for narrow.
5. Books such as Galatians and Romans present the gospel to Christians to make sure they remain clear on the gospel. However, no other book is written to tell unbelievers how they might have eternal life. All other books in Scripture are addressed to believers.
6. Of course, some don't think of it in these terms. They may think they believe it simply because they were told that it was true. Their elementary school teacher told them that George Washington was the first president and they believed her. However, that is believing evidence. Taking a teacher at her

word is not really any different than taking God at His word. The issue is the trustworthiness of the one making the statement or promise. Of course, elementary school students have lots of additional evidence to convince them that Washington was the first president. Our textbooks say so. Our national capitol and one of our States are named after him. And his likeness appears on the dollar bill and the quarter.

7. Jesus is called the Son of Abraham in Matthew 1:1. The promise that Abraham believed did not merely concern the birth of Isaac. It also concerned the birth of Abraham's ultimate Son, the Messiah, the Savior, and the Giver of eternal life. Abraham believed in this coming Son for eternal life (Genesis 15:6; John 8:56; Romans 4:21-22; Galatians 3:6-14). That is, Abraham believed in Christ long before the incarnation. That is why Paul could rightly say that Abraham is the father of all who believe in Christ. And that is why Jesus Himself could truly say, "Abraham rejoiced to see My day" (John 8:56).

8. There is one sense in which continuing in *un*belief can be a choice, when one refuses to even look at the evidence. A person might choose not to read the Bible, attend church, listen to Christians, or read Christian books. While, of course, God could upset those plans and bring a witness into one's life that was unexpected and unavoidable, apart from such intervention a person might indeed be able to choose to remain in unbelief. However, even then, the unbelief is based on a conviction that Christianity is wrong.

9. There might even be more workers on the mission field than there are in the home churches!

10. If a person came to believe the gospel while he was praying a prayer, he would be saved. However, it is not a good idea to ask a person to pray something that he doesn't already believe. And, if he already believes it, then he is already saved without the prayer.

11. Of course, if a person comes forward and a counselor is used of God to convince him that Jesus guarantees eternal life to all who believe in Him, then he would end up being saved. However, coming forward is not a condition, any more than coming to church in the first place is a condition. A person can be saved at school, at work, in her car, in a foxhole, on a basketball court, or anywhere, with or without an aisle or a preacher!

12. See appendix 3 for a more detailed discussion of repentance.

13. In my early days in evangelism I used this appeal. I remember one student at my college who invited Christ into his life. I gave him some material to read and scheduled an appointment for the next week. When we met for follow-up, he told me that the material I had given him said that Jesus was the only way to God, but that he didn't believe that. "Really," I said. "Then why did you invite Jesus into your heart?" He told me that he was a Bahai and that he had invited Jesus into his heart because he wanted all of the prophets in his heart.

14. Of course, this approach is futile. Each time the person doubts, he invites Jesus in "one last time." It becomes more difficult to do this sincerely since it

seems so hypocritical. The only way to be sure that Christ is in your life and that you are eternally secure is to believe Jesus' promise that all who simply believe in Him have eternal life.

15. John F. MacArthur, Jr., *Faith Works: The Gospel According to the Apostles* (Dallas: Word Publishing, 1993), 42.

16. Bernard Koerselman, *What the Bible Says About a Saving Faith* (Chandler, AZ: Berean Publishers, 1992), 138-39, 143, 160. Note: the cited statements are all headings of sections in a chapter entitled "A Saving Faith." See also Curtis I. Crenshaw, *Lordship Salvation: The Only Kind There Is! An Evaluation of Jody Dillow's* The Reign of the Servant Kings *And Other Antinomian Arguments.* (Memphis: Footstool Publications, 1994), 58-59; James Montgomery Boice, *Christ's Call to Discipleship* (Chicago: Moody Press, 1986), 113-14; Kenneth L. Gentry, Jr., *Lord of the Saved: Getting to the Heart of the Lordship Debate* (Phillipsburg, NJ: Presbyterian and Reformed Publishing Company, 1992), 19.

17. There is a tract called "Missing Heaven by Eighteen Inches." It argues that you would miss heaven if you believed the gospel with your *head* rather than with your *heart*. *Head faith* is dangerous, it suggests, because you may think you are saved simply because you believe the facts of the gospel. Yet without the heart commitment, that "faith" is not saving faith at all.

18. The word *head* occurs approximately 330 times in the Bible. Of those, the vast majority refers literally to the head. The figurative uses include *lifting up the head*, which refers to being placed in a position of honor or having one's former status reinstated (Genesis 40:13; Job 10:15), *blood* or *wickedness* being *on the head*, which refers to guilt and judgment coming against persons for their wicked deeds (1 Kings 2:37, "your blood shall be on your own head," 1 Samuel 25:39, "the Lord has returned the wickedness of Nabal on his own head"), and *head* as ruler or authority over others (2 Samuel 22:44, "head of the nations," 1 Corinthians 11:3, "the head of every man is Christ, the head of woman is man, and the head of Christ is God"). There is absolutely no biblical warrant for speaking of *head faith*.

19. For example, "Thus my *heart* was grieved, and I was vexed in my *mind*" (Psalm 73:21). There is synonymous parallelism here. That is, the two halves of the verse are saying the same thing using synonyms. To be grieved in your heart is to be vexed in your mind. The same thing is evident in Hebrews 8:10, "I will put My laws in their *mind* and write them on their *hearts*." *Mind* and *heart* are used synonymously there.

Another example is found by comparing Luke 24:25 and Luke 24:45:

"O foolish ones, and slow of *heart* to believe in all that the prophets have spoken."

"And He opened their understanding [lit. *mind*], that they might comprehend the Scriptures."

Those two passages are talking about the same thing. The disciples were *slow of heart* to believe the prophetic teaching of the Old Testament Scriptures regarding His resurrection. So what did Jesus do? He *opened their mind* that they might comprehend those Scriptures. There is no difference whatsoever here between believing in the heart or believing in the mind. Compare also 1 Samuel 2:35; Psalm 26:2; Jeremiah 11:20; 20:12; and Ephesians 4:17-18.

20. The *mind* is associated with believing in at least three passages (Luke 24:45; Romans 14:5; Ephesians 4:17-18). In these three passages the words *believe* and *faith* do not occur. However, synonyms are present. Luke 24:45 is discussed in the immediately preceding note. In that text, opening of the mind is shown to be antithetical to being "slow of heart to believe" (verse 25). Romans 14:5 reads, "Let each be *fully convinced* in his own *mind*." Ephesians 4:17-18, which, like Luke 24:45, equates the heart and mind, says, "The Gentiles walk in the futility of their *mind*, having their *understanding* darkened…because of the blindness of their *heart*."

21. One passage, Romans 10:9-10, directly speaks of "believ[ing] in your heart." That is set in contrast with "confess[ing] with your mouth." The former is internal; the latter external. The former is by faith alone. The latter includes works. "Confessing with your mouth the Lord Jesus" is the action that involves commitment, obedience, and turning from sins, not "believing in your heart that God raised Him from the dead." Nor is believing with your heart defined as some special kind of faith that might rightly be called *heart faith*. Paul is merely indicating that saving faith takes place internally, as opposed to confessing Christ in word and deed, which takes place externally. Romans 10:9-10 is dealing with salvation from the wrath of God, both eternally and temporally. Believing the gospel is the condition of escaping the wrath of God eternally ("with the heart one believes unto righteousness"— [all righteous people go to heaven]). Confessing Christ is the condition of escaping the wrath of God here and now ("with the mouth confession is made unto salvation" [from God's temporal wrath]). For a discussion of Romans 10:9-10, see Zane C. Hodges, *Absolutely Free! A Biblical Reply to Lordship Salvation* (Dallas and Grand Rapids: Redención Viva and Zondervan Publishing House, 1989), 197-98, and Larry Moyer, *Free and Clear: Understanding & Communicating God's Offer of Eternal Life* (Grand Rapids: Kregel Publications, 1997), 116-23. See also note 10 in chapter 4.

Four other passages, none of which is dealing with saving faith, indicate indirectly that belief takes place in the heart (Mark 11:23; 16:14; Luke 8:12; 24:25). However, in each of those verses the point is just that belief takes place internally. And, as we have already seen, in the last of those passages believing in the heart is equated with believing with the mind.

See also note 20 for three passages that indicate that believing takes place in the mind.

Chapter 2: The Original Nic at Nite (John 3:16)

1. The pastor tells new converts: "You must be saved for at least three years before you have accumulated enough good works to be sure that you are truly saved and not just a stony-ground hearer" (Donald Dunkerly, "Hyper-Calvinism Today," *The Presbyterian Journal* [Nov. 18, 1981]: 15). Such a mistaken view of John 3:16 and of assurance stems from a faulty view of the gospel itself. The pastor in question did not believe that a person is saved merely by believing in Christ for eternal life. He felt that commitment and obedience were also required. As a result, a verse like John 3:16 seems very difficult, for it contains only one requirement—believing in Christ for eternal life.

2. The condition for Nicodemus and for us today is no different than it was for Abraham: "[Abraham] believed in the Lord, and He accounted it to him for righteousness" (Genesis 15:6). Abraham believed what the Lord said about giving him an Heir, from his own body, who would provide eternal salvation to all who believed in Him. Compare John 8:26; Romans 4:1-8; and Galatians 3:6-14.

Chapter 3: Faith on the Rocks (Luke 8:11-13)

1. Some would say that those who lose their faith also lose their salvation. Others would say that those who lose their faith never had real saving faith in the first place. Both would agree, however, that if faith fails, heaven is out of the question.

2. John Martin, "Luke," in *The Bible Knowledge Commentary*, New Testament Edition (Wheaton: Victor Books, 1983), 225. See also, Walter L. Liefeld, "Luke," in *Zondervan NIV Bible Commentary,* Vol. 2, New Testament (Grand Rapids: Zondervan Publishing House, 1994), 238.

3. See, however, Bernard Koerselman, *What the Bible Says About a Saving Faith* (Chandler, AZ: Berean Publishers, 1992), 223. He writes, "Jesus taught that to be saved we must persevere, standing firm to the end. The cowardly do not stand firm. Jesus predicted such falling away in the parable of the sower: 'Those on the rock are the ones who receive the word with joy when they hear it, but they have no root. They believe for a while, but in time of testing they fall away' [Luke 8:13]. These are the cowardly."

4. The Greek expression is *dechomai ton logon.*

5. For Jesus' teaching on eternal security, see John 5:24; 6:38-40; 10:25-30; 11:25-27.

6. That the endurance spoken of concerns continuance in our profession of faith is clear from the second half of verse 12: "If we deny Him, He will also deny us." That is an allusion to Matthew 10:33. The first half of the verse is an allusion to Matthew 10:32, which says, "Whoever confesses Me before men,

him I will also confess before My Father who is in heaven." It is thus clear that "if we endure" refers to enduring in our confession of Christ before men. The author of Hebrews similarly urged his readers, "Let us hold fast the confession of our hope without wavering" (10:23). The believer who endures in his confession of Christ will be confessed by Christ at His Judgment Seat as one who is indeed worthy to reign with Him (compare Luke 19:11-27).

7. See chapter 16 for a discussion of what I call *perseverance prizes*.

8. For a discussion of 1 Timothy 1:18-20 and the issue of apostasy see Hodges, *Absolutely Free! A Biblical Reply to Lordship Salvation* (Dallas and Grand Rapids: Redención Viva and Zondervan Publishing House, 1989), 108-113.

Chapter 4: Will the Real Believer Please Stand Up? (John 12:42-43)

1. Another way of saying this is that there are many professors, but few possessors.

2. See chapter 11.

3. D. A. Carson, *The Gospel According to John* (Grand Rapids: Wm. B. Eerdmans Publishing Co., 1991), 450-51.

4. There isn't space here to give a detailed response to the various passages cited by Carson in the preceding note. For a discussion of John 8:30-32, see chapter 5. For a discussion of John 2:23-25, see my newsletter article, "Saints: Spurious or Secret," *Grace in Focus* (November–December 1996).

   Regarding the "searing indictment" of John 5:44, whatever it means, it doesn't contradict John 12:42-43. Most likely John 5:44 is the statement of the general principle that seeking honor from God moves Him to open one's heart to the gospel (Cornelius in Acts 10:1-48 and Lydia in Acts 16:14) and that seeking honor from men disinclines Him to do so. However, there are exceptions. Saul of Tarsus, of course, fell under this indictment, yet came to faith in Christ. So did the rulers in John 12:42-43. In His grace He sometimes opens the eyes of even His most ardent opponents.

5. The other uses of this expression in John are in 7:5, 48; 8:30; 9:36; 11:48; and 12:37. All of these also refer to saving faith—two negatively, in reference to those who didn't believe savingly (7:5; 12:37), one hypothetically (11:48), and two interrogatively (7:48; 9:36).

   In addition, the related expression "believing in Me" refers to saving faith as well. See 6:35, 47; 7:38; 11:25-26; 12:44, 46—immediately following 12:42(!); 16:9 (used negatively); and 17:20.

6. John 3:16 has an articular present participle and John 12:42 has an aorist indicative. The former is referring *generally* to anyone who comes to faith in Christ. The latter is referring *specifically* to a group of people who had already come to faith in Him.

7. While it is hypothetically possible that he was an unbelieving disciple—see John 6:64, there is no hint of this in the context. Indeed, the unbelieving disciples of John 6:64 were openly following Jesus until that

point. Nicodemus had never done this. Yet he is called a disciple of Jesus. This naturally suggests that he was one of the rulers spoken of in John 12:42 who "believed in Him, but…did not confess Him."

8. Nicodemus is John's prime example of a secret believer. All three times John speaks of him he mentions that he came at night (3:2; 7:50; 19:39). Nicodemus evidently came to faith in Christ during his night interview with Jesus (John 3:1-18). While he never comes right out and directly asserts his faith in Christ, there is a gradual opening of the door evident in 7:45-52 and 19:38-42.

    The conclusion of some that Nicodemus and Joseph of Arimathea were not yet born again (see note 7) is not derived from the text of John. It is based on a theological presupposition that all truly saved people confess Christ. If that presupposition is wrong, and John 12:42-43 shows that it is, then the reader of John's Gospel is free to draw the obvious conclusion that Nicodemus and Joseph of Arimathea were secret disciples of Christ.

9. There are two ways in which this can occur. Some false professors really think they are believers but are not, because they don't understand and believe the true gospel. Other false professors are con artists who know they don't believe, but profess to believe so that they can gain an advantage in panhandling, in business, etc.

10. Some do, however, suggest that passages like Matthew 10:32-33 (which is parallel with Luke 12:8-9; see also Mark 8:38 and Luke 9:26) and Romans 10:9-10 teach that confessing Christ is indeed a condition of eternal salvation. Yet a careful consideration of these texts proves otherwise, as I have shown in newsletter articles, which are available at our website at www.faithalone.org. Briefly, in the former passage the Lord says that He will confess before the Father and the angels those believers who confessed Him before men. This refers to the public praise of those believers who, by their words and deeds, confessed Christ and proved to be worthy to rule with Him. Those whom Jesus does not confess, those He denies, are believers who will not reign with Him, as Paul makes clear in 2 Timothy 2:11-13, especially verse 12. While all believers will be in the kingdom, only those who endure in the faith will rule with Christ.

    Romans 10:9-10 can only be rightly understood if we recognize that Romans is about deliverance both from God's eternal and His temporal wrath. One escapes God's wrath eternally by believing in Jesus. One escapes God's wrath here and now by confessing Christ in word and deed on an ongoing basis. This is precisely what Romans 10:9-10 says. When one believes in Christ he is immediately declared righteous: "For with the heart one believes unto righteousness." There are no righteous people in hell. However, added to this internal act must be ongoing external actions if one is to obtain continuing deliverance from God's *temporal* wrath: "and with the mouth confession is made unto salvation [deliverance]." Verses 13-14 clarify the latter half of verse 10: "For 'whoever calls upon the name of the Lord shall be saved.' How then shall they call on Him in whom they have not believed?"

Clearly, the ones doing the calling upon the Lord are *believers*. Thus the salvation of verses 10 and 13 is the salvation of believers from God's temporal wrath. Larry Moyer has a very helpful discussion of Romans 10:9-10 in his excellent new book, *Free and Clear: Understanding & Communicating God's Offer of Eternal Life* (Grand Rapids: Kregel Publications, 1997), 116-23.

11. So did the Lord Jesus and John's fellow apostles. There are many commands, explicit and implicit, for believers to love God's praise and to confess Christ. These commands are often linked with eternal rewards which faithful believers will receive at the Judgment Seat of Christ. See Matthew 10:32-33; John 12:42-43; 1 Corinthians 9:24-27; 2 Corinthians 5:9-10; Galatians 1:10; 6:6-10; 2 Timothy 1:8, 12; 4:6-10; 1 Peter 5:1-4; 2 Peter 3:14-18; and 1 John 2:28. There would be no need of this if all believers automatically confessed Christ, sought God's praise, and received eternal rewards.

12. That praise will not be received by all believers. Only those who persevere in confessing Christ in word and deed will be so honored (Luke 19:11-26; 2 Timothy 2:12, compared to Matthew 10:32-33).

Chapter 5: Free at Last! (John 8:30-32)

1. It is true, *in a positional sense* that all believers are free from bondage to sin. Romans 6:18 says, "Having been set free from sin, you became slaves of righteousness." However, that doesn't mean that believers are free from sin's bondage *in their experience*. Romans 6 makes this clear by commanding those who are already free, "Do not let sin reign in your mortal body" (6:12); "Do not present your members as instruments of unrighteousness to sin, but present yourselves to God as being alive from the dead, and your members as instruments of righteousness to God" (6:13); and "Now present your members as slaves of righteousness for holiness" (6:19).

Chapter 6: Assurance in Focus

1. "Reasonably confident" is not the same as absolutely certain. People who believe that they can lose their salvation can't be absolutely sure that they have it right now, since they don't know for sure if they have done something bad enough to cause them to lose their salvation.

2. The term *Calvinist* is somewhat like the term *Evangelical*. Both are used today to describe an extremely wide range of people. Most modern Calvinists understand assurance as I have described it here. However, Calvin himself did not hold that view of assurance. He believed that assurance is of the essence of saving faith—that is, that when one believes in Christ, that person is absolutely sure he is saved, simply based on the objective promises of God (see Calvin's *Institutes of the Christian Religion,* 2 Vols. [Grand Rapids: Wm. B. Eerdmans Publishing Co., 1975], 3.2.16). So, too, there are some

Calvinists today who accept Calvin's view of assurance, contrary to the prevailing Calvinist view of assurance.

3. This is contrary to Calvin himself.

4. This account appeared originally in the *Sword of the Lord* (October 28, 1988), under the title, "A Conversation Between J. Wilbur Chapman and D. L. Moody." It was later used by permission and reprinted in the February 1989 issue of the Grace Evangelical Society newsletter (which was then called *The GES News;* now it is called *Grace in Focus*).

5. Actually 1 Corinthians 3:10-15 directly speaks to the building of the church. Church leaders (and ultimately every member of a church) are to be careful to build on it with the materials that God has said will endure. However, the passage also has application to the way in which we each build up the structure of our lives.

6. For further discussion of this point see Hodges, "Assurance: Of the Essence of Saving Faith," *Journal of the Grace Evangelical Society* 10 (Spring 1997): 3-17.

Chapter 7: Assurance and God's Approval (2 Corinthians 13:5)

1. For a defense of the doctrine of eternal security, see chapter 11.

2. John F. MacArthur, Jr., *The Gospel According to Jesus: What Does Jesus Mean When He Says, "Follow Me"?* Revised and Expanded Edition (Grand Rapids: Zondervan Publishing House, 1988, 1994), 214.

3. Ibid., 215.

4. *The New Geneva Study Bible: Bringing the Light of the Reformation to Scripture,* edited by Luder Whitlock, Jr., R. C. Sproul, Bruce Waltke, Moisés Silva, et al. (Nashville: Thomas Nelson Publishers, 1995), 1844.

5. Calling people to look to their works for assurance is unbiblical and counter-productive. The Scriptures tell us to look to Christ for assurance. Since no one's works are infallible (1 John 1:8, 10), no believer could ever be sure of his salvation if his assurance were based on self-examination.

   As to the charge that assurance apart from works promotes sin, I would say that the opposite is true. Assurance by looking to Christ and Him alone promotes love and a desire to please God in the heart of the grateful believer. "We love Him because He first loved us" (1 John 4:19). "The love of Christ compels us" (2 Corinthians 5:14). The opposite result occurs when people look to their works for assurance. When Christians take their eyes off Christ and look within themselves for assurance, discouragement and despair usually follow.

6. Paul twice used the expression without the preposition (*tē pistei* instead of *en tē pistei*) where it clearly referred to "in the faith" (Romans 14:1; and Colossians 1:23). Three times he used the expression without the definite article (*en pistei* instead of *en tē pistei*) where it could mean "in the faith," but might well simply mean "in faith" (1 Timothy 1:2; 3:13; 3:15). There is also

one New Testament use of this expression outside of Paul's epistles (2 Peter 1:5); however, the sense there is not "in the faith" but *to* your faith" ("add to your faith..."). There are also three uses of the expression outside of Paul's epistles without the preposition where it clearly refers to "in the faith" (Acts 14:22; 16:5; and 1 Peter 5:9).

7. While the word *established* is a participle, not an imperative, it is dependent upon an imperative from the previous verse, "walk in Him..."

8. David K. Lowery, "First Corinthians," in *The Bible Knowledge Commentary*, New Testament Edition (Wheaton: Victor Books, 1983), 584-85 (italics original).

9. The youth ministry, AWANA, bases its name on this verse. AWANA stands for *Approved Workmen Are Not Ashamed*. AWANA aims to lead children to faith in Christ, and then to build them up in the faith so that they will not be ashamed of themselves when the Lord returns.

10. At the very end of his life, as he was about to be martyred, Paul was certain that he would have this approval. See 2 Timothy 4:6-8.

Chapter 8: The Place of Feelings in Assurance (Romans 8:15-16)

1. Chapter 18, Section 2. It might be more accurate, however, to say that the Westminster Confession says that there are two *or* three grounds of assurance. After mentioning the promises of salvation and the inward evidences of grace as two grounds of assurance, the Westminster Confession of Faith states that assurance is also grounded upon "the testimony of the Spirit of adoption witnessing with our spirits that we are children of God." It merely paraphrases Romans 8:16 without comment. The reason for this is that among those who drew up the Confession, there was a difference of opinion on this issue. Some felt there were only two grounds of assurance. They regarded the so-called "inner witness of the Spirit" as being part of the second ground, the works evident in the life of a believer. That is, they felt the Holy Spirit testified to believers through their works. Others felt that there was a separate, powerful, subjective experience whereby the Spirit testified internally to some or all believers that they were children of God. For further information on this point see Joel R. Beeke's, "Personal Assurance of Faith: English Puritanism and the Dutch 'Nadere Reformatie:' From Westminster to Alexander Comrie (1640-1760)." Unpublished doctoral dissertation, Westminster Theological Seminary, 1988.

2. Some suggest, however, that the preposition does not in this case carry the force of "with," but that it merely serves to *intensify* the sense of the verb. Thus they argue that Paul is indeed talking about a witness "to" our human spirits. This suggestion, however, is not supported by the context. As we shall see, Paul is talking about a dual witness that takes place whenever we pray. In keeping with the Old Testament principle that two or three witnesses confirm a matter, Paul gives two witnesses here. In addition, the word

occurs only two other times in the New Testament, in Romans 2:15 and 9:1, also dealing with dual witnesses (works and conscience in 2:15, and Paul's words and his conscience in 9:1).

3. Of course, these good feelings are related to our eternal destiny and to the attending blessings such as spiritual life now, access to God in prayer, the indwelling of God's Spirit, the love that God has for me, etc. Though a believer who dwells on these truths will experience joy, he may not necessarily be *happy*. Joy and happiness are not the same thing. Happiness is dependent on circumstances. Joy is independent of our circumstances. So a believer might be discouraged, or even depressed, and yet experience joy if he abides in Christ and in the certainty of his eternal salvation.

Chapter 9: Confirming Your Call and Election (2 Peter 1:10-11)

1. Curtis I. Crenshaw, *Lordship Salvation: The Only Kind There Is! An Evaluation of Jody Dillow's* The Reign of the Servant Kings *And Other Antinomian Arguments* (Memphis: Footstool Publications, 1994), 114-15.

2. John F. MacArthur, Jr., *Faith Works: The Gospel According to the Apostles* (Dallas: Word Publishing, 1993), 158, italics his. See also, *The New Geneva Study Bible: Bringing the Light of the Reformation to Scripture*, edited by Luder Whitlock, Jr., R. C. Sproul, Bruce Waltke, Moisés Silva, et al. (Nashville: Thomas Nelson Publishers, 1995), 1980: "While God's choice of the elect is firm and certain in God (2 Tim. 2:19), it may not always be obvious to the individual Christian. Assurance of God's call comes through the evidence of the Holy Spirit's work in our lives (1 John 3:10, 14) as well as through the internal testimony of the Spirit in our hearts (Gal. 4:6)."

3. Of course, if that sort of understanding is true, then certainty of one's election is impossible prior to death, since no one achieves absolute holiness in this life. This in itself ought to make one rethink the interpretation.

4. This, of course, can only apply to born again persons. No unregenerate person has been "cleansed from his old sins."

5. It is used only three other times in the New Testament: "Let the word of Christ dwell in you *richly*" (Colossians 3:16); "God gives us *richly* all things to enjoy" (1 Timothy 6:17); "the Holy Spirit, whom He poured out on us *abundantly* [or richly]" (Titus 3:5-6).

6. See *A Greek-English Lexicon of the New Testament and Other Early Christian Literature,* by William F. Arndt and F. Wilbur Gingrich, Second edition, revised and augmented by F. Wilbur Gingrich and Frederick W. Danker from Walter Bauer's Fifth Edition, 1958 (Chicago: The University of Chicago Press, 1979), 673. See also Revelation 2:9.

7. Paul is referring to our *eternal* IRA. Every believer has an "account" to which we can add by the deeds we do. The wise believer makes frequent deposits to this account.

8. See, for example, Acts 10:1-6, especially verse 4, "your prayers and your alms have come up for a memorial before God." Cornelius was genuinely seeking God and as a result God sent an angel to tell him to call for the apostle Peter who would tell him what he must do to be saved. See also Acts 17:27.

9. If that is the case, then Peter's point is that by adding godly character to our faith we confirm to others that we are believers. Peter's readers were already sure that they had eternal salvation (see 2 Peter 1:1-4).

10. The third passage is Revelation 17:14. It pictures the Second Coming of Christ to vanquish the enemies of God at Armageddon. The King of kings is surrounded by a coterie of approved believers: "Those who are with Him are called, chosen, and faithful." Unfaithful believers are not mentioned. They will not be numbered among Jesus' partners or companions (*metochoi*, see Hebrews 1:9). This is in keeping with the imagery of Psalm 45. The king rides in majesty and overcomes his enemies. He then rules forever: "Your throne, O God, is forever and ever." That king is none other than the Lord Jesus (compare Hebrews 1:8-9). God the Father will anoint Him "with the oil of gladness more than [His] companions" (Psalm 45:7; Hebrews 1:9). Of course, the Lord Jesus will rightly have the superlative experience of joy. Yet His companions will also be given a special measure of gladness forever.

11. For more discussion of the latter parable see, Gregory Sapaugh, "A Call to the Wedding Celebration: An Exposition of Matthew 22:1-14," *Journal of the Grace Evangelical Society* 5 (Spring 1992):11-34, and Michael G. Huber, "The 'Outer Darkness' in Matthew and Its Relationship to Grace," *Journal of the Grace Evangelical Society* 5 (Autumn 1992):11-25.

12. James has a similar exhortation: "Who is wise and understanding among you? Let him show by good conduct that his works are done in the meekness of wisdom" (3:13).

13. Zane C. Hodges, "Making Your Calling and Election Sure: An Exposition of 2 Peter 1:5-11," *Journal of the Grace Evangelical Society* 11 (Spring 1998): 32, italics his.

14. Compare 1:10, "For if you do these things you will never stumble," and 3:17-18, "You therefore, beloved, since you know this beforehand, beware lest you also fall from your own steadfastness, being led away with the error of the wicked; but grow in the grace and knowledge of our Lord and Savior Jesus Christ." Clearly failure is possible for believers.

Chapter 10: Believer, Do You Know God? (1 John 2:3-6)

1. Many pastors hold this view as well. For example, in his book, *Saved Without a Doubt: How to Be Sure of Your Salvation* (Wheaton: Victor Books, 1992), John MacArthur writes, "First John 2:3 couldn't be clearer: 'By this we know that we have come to know Him, if we keep His commandments.' If you want

to know whether you're a true Christian, ask yourself whether you obey the commandments of Scripture…The Greek word translated 'keep' in verse 3 speaks of watchful, careful, thoughtful obedience. It involves not only the act of obedience, but also the spirit of obedience—a willing, habitual safeguarding of the Word, not just in letter but in spirit" (72-73).

2. Robert Law, *The Tests of Life: A Study of the First Epistle of St. John* (Edinburgh: T. & T. Clark, 1909).

3. In the majority of manuscripts that is only the first half of the verse. Most manuscripts also say (as reflected in the KJV and NKJV translations), "and that you may continue to believe in the name of the Son of God."

4. John Mitchell, J. Dwight Pentecost, and Zane Hodges have written commentaries advocating this view.

5. See, for example, Galatians 1:8-9 and James 1:19-20.

6. See, for example, John 17:3 ("This is eternal life, that they may know You, the only true God, and Jesus Christ whom You have sent"); Galatians 4:8-9; 1 Thessalonians 4:5; 2 Thessalonians 1:8.

7. See, for example, Titus 1:16; 2 Peter 1:8; 2:20; 3:18; 1 John 3:6; 4:6, 8. See also the book *Knowing Christ* (Chicago: Moody Press, 1980), by S. Craig Glickman in which he challenges believers to know Christ in their daily experience.

8. This verse clearly doesn't mean that anyone who sins has never been born again. Compare 1 John 1:8, 10. All believers sin. Perfect tenses are used here. They refer to past action with an abiding result. In this case they refer to the fact that one who sins doesn't have the abiding result of seeing and knowing Christ. When we sin, we take our eyes off Christ. When we sin, we fail to know Christ in that experience. It is not to say that those who sin are necessarily out of fellowship with God. It means that sin is never an expression of knowing God.

9. Zane C. Hodges, "Is God's Truth in You? (1 John 2:4b)," *The GES News* (July 1990): 3.

10. Verses 9 to 11 amplify this point. Any believer who hates his brother is walking in darkness and, conversely, any believer who loves his brother is walking in the light. That is, loving our Christian brothers and sisters is an expression of walking in the light and walking in fellowship with God.

The word *fellowship* (Greek: *koinōnia*) actually means "sharing." Fellowship with God is a *sharing* of His character and nature in our experience. Love is a reflection of the character of God. Hatred is not.

In Ephesians 5:2 Paul said, "And walk in love, as Christ also has loved us and given Himself for us." A few verses later Paul continued on that theme by saying, "For you were once darkness, but now you are light in the Lord. Walk as children of light" (verse 8). In this verse Paul appeals to the believers' position ("you are light in the Lord") and asks them to live in keeping with that reality: "walk as children of light." Believers don't automatically live in a manner consistent with their position.

11. Compare also James 2:23; 4:4; and 1 John 2:15.
12. Only Abraham specifically has that title (2 Chronicles 20:7; Isaiah 41:8; James 2:23). It is implied of others. For example, David is called "a man after My own heart" (Acts 13:22) and of Enoch we read that, "he pleased God" (Hebrews 11:5; compare Genesis 5:22-24).
13. See Romans 8:6; 12:1-2; and 1 Corinthians 2:14–3:3.

Chapter 11: Eternal Security in Focus

1. Exactly which sins those are is not always clear. Are jealousy, envy, and covetousness major sins? What about lying and outbursts of anger? What of hatred? And so on.
2. That means, for example, that under this thinking any Christian committing suicide loses his salvation.
3. Even many who don't believe in hell are concerned that it might exist and that they might end up there.
4. This is why the proclamation of eternal security is not an optional extra in evangelism. We need to tell people that Jesus guarantees *eternal life*, an eternally secure life, to all who believe in Him for it. Otherwise, we are not proclaiming the life-giving message clearly.
5. Other motivations include fear of God's discipline, desire for God's blessings, and a realization that the fullness of our eternal experience in God's kingdom is dependent on the life we now live. Believers who walk in sin miss out on an abundant life now, and, if they continue in that walk, they will miss the abundant life forever. While all believers have life, only faithful ones have it more abundantly (John 10:10).
6. You might also wish to read some books that exclusively address this question. There are several excellent books available on the subject. See, for example, Charles Stanley's *Eternal Security: Can You Be Sure?* (Nashville: Oliver Nelson, 1990); R. T. Kendall's *Once Saved, Always Saved* (Chicago: Moody Press, 1983); and H. A. Ironside's *Full Assurance: How to Know You're Saved* (Chicago: Moody Press, 1968, revised edition). You might also wish to read the section entitled "The Security of the Believer," in Charles C. Ryrie's *Basic Theology* (Wheaton: Victor Books, 1986), 328-34.

Chapter 12: A Punishment Worse Than Death (Hebrews 10:26-31)

1. Zane C. Hodges, "Hebrews," in *The Bible Knowledge Commentary*, New Testament Edition (Wheaton: Victor Books, 1983), 806.
2. We live in a time which makes this especially easy to do. The importance of sound doctrine is minimized and *toleration* and *unity* are the bywords of the day. In his book *No Place for Truth, Or Whatever Happened to Evangelical Theology?* (Grand Rapids: Wm. B. Eerdmans Publishing Company, 1993), David Wells gives a sober warning: "Theology is disappearing" (12). Why is

this happening? Because, he says, while "the great sin in fundamentalism is to compromise," "the great sin in evangelicalism is to be narrow" (129).

3. Philip Edgcumbe Hughes, *A Commentary on the Epistle to the Hebrews* (Grand Rapids: Wm. B. Eerdmans Publishing Company, 1977), 426, italics added. It should be noted that Hughes does not adopt the view that temporal judgment is in view. However, his comment is equally valid and helpful for those who adopt the temporal-judgment view.

Chapter 13: The Burned Branches (John 15:6)

1. Although *pur* is a common word in the Synoptic Gospels, occurring 27 times, this is its only use in John's Gospel. John never cites any of the occasions when Jesus spoke of "everlasting fire" (Matthew 18:8) or of "unquenchable fire" (Matthew 3:12; Mark 9:44-48; Luke 3:17). John's common words for the fate of the lost are "perishing" (e.g., John 3:15, 16; 6:39; 10:28; 17:12; 18:9) and "condemnation" (e.g., John 5:24, 29), neither of which occur in this context.

2. In addition, the expression "the lake of fire" always refers to eternal judgment.

3. James Montgomery Boice, *The Gospel of John*, (Grand Rapids: Zondervan Publishing House, 1978) 5 Volumes, 4:238. This statement is particularly significant since Boice believes that all genuine believers persevere in good works. In spite of that, he doesn't believe that this particular verse supports that doctrine.

4. See, for example, the *New Geneva Study Bible: Bringing the Light of the Reformation to Scripture*, edited by Luder Whitlock, Jr., R. C. Sproul, Bruce Waltke, Moisés Silva, et al. (Nashville: Thomas Nelson Publishers, 1995), 1694.

5. God chastens believers who persist in willful disobedience. There are many biblical examples of this (Leviticus 10:1-7; Psalm 32:3-5; Acts 5:1-11; 1 Corinthians 11:30; see also, Hebrews 12:3-11; James 5:20).

6. Of course, care should be taken to avoid obsessing about minor (or even major) problems and introspecting in an unhealthy manner. Overly sensitive people are prone to false guilt and undue self-examination. We should let God show us if there is some problem in our lives.

Chapter 14: Falling from Grace (Galatians 5:4)

1. Thomas F. Torrance, *The Doctrine of Grace in the Apostolic Fathers* (Edinburgh: Oliver, Ltd., 1948).

2. The apostolic fathers were Clement of Rome, Ignatius of Antioch, Hermas, Polycarp, Papias, and the authors of the Epistle of Barnabas, the Epistle of Diognetus, and the Didache.

3. Prior to this new formulation toward the end of the second century, some of the apostolic fathers were saying that there was only one opportunity for repentance after baptism. The result was that people then waited until their deathbeds to confess their sins to a priest and to repent and receive absolution.

4. As the tract cited suggests.

5. See *The New Geneva Study Bible: Bringing the Light of the Reformation to Scripture,* edited by Luder Whitlock, Jr., R. C. Sproul, Bruce Waltke, Moisés Silva, et al. (Nashville: Thomas Nelson Publishers, 1995), 1855n. Commenting on Galatians 5:4 it says, "Those who are chosen in Christ will be kept from such a renunciation of the gospel...There may be those, however, who appear to be true members of Christ who will abandon the gospel (Romans 11:22; 1 John 2:19)."

6. A person who thinks that eternal salvation can be lost, or that he can prove he never had it in the first place, does not believe that "he who believes in Me has everlasting life" (John 6:47) or that the one who "believes on the Lord Jesus Christ...shall be saved" (Acts 16:31). The only way such a person can be born again, then, is if at some time in the past he believed the gospel. Sadly there are multitudes of well-meaning people who never have believed the gospel. They have rejected apostolic doctrine and their hope of eternal salvation is built on the sand of their own good works. It is my sincere prayer that this book might be used to help many see that their view of the gospel is wrong, that eternal life is both eternal and free.

7. The expression *you have become estranged from Christ* refers to a break in fellowship. Believers who fall prey to legalism are like husbands who aren't on good terms with their wives. They became estranged because of something that one of them said or did. So, too, there is a break in fellowship between believers and Christ whenever they stop looking to Him alone for salvation and assurance. See *katargeō* in *A Greek-English Lexicon of the New Testament and Other Early Christian Literature,* by William F. Arndt and F. Wilbur Gingrich, Second edition, revised and augmented by F. Wilbur Gingrich and Frederick W. Danker from Walter Bauer's Fifth Edition, 1958 (Chicago: The University of Chicago Press, 1979), 417.

8. Those who believe you can lose your eternal salvation have obvious trouble explaining these verses. Grasping for straws, they sometimes point to this last expression, "nor any other created thing," and say something like this: "The word *other* in 'nor any other created thing,' is crucial. Paul means that no one other than we ourselves can separate us from God's love in Christ."

Such a view is self-contradictory, however. Since Paul has already said that nothing in life and nothing to come can separate us from Christ, then that *must* include anything that I myself might do. In addition, the word *other* in context is not speaking of created things (e.g., fallen angels) other than oneself. Rather, it is speaking of created things other than those already mentioned (life, death, angels, fallen angels, space). In other words, Paul is using a catchall expression at the end to say, "and if there is any other created thing which you might fear can separate you from the love of God, forget it. Nothing can."

9. Donald K. Campbell, "Galatians," *The Bible Knowledge Commentary*, New Testament Edition (Wheaton: Victor Books, 1983), 605. See also *A Greek-English Lexicon of the New Testament and Other Early Christian Literature*, 244.

10. "Barren intellectual formalism" is a highly pejorative expression. Zane Hodges defines faith as a conviction that something is true. Thus he says that saving faith is being convinced that the gospel is true, that Jesus gives eternal life to all who believe in Him for it. See *Absolutely Free! A Biblical Reply to Lordship Salvation* (Dallas and Grand Rapids: Redención Viva and Zondervan Publishing House, 1989), 25-33. That is not "barren intellectual formalism." *Barren* suggests infertility and lack of productivity. Yet believing in Christ for eternal life is fertile and productive. The one who believes is born of God and has eternal life! *Intellectual*, while not necessarily pejorative in itself, is often used in our society to suggest detachment and disinterest. However, saving faith is neither detached nor disinterested (see *Absolutely Free*, 29-32). *Formalism* is practically an evangelical curse word. It pictures strict excessive observance to form and implies that the form in question is an unbiblical man-made creation. For if the form were biblical, then observing it would not be negative. Hodges's view of saving faith is not, however, unbiblical or man-made.

11. J. I. Packer, "Understanding the Lordship Controversy," *TableTalk* (May 1991): 9, emphasis added.

12. He admits in the quote cited that he "once" believed the gospel Hodges preaches, but no longer. That is precisely what falling from grace is, ceasing to believe the gospel of grace and instead believing in a legalistic faith-plus-works "gospel."

13. Lordship Salvation people cannot say this of any Free Grace people, whether they once believed the Lordship Salvation gospel or not. That is because according to Lordship Salvation anyone who ceases to believe that message proves he was never saved in the first place. A careful examination of Packer's statement indicates that he considers Zane Hodges and all Free Grace believers to be lost: "God mercifully made me aware of my *unconverted state… I almost lost my soul* through assuming what Hodges teaches" (emphasis added). What can this mean but that all who believe the gospel which Hodges preaches are unsaved?

Chapter 15: Erasers in Heaven? (Revelation 3:5)

1. To receive a free subscription to *Grace in Focus*, or to sign up someone else you believe would like to receive it, please write us at GES, PO Box 167128,

Irving, TX 75016-7128 or e-mail us at ges@faithalone.org. You can also browse all back issues of our newsletter at our website: www.faithalone.org.

2. See also John 5:24; 10:27-28; and 11:25-26.

3. John F. MacArthur, Jr., *The Gospel According to Jesus: What Does Jesus Mean When He Says "Follow Me"?* Revised and Expanded Edition (Grand Rapids: Zondervan Publishing House, 1988, 1994), 253.

4. Ibid.

5. Ibid., 252-54. See also 123-33, 134-40, 141-48, 164-72, 188-94.

6. See Robert N. Wilkin's, *An Exegetical Evaluation of the Reformed Doctrine of the Perseverance of the Saints*, an unpublished master's thesis (Dallas Theological Seminary, 1982).

7. Compare Matthew 24:45-51; 25:1-13; and 1 Peter 5:1-11.

8. This is the same Greek verb *(gregoreō)* as the word translated "watch" in Revelation 3:3. This word also appears in 1 Thessalonians 5:6, where it is translated "watch."

9. The verb translated "blot out" occurs four other times in the New Testament. In those uses, the things blotted out are: "sins" (Acts 3:19), "the handwriting of requirements that was against us, which was contrary to us" (Colossians 2:14), and "every tear" (Revelation 7:17; 21:4).

10. A few Old Testament references refer to blotting out people's names. Some of these are general: "Let Me alone, that I may destroy them and blot out their name from under heaven" (Deuteronomy 9:14; see also Deuteronomy 29:20 and 2 Kings 14:27). After the golden calf incident, God contemplated destroying the nation and making a new nation from the descendants of Moses: "and I will make of you a nation mightier and greater than they" (Deuteronomy 9:14). In these cases, the blotting out of one's name refers to his physical death. Some Old Testament references are specific and refer to blotting out *from God's book*. Again, physical death is meant. In the Exodus account of the golden calf incident, Moses said to God, "If You will forgive their sin— but if not, I pray, blot me out of Your book which You have written" (Exodus 32:32). Then God responded, "Whoever has sinned against Me, I will blot him out of My book" (Exodus 32:33).

11. This number does not count Revelation 22:19, which in the vast majority of manuscripts reads *tree of life*, not Book of Life.

12. In the lone other biblical reference to the Book of Life, Paul speaks of his fellow workers "whose names are in the Book of Life" (Philippians 4:3). This confirms the understanding that the Book of Life contains the names of all born again people. Luke 10:20, though it doesn't specifically mention the Book of Life, alludes to it and confirms this understanding as well: "Rejoice because your names are written in heaven."

13. J. William Fuller has suggested, however, in an article entitled "I Will Not Erase His Name from the Book of Life," *Journal of the Evangelical Theological Society* 26 (September 1983): 297-306, that "name" (Greek: *onoma*) refers here not to one's given name, but to one's *reputation*. Compare

3:1. If that were true, then blotting out of one's name would not refer to a removal of one's entry from the Book of Life, but to a blotting out of one's good reputation. A major difficulty is that other references in the Book of Revelation (and in Luke 10:20 and Philippians 4:3) suggest that if your name isn't in the Book of Life, you are not saved. Thus this view would require that the word *name* refers to *reputation* in Revelation 3:5, but not in any of the other passages which deal with the Book of Life. While possible, that seems unlikely.

14. A number of authors argue that Jesus is here promising to reward the overcoming believer, though they don't specifically see this as a literal promise to highlight the name of the overcomer in the Book of Life. Proponents of this view include Zane C. Hodges, *Grace in Eclipse* (Dallas: Redención Viva, 1987), 109-111 and 119-20; Martyn Lloyd-Jones, *Romans Chapter 8:17-39: The Final Perseverance of the Saints* (Grand Rapids: Zondervan Publishing House, 1975), 314ff; Joseph Dillow, *The Reign of the Servant Kings: A Study of Eternal Security and the Final Significance of Man* (Hayesville, NC: Schoettle Publishing, 1992), 485-86.

15. *The American Heritage Dictionary of the English Language*, New College Edition (Boston: Houghton Mifflin Company, 1976), 763.

16. If the second promise is that vague, then the specificity comes in the third promise in the verse, the promise to confess the overcomer's name at the Judgment Seat of Christ.

17. Most likely there will be a worldwide phone book in the kingdom. If so, maybe the Book of Life will be that book. It could list the name, address, and phone number of every saint in the kingdom.

18. It is likely that this emphasis will not be merely all or nothing. In light of passages like Luke 19:11-16, there will probably be many different types of emphases. For example, there could be more than one crown (or asterisk) present at the front of an entry. Someone like King David might get ten crowns in front of his name. Someone else might get nine, another eight, and so on, down to the person who receives one crown. There might also be different colors of ink, different degrees of boldness, etc.

19. And it is noteworthy that the last two promises concern the exaltation of the overcomer's *name*. If the view suggested here is correct, the overcomer's name will be exalted both verbally and in print.

20. J. William Fuller, "I Will Not Erase His Name from the Book of Life," *Journal of the Evangelical Theological Society* 26 (September 1983): 299.

21. The superlative experience referred to in Revelation 3:5 (and in Galatians 6:9) certainly includes ruling with Christ, which is a privilege reserved only for those who persevere in the faith. Compare 1 Corinthians 9:27; 2 Timothy 2:12; Revelation 2:26; 3:21.

Chapter 16: Perseverance in Focus

1. This is normally called the Reformed doctrine of the perseverance of the saints. Some, however, prefer to call it the Reformed doctrine of the *preservation* of the saints since preservation puts the focus on God rather than on us. Whatever it is called, it suggests that all truly regenerate people persevere in good works.
2. There is decided ambiguity in this. Most Calvinists would say that a genuine believer will not live in such a way as to have a life characterized by sinful actions, which we might call carnality (1 Corinthians 3:1-3). The proviso is normally added, however, that for short periods of time this might even be true of a believer. How long this might go on is not made clear, since there is no verse that gives a time limit. Most would also say that perseverance means that at the point of death or the Rapture no believer would be in a state of carnality.
3. Eternal security is the doctrine that once a person is born again he forever remains born again. Some refer to this as "Once saved, always saved" (see chapter 11). The fifth point of Calvinism is really only formal belief in eternal security, since anyone who fails to persevere is said to be unsaved. This is essentially no different from the view that those who fail to persevere lose their salvation. In both cases the backslider goes to hell.
4. Calvinists object to this charge, saying that it is God who causes the believer to persevere in good works. In this way they think they are eliminating any ground for boasting. This does not eliminate room for boasting, however, because Calvinists see all of the commands to persevere and warnings against falling away as being God's way of motivating believers to make every effort to persevere. This shows that any resulting good works are not solely a work of God. The believer must exert effort.
5. Jesus did make statements indicating that *some* Tribulation believers would persevere. In Matthew 24:12 He said, "He who endures to the end shall be saved." The context makes it clear that "the end" of which Jesus was speaking was the end of the Tribulation, not the end of their lives. Verse 22 shows that the "salvation" of verse 12 refers to surviving the Tribulation alive, not to deliverance from hell. Verse 22 has the only other use of the word *save* in the context: "Unless those days were shortened, no flesh would be saved." Clearly that is speaking of temporal deliverance, not eternal salvation.

    According to Matthew 25:31-46, all of the believers who survive the Tribulation will have been faithful and will be rewarded. Thus, Jesus' point in Matthew 24:12 is that the only believers who will survive the Tribulation are those who have endured. Unfaithful believers will be taken home prematurely by the Lord during that time.

    The Book of Revelation also gives some statements regarding Tribulation believers who persevere. According to Revelation 6:9-11 many believers during the Tribulation will be "slain for the word of God and for the testimony which they held."

6. That Paul was uncertain he would persevere has led a number of Calvinists to conclude that Paul was not sure he had eternal life! For example, a few years back at a national meeting of about 1,000 Bible scholars, I heard a renowned seminary professor make this very point based on 1 Corinthians 9:24-27. I was chagrined to see that none of the other scholars in the audience expressed any discomfort with his position. Any theological position that necessitates the conclusion that the apostle Paul was unsure of his salvation is patently false.

7. Oppositely, the carnal believer frustrates the lives of those around him. His family, friends, neighbors, and co-workers find it more difficult to walk with God and to be content and fulfilled because of his ungodly influence in their lives.

Chapter 17: Are Believers Free of All Bad Habits? (2 Corinthians 5:17)

1. My friends who quoted this verse did not believe in sinless perfection. They never really made it clear how they understood 2 Corinthians 5:17. However, the impression I got was that they were saying that Christians were, from the moment of spiritual birth onward, without the encumbrances of sinful thoughts and actions.

2. For instance, John MacArthur says, "Receiving Christ does not mean that we can merely add Jesus to the refuse of our lives. Salvation is a total transformation: 'If any man is in Christ, he is a new creature; the old things passed away; behold, new things have come' (2 Cor. 5:17). What could be clearer than that? Old things pass away. Sin and selfishness and worldly pleasure are replaced by new things. This is the whole point of salvation: it produces a changed life" (*The Gospel According to Jesus: What Does Jesus Mean When He Says "Follow Me"?* Revised and Expanded Edition. [Grand Rapids: Zondervan Publishing House, 1988, 1994], 207; see also 275-76).

3. Luis C. Rodriguez, "Saturday Mornings: The Rough Road of a Carnal Christian," *The GES News* (December 1988):1, 4.

4. The verb *is* does not occur in the Greek. Literally the Greek just says, "If anyone in Christ."

5. The *New King James Version* reads, "*he is* a new creation." However, it places the words *he is* in italics, showing that those words are supplied.

6. Even if Paul meant that a believer is a new creation, we would still need to consider the context to see what that meant in terms of behavior.

7. *The New Geneva Study Bible: Bringing the Light of the Reformation to Scripture,* edited by Luder Whitlock, Jr., R. C. Sproul, Bruce Waltke, Moisés Silva, et al. (Nashville: Thomas Nelson Publishers, 1995), 1835. *The New English Bible* (N.p.: Oxford University Press and Cambridge University Press, 1961, 1970) essentially has this translation as well, reading, "There is a new world."

8. The Greek has *ta panta,* the exact same wording as in 2 Corinthians 5:17, four times (verses 16 twice, 17, 20). The other two are *pantōn* and *pasin* (verses 17, 18).
9. Both Second Corinthians 5 and Colossians 1 speak of all things being reconciled through Christ. This refers to Christ's finished work on the cross. He has already paid the full price for the reconciliation of every person who has lived and who will ever live. All are reconcilable because of the cross. Reconciliation occurs the moment a person believes in Christ for eternal life. Thus we are to implore people on Christ's behalf to be reconciled to God (2 Corinthians 5:20).
10. Paul goes on to say that Christ "died for us, that whether we wake or sleep, we should live together with Him" (1 Thessalonians 5:10). Clearly this shows that believers might not be watchful and sober. Christians might be morally asleep at the switch, unprepared for Christ's return. Yet they too will live together with Him forever!
11. See Stephen Spencer's article, "Why Can't I Change?" *Kindred Spirit* (Spring 1998): 4-5. He says, "We all have more than a token presence of fleshliness in us. Even as mature Christians, we have abundant capacity for wickedness and a pervasive taint on even our best motives and accomplishments. Even then, we are acceptable to God only in Christ's righteousness."

Chapter 18: The Danger of Falling Away (Hebrews 6:4-8)

1. The word *tasted,* which occurs in three of these five descriptions, is used on only one other occasion in Hebrews. In Hebrews 2:9 the author says that Jesus by His death on the cross *tasted* death for everyone. To suggest, as some do, that *tasted* in Hebrews 6:4-5 refers to something less than a full experience is thus untenable.
2. I. Howard Marshall, *Kept by the Power of God: A Study of Perseverance and Falling Away* (London: Epworth Press, 1969), 138.
3. Homer A. Kent, Jr., *The Epistle to the Hebrews* (Grand Rapids: Baker Book House, 1972), 110.
4. See, for example, Matthew 11:21; 12:41, where the same word is used.
5. See appendix 3 for a discussion of the issue of repentance and eternal salvation.
6. This is a type of metonymy called metonymy of cause for the effect. The cause is repentance. The effect is fellowship with God.
7. In other words, once a believer has gone to the extreme of turning his back on the gospel (in this case, offering animal sacrifices again because they no longer believed the death of Christ was sufficient to atone for their sins), it is humanly impossible to get them to decide to turn back.
8. See, for example, Philip Edgcumbe Hughes, *A Commentary on the Epistle to the Hebrews* (Grand Rapids: Wm. B. Eerdmans Publishing Company, 1977), 221-22; F. F. Bruce, *The Epistle to the Hebrews.* The New International

Commentary on the New Testament (Grand Rapids: Wm. B. Eerdmans
Publishing Company, 1964), 122-24.

9. See the reference in Pliny the Elder, *Historia Naturalis,* XVII.300.72.

10. *A Greek-English Lexicon of the New Testament and Other Early Christian
Literature,* by William F. Arndt and F. Wilbur Gingrich, Second edition,
revised and augmented by F. Wilbur Gingrich and Frederick W. Danker from
Walter Bauer's Fifth Edition, 1958 (Chicago: The University of Chicago Press,
1979). All believers will also experience judgment at the Judgment Seat of
Christ after this life. There will be a comprehensive evaluation and
recompense for the deeds we did as believers (1 Corinthians
9:24-27; 2 Corinthians 5:9-10; 2 Timothy 2:12; 4:7-8; 1 Peter 5:1-4). While
all believers will have a joyful, pain-free eternity, some believers will have
more abundant experiences than others. How we live now will have a direct
bearing on the abundance of our eternal experience.

11. See *A Greek-English Lexicon of the New Testament and Other Early
Christian Literature,* 18.

12. Of course, all of these things will come to no avail if the believer fails to
center his life on Christ. "I have been crucified with Christ; it is no longer I
who live, but Christ lives in me; and the life which I now live in the flesh I
live by faith in the Son of God, who loved me and gave Himself for me"
(Galatians 2:20). The successful Christian life is lived by faith, not by legalism. Though there are commandments, they are not the key to the Christian
life. Christ is. Apart from Him we can do nothing (John 15:5).

Chapter 19: Dangerous Road Ahead (2 Peter 2:18-22)

1. Note that Peter is saying that they *are* overcome, not that they overcome. The
people in question are entangled in the pollutions of the world and are
overcome by them. Don't confuse Peter's statement here with the overcomer
statements of Revelation 2–3. In the Second Peter passage the world overcomes believers. In the Revelation 2–3 passages believers overcome the world.

2. Of course, not only Peter, but the Lord Jesus and all of His other apostles also
taught eternal security. Compare, for example, John 5:24; 10:28-29; Romans
8:38-39; Hebrews 13:5; James 1:17-18.

3. See, for example, Kenneth L. Gentry, *Lord of the Saved: Getting to the Heart
of the Lordship Debate* (Phillipsburg, NJ: Presbyterian and Reformed Publishing Company, 1992), 89: "The dog returns to his own vomit and the swine
to the mud, but the believer stands in a new relationship to God (2 Peter 2:22;
2 Corinthians 2:17)." See also John F. MacArthur, Jr., *The Gospel According
to Jesus: What Does Jesus Mean When He Says, "Follow Me"?,* Revised and
Expanded Edition (Grand Rapids: Zondervan Publishing House, 1988, 1994),
112: "Inevitably, true disciples will falter, but when they fall into sin, they
will seek cleansing. They will not wallow in the mire (cf. 2 Peter 2:22). Their
faith is neither fragile nor temporary; it is a dynamic and ever-growing
commitment to the Savior."

4. While a believer could become a false teacher, Peter was writing about specific false teachers. These false teachers were unbelievers and had not yet come on the scene when Peter was writing. In 2 Peter 2:2 he was prophesying about those who would soon threaten the spiritual health of his readers: "There *will be* false teachers among you" (emphasis added).

5. See also 1:1, 9 and 3:1, 8, 14, 17-18 for further proof that Second Peter is addressed to believers.

6. When Peter referred to knowing Christ and to knowing the way of righteousness, he was not speaking about becoming Christians. While all believers know Christ in one sense (John 17:4), only spiritual believers know Him in their experience (1 Corinthians 2:15-16). For further discussion of this point, see the section which follows, entitled, "Peter Warns Christians of Judgment Here and Now."

7. Some might object that the parable deals with the issue of demon possession and only unbelievers can be demon possessed. However, that is to confuse the issue. Clearly an expression such as this one can be used, as Peter does here, in a different context. In Peter's context it can, and does, refer to believers.

8. John Long, "Death Grip," *Reader's Digest* 146 (February 1995): 128.

Chapter 20: Obedience and Disobedience (John 3:36)

1. See also Acts 6:7; Romans 1:5; 16:26; 1 Peter 1:22; 2:7.

2. For a more detailed discussion on the issue of perseverance, see chapter 16.

3. The others are, with the number of occurrences listed in parenthesis, Matthew 5:20 (6); 7:21-23 (6); 9:13 (5); Luke 19:10 (7); John 6:37 (5); Romans 6:23 (5); 10:9-10 (7); Titus 1:15-16 (6); James 2:19 (5); and 1 John 2:19 (5). He cites John 3:36 five times, on pages 39, 53, 59, 191, and 194.

4. John F. MacArthur, Jr., *The Gospel According to Jesus: What Does Jesus Mean When He Says "Follow Me"?* Revised and Expanded Edition (Grand Rapids: Zondervan Publishing House, 1988, 1994), 53.

5. Ibid., 191.

6. John H. Gerstner, *Wrongly Dividing the Word of Truth: A Critique of Dispensationalism* (Brentwood, TN: Wolgemuth & Hyatt, Publishers, Inc., 1991), 210, italics his.

7. Ibid., 256.

8. See, for example, MacArthur, *The Gospel According to Jesus*, 39.

9. The Greek words for obedience are *hupakoē, hupakouō, eisakouō, peithō,* and occasionally *akouō,* which refers to hearing and hence is occasionally used figuratively to refer to obedience (James 1:19). None of those first four words occur in John. The fifth does occur frequently, but most often in the literal sense of hearing. Among its figurative uses, it is translated as "hear" or "listen," and in those cases it seems to have the sense of "believing," rather than "obeying" (cf. 5:24, 25, 28, 37; 8:43, 47; 9:27; 10:16; 18:37), though, as

we shall soon see, believing the gospel is obeying God's command to believe it.

10. The concept of obeying God's commands does occur in John's gospel using other terms (for example, John 14:15, "If you love me, *keep* My commandments"; see also 15:14). However, none of those are connected with obtaining eternal salvation or of guaranteed perseverance. There is no promise in John that those who believe in Christ will persevere in good works. In fact, there are warnings that they might not (John 15:6).

11. *A Greek-English Lexicon of the New Testament and Other Early Christian Literature,* by William F. Arndt and F. Wilbur Gingrich, Second edition, revised and augmented by F. Wilbur Gingrich and Frederick W. Danker from Walter Bauer's Fifth Edition, 1958 (Chicago: The University of Chicago Press, 1979), 82.

12. The sixteen uses are John 3:36; Acts 14:2; 17:5; 19:9; Romans 2:8; 10:21; 11:30, 31; 15:31; Hebrews 3:18; 11:31; 1 Peter 2:7, 8; 3:1, 20; 4:17.

13. Roger M. Raymer, "First Peter," in *The Bible Knowledge Commentary,* New Testament Edition (Wheaton: Victor Books, 1983), 845, italics supplied by Raymer.

Appendix 1: Lordship Salvation

1. John F. MacArthur, Jr., *Faith Works: The Gospel According to the Apostles* (Dallas: Word Publishing, 1993), 23, italics his.

2. John F. MacArthur, Jr., *The Gospel According to Jesus: What Does Jesus Mean When He Says, "Follow Me"?*, Revised & Expanded Edition (Grand Rapids: Zondervan Publishing House, 1988, 1994), 27.

3. Kenneth L. Gentry, Jr., *Lord of the Saved: Getting to the Heart of the Lordship Debate* (Phillipsburg, NJ: Presbyterian and Reformed Publishing Company, 1992), 19, italics his.

4. James Montgomery Boice, *Christ's Call to Discipleship* (Chicago: Moody Press, 1986), 114, italics his.

5. MacArthur, *The Gospel According to Jesus,* 147.

6. Boice, *Christ's Call to Discipleship,* 112.

7. See, for example, the testimony to personal lack of assurance, and to the impossibility that anyone can be sure prior to death, by R. C. Sproul in his article, "Assurance of Salvation," *TableTalk* 13 (November 1989): 20.

8. Sinless perfection is a logical application of this view; if God guarantees holiness on the part of the justified, logically He would guarantee complete sinlessness. If justification and sanctification are inseparably linked, believers would experience ultimate sanctification the moment they believed in Christ.

Appendix 2: Baptism and Salvation

1. Other passages sometimes given are John 3:5, Romans 6:3-4, Galatians 3:27, and Ephesians 4:5. In John 3:5 Jesus said that one must be born of water and the Spirit to enter the kingdom of God. In Romans 6:4 Paul said, "We were buried with Him through baptism into death." In Galatians 3:27 Paul said, "As many of you as were baptized into Christ have put on Christ." Finally, in Ephesians 4:5 Paul said that there is "one Lord, one faith, one baptism." See note 7 below for a brief explanation of each.

2. See *A Greek-English Lexicon of the New Testament and Other Early Christian Literature,* by William F. Arndt and F. Wilbur Gingrich, Second edition, revised and augmented by F. Wilbur Gingrich and Frederick W. Danker from Walter Bauer's Fifth Edition, 1958 (Chicago: The University of Chicago Press, 1979), 132.

3. This was also the case in the Old Testament. All Old Testament believers were born again, for to be born again is to have eternal life (see John 1:12-13). However, they did not receive the Spirit, were not indwelt by Him, and were not baptized into the Body of Christ, the Church (which wasn't born until after Jesus' resurrection). This was true of the disciples, as well, until Pentecost. They were born again, yet they had not yet received the Holy Spirit (see John 7:39).

4. See, for example, Lewis Sperry Chafer, *Systematic Theology* (Dallas: Dallas Seminary Press, 1948), 8 Volumes, 6:150-51.

5. Zane C. Hodges, *The Gospel Under Siege*, Revised and Enlarged Edition (Dallas: Redención Viva, 1981, 1992), 123.

6. Though he takes a different view of Mark 16:16, R. T. Kendall also sees a link between Romans 10:9-10 and Mark 16:16 in his book *Once Saved, Always Saved* (Chicago: Moody Press, 1983), 41-42. He suggests that while confessing Christ is not a condition of eternal life (compare his remarks on page 88), all who believe will confess Christ, at least to one individual, if given enough time and opportunity to do so.

7. The other passages cited in note 1 above, John 3:5, Romans 6:3-4, Galatians 3:27, and Ephesians 4:5, also do not teach that baptism is a condition of eternal life. In John 3:5 the expression *born of water* most likely refers to physical birth. It certainly doesn't refer to Christian baptism since it didn't even exist until years after Jesus spoke with Nicodemus and since Jesus nowhere conditions entering the kingdom upon water baptism. Romans 6:3-4 and Galatians 3:27 refer to Holy Spirit baptism, when the Holy Spirit places believers into the Body of Christ. Compare 1 Corinthians 12:13. Ephesians 4:5 could refer either to Holy Spirit baptism or to Christian water baptism. In either case, Paul is not denying that both baptisms exist, for he speaks of both. In addition, the fact that Christian water baptism exists in no way proves that it is a condition of eternal life.

Appendix 3: Repentance and Salvation

1. See Charles C. Ryrie, *Balancing the Christian Life* (Chicago: Moody Press, 1969), 171-72, for a more detailed discussion of the importance of this passage to evangelism.

2. This is true as well in 2 Peter 3:9, "The Lord is…not willing that any should perish, but that all should come to repentance." That isn't talking about eternal condemnation. The only other use of the word *perish* in Second Peter occurs three verses earlier and there it unequivocally refers to the physical death which occurred when God sent a worldwide flood upon Noah's generation: "The world that then existed perished, being flooded with water" (2 Peter 3:6).

3. Of course, as John makes clear in his First Epistle, for the believer who is already in fellowship with God, the conditions are faith and *openness* before God (i.e., confessing our sins, 1 John 1:9). John doesn't even speak of repentance in First John because his readers were already in fellowship with God (see 2:12-14). Repentance is the condition for believers out of fellowship with God to get back in fellowship.

Appendix 4: My Approach to Understanding God's Word

1. In the NKJV, only John 10:24 translates *psychē* as a personal pronoun. However, in addition to that text, the KJV translates *psychē* in 2 Corinthians 12:15 with a personal pronoun. In addition to both of those texts, the NIV also translates *psychē* with a personal pronoun in Matthew 12:18.

2. This varies, obviously, by translation. For the KJV it is approximately 57 to 40. For the NKJV 52 to 27.

3. There is a new ad out by the car maker Volvo. They are promoting a new off-road vehicle with this line, "A Volvo that can save your soul." That is akin to the New Testament concept of the saving of one's *psychē*.

4. In the context—see especially verse 23—to believe in the Father is to believe in the Son since the Father sent Him and commands all to believe in Him. Thus the words "He who hears My words and believes in Him who sent Me" do not express two conditions of eternal life, but one. Both expressions refer to faith in Christ.

5. This doesn't mean that we shouldn't be open to changing our views. We should. For example, I recently changed my view on repentance, going against the position I advocated in my doctoral dissertation. (See appendix 3.) However, if we have carefully studied the Word of God on a subject, we should certainly be cautious about changing our view. We need to search the Scriptures to see if any new view is correct (Acts 17:11). We should adopt a new interpretation or theological belief only when convinced by Scripture and the Holy Spirit.

SUBJECT INDEX

Abiding in Christ, 40–43, 65, 83–87, 98, 105–109, 224, 257
Abraham, 5, 6, 248, 251, 260
Antinomianism, 171, 219
Apostasy, 102, 152, 156, 252
Approval (*Dokimos*), 65, 66, 156, 255
Arminianism, 47, 92, 93, 219, 247
Assurance of salvation, 47–59, 64, 69, 70, 74, 82, 96, 116, 136, 174, 179, 184, 220, 255

Backsliding, 58
Baptism and Salvation, 111, 112, 187-98, 204, 220
Baptismal regeneration, 187, 188, 189, 194
Believe. *See* Faith.

Calvin, John, 48, 54, 112, 132, 220, 254
Calvinism, 48, 132, 219, 220, 226, 247, 254, 266
Carnality, 139, 221
Cheap grace, 113, 221
Co-heirs, 223
Commitment, 3, 4, 10–13, 21, 113, 166, 180, 185, 197, 221, 224, 250
Confessing Christ, 31–36, 169, 196, 221, 250, 253
Confession, 29, 221
Confidence, 74, 87, 107
Conversion, 165, 183
Cost of salvation, 179, 181, 184
Cross, 12, 20, 21, 34, 36, 58, 145, 153, 184, 190, 191, 212, 220, 222, 268

Death, 7, 8, 51, 93, 94, 99, 101, 102, 107, 108, 137, 139, 162, 197, 205, 217

Death of Christ, 14, 20–23, 58, 145, 152, 175, 189, 190, 212
Denying Christ, 251
Disapproval (*Adokimos*), 65, 66, 134, 156
Discipleship, 25–29, 37–43, 73–80, 131–41, 159–68, 193, 194, 204
Divine discipline, 35, 101, 137, 155, 260
Doubt, 11, 25, 55, 56, 64, 184, 186

Easy believism, 113, 221
Election, 73–80
Eternal life, 3–15, 17–23, 91–98
Eternal rewards, 29, 53, 65, 76, 77, 96, 101, 113, 121–124, 127, 138, 154, 225, 254
Eternal security, 47, 54, 57, 59, 91–98, 132, 153, 222, 266
Evangelism, 179, 260, 273

Faith, 5–7, 220
    head, 13, 249
    heart, 9, 13, 250
    not a decision, 6, 7
    saving, 3–15, 21, 27, 28, 29, 32, 38, 54, 56, 76, 96, 133, 174, 179, 180–83, 220
False professor, 38, 39, 253
Fear of hell, 135
Fellowship, 140, 153, 157, 162, 167, 204, 207, 210, 225, 259
Fire, 106, 155, 213
Flesh, 18, 59

Great White Throne Judgment, 96, 222–23

Holiness, 98, 135
Holy Spirit, 53, 64, 69–71, 95, 100, 113, 114, 139, 147, 152, 188–97, 226

SCRIPTURE INDEX

A WORD ABOUT GRACE EVANGELICAL SOCIETY

Grace Evangelical Society (GES) was founded in 1986 by Dr. Bob Wilkin as an educational and motivational networking ministry. The purpose of GES is to promote the clear proclamation of God's free salvation and related, yet distinct, discipleship issues. GES accomplishes this purpose by the following means:

- a free bimonthly newsletter,
- a semiannual journal,
- commentaries on New Testament books,
- evangelistic and discipleship booklets,
- books by writers such as Zane Hodges, Jody Dillow, and Bob Wilkin,
- audio tapes,
- conferences and seminars, and
- a non-resident seminary.

If you would like to receive our free newsletter or would like more information about the various ministries and publications listed above, you can contact us in any of the following ways:

- 972-257-1160 (phone),
- 972-255-3884 (fax),
- ges@faithalone.org (email),
- www.faithalone.org (website), or
- PO Box 167128, Irving, TX 75016-7128.

If you have come to faith or have regained assurance of your salvation through reading this book, we would especially like to hear from you.